Children's Rights and International Development

Children's Rights and International Development

Lessons and Challenges from the Field

Edited by

Myriam Denov, Richard Maclure, and Kathryn Campbell

palgrave
macmillan

CHILDREN'S RIGHTS AND INTERNATIONAL DEVELOPMENT

First published in 2011 by
PALGRAVE MACMILLAN®
in the United States—a division of St. Martin's Press LLC,
175 Fifth Avenue, New York, NY 10010.

Where this book is distributed in the UK, Europe and the rest of the world, this is by Palgrave Macmillan, a division of Macmillan Publishers Limited, registered in England, company number 785998, of Houndmills, Basingstoke, Hampshire RG21 6XS.

Palgrave Macmillan is the global academic imprint of the above companies and has companies and representatives throughout the world.

Palgrave® and Macmillan® are registered trademarks in the United States, the United Kingdom, Europe and other countries.

ISBN: 978–0–230–60682–1

Library of Congress Cataloging-in-Publication Data

Children's Rights and International Development / edited by Myriam Denov, Richard Maclure, and Kathryn Campbell.
p. cm.
ISBN-13: 978–0–230–60682–1
ISBN-10: 0–230–60682–2
1. Children's rights—Developing countries—Case studies. I. Denov, Myriam S., 1970– editor of compilation. II. Maclure, Richard Alexander, 1951– editor of compilation. III. Campbell, Kathryn M. (Kathryn Maria), 1960– editor of compilation. IV. Seneviratne, Dharshini. Home truths.

HQ792.2.C45 2011
323.3′52091724—dc22 2010049483

A catalogue record of the book is available from the British Library.

Design by Newgen Imaging Systems (P) Ltd., Chennai, India.

First edition: June 2011

10 9 8 7 6 5 4 3 2 1

Printed in the United States of America.

Contents

Figures

Tables

Acknowledgments

We would like to thank the Canadian International Development Agency (CIDA) who generously supported many of the research projects featured in this book, as well as this book-writing endeavor. Without CIDA's assistance through the Child Protection Research Fund, these projects, as well as the completion of book, would not have been possible.

In 2006, a conference entitled "Children's Rights and International Development: Research, Challenges and Change" was held in Ottawa, Canada, through the support of CIDA. We are grateful to the conference participants, many of who have written chapters for this book, and especially to the young people from around the world who participated in the conference and were involved in the conference's youth forum. Their insightful presentations and contributions provided much inspiration for this larger book-writing project. Special thanks go to Inbal Solomon whose work and commitment to both the Ottawa conference and to this book were invaluable.

Many individuals provided vital help along the way. We are grateful to Bree Akesson, Tamsyn Farr, Osnat Fellus, Lindsay Jones, and especially Ahila Poologaindran for the excellent support and assistance.

Our families have provided much needed laughter and encouragement. We are grateful for the love and support of Craig, André, Léoni, Sumaya, Sara, and Malaika.

Our deepest thanks and appreciation go to the children whose lives are featured in the chapters of this edited collection. In the face of great adversity, these children exude strength and courage and their stories embody extraordinary resilience and capacity. We are grateful to all of them for sharing their perspectives and their stories. This book is dedicated to them, and to children like them, who survive, and in some cases, thrive under unimaginable hardship.

Introduction

Kathryn Campbell, Myriam Denov, Richard Maclure, and Inbal Solomon

Children[1] and young persons the world over require special considerations and protections, due to their limited cognitive, emotional, and social development, as well as their relative lack of political power. However, a child's arbitrary place of birth determines to a great measure the extent to which their basic needs will be met and their overall rights respected. The so-called North-South hemispheric divide, where the industrialized North possesses vastly greater access to resources and power than the developing South (Malone & Hagman, 2002), is nowhere more evident than in the area of children's rights and children's protection. Many children from the developing South face a myriad of hardships, including, *inter alia*, poverty, limited basic health care, illiteracy and restricted educational opportunities, hunger and malnutrition, abuse, exploitation, and discrimination. In addition, contexts of armed conflict and pandemics of diseases such as HIV/AIDS have greatly contributed to the unraveling of children's social support networks and diminished their sense of safety and security. All of these circumstances, which are invariably shaped by children's age, gender, ethnicity, mobility, and socioeconomic status, jeopardize their fundamental rights and protections.

The global children's rights movement, which has struggled to reduce many of the above-noted circumstances, has a long history. Yet, the idea that children can possess and exercise rights is a paradoxical one, as rights-bearers are more often considered as capable of mobilizing autonomously to champion their own rights (e.g., women's associations, ethnic minorities, and indigenous peoples). Children, however, are different. Until recently, children were viewed largely as passive recipients of rights and protections that supervising adults deemed they deserved. Yet over the latter half of the twentieth century, children and adolescents have come to be regarded as subjects *with* rights, rather than simply objects *of* rights or objects of protection. This changing attitude has been accompanied by attendant policy and legislative changes, on both national and international levels. Nevertheless, because of their biological and social development, children are largely dependent on an adult world, and only gradually attain self-sufficiency and the skills necessary to exercise agency in defense of their rights (Woodhouse, 2000). Given their relative dependence, notions of children's rights encapsulate not only capacity-based rights, but also needs-based rights, which are reliant on adult determinations and adult institutions to facilitate their exercise. Indeed, some argue that it is impossible to separate children's rights from those of adults, and that when adults invoke children's rights it is simply to promote adults' agendas (Guggenheim, 2005).

The UN Convention on the Rights of the Child: Rights or Rhetoric?

The primary document aimed solely at protecting children and promoting their rights is the United Nations Convention on the Rights of the Child (CRC). Adopted in 1989 and currently ratified by 192 signatory member states (UNICEF, 2006),[2] the scope of its applicability is "every human being below the age of eighteen years" (CRC, Article 1). A hallmark of the CRC is its integration of broad categories of rights, including civil and political rights (e.g., to self-determination, and to protection from arbitrary arrest, torture, and compulsory labor) and economic, social, and cultural rights (e.g., to basic economic welfare, health care, education, and freedom of religion). The CRC applies to all children, regardless of their circumstances, as well as those who are in special situations, including refugees, children with disabilities, orphans, minority, and indigenous children.

The application of the CRC is guided by four fundamental principles. The first is that a primary consideration underlying all actions undertaken on behalf of children must be in their best interests, and not those of state parties or other adults in their lives. The second principle stipulates that children have the right to nondiscrimination, and that state parties must ensure protection from any form of discrimination. The third principle articulates every child's basic right to life, survival, and development, which state parties must ensure to the maximum extent possible. Finally, the CRC recognizes that all children have the right to participation, including the right to be heard in any proceedings or tribunals affecting them.

The nature and extent of the rights that are recognized and promoted by the CRC are far-reaching, and once adopted, it was heralded as revolutionizing the concept of children's rights throughout the world (Bisht, 2008). Unfortunately, however, the CRC does not have the legal status of a statute and cannot, therefore, be imposed to override national laws of signatory nation states. For example, in Canada, the CRC is recognized as an "interpretive guide" for situations where legislation is ambiguous or silent (Denov, 2005). Moreover, there is no permanent international monitoring mechanism for implementation of the CRC. While nation states are required to provide periodic reports to the United Nations Committee on the Rights of the Child regarding the extent to which their legislation and policy meet the protections outlined in the CRC, there is little clout or substantive consequences attached to this process, and the continual risk is that the CRC is relegated to the margins of policy as merely a symbolic instrument.

In the current context of rapid global change and widening gaps between the rich and the poor, this is a profound & tangible risk. In the past 20 years since the CRC was enacted, children and young persons throughout the world continue to be abused, neglected, exploited, and suffer discrimination. It is unacceptable that state parties that formally claim to respect children's rights by virtue of their ratification of the CRC subject them to horrific conditions, through omission or commission, such that their survival and long-term development is appallingly compromised. Yet throughout much of the world, particularly in countries of the South, socioeconomic realities are such that the rights of children to protection and participation are generally subsumed by preoccupations of economic development, fluctuating power arrangements, and allocation of scarce resources for basic welfare provisions. In effect, profound socioeconomic and political constraints have prevented many countries from implementing the provisions of the CRC. In particular, the realities of civil war, HIV/AIDS, and the necessity of child labor in many developing countries have severely limited the ability of state parties to protect and promote the rights of children.

Notions of what constitutes "childhood" and children's rights are similarly problematic. As revealed in the chapters of this volume, the concept of childhood is itself a social construct that varies a great deal in form and content across culture, social groups, local understandings, and values (Denov, 2010). When childhood is defined solely by age, as seen in the CRC, it downplays the importance of other salient factors such as culture, gender, and socioeconomic status. Arguably, the vision of childhood and children's rights envisaged by the CRC is an idealized, modern, Western one, which consequently has limited application in other cultures. Moreover, the contexts of deprivation in which many children around the world live force them to take on adult roles and responsibilities much earlier than many would deem acceptable in view of their evolving psychological and social development. Given these realities, the definition of a child is thus complex and involves a "process of negotiations between individuals, family members, peer groups and the wider community in the context of life events and rights of passage" (Mawson, 2004, p. 226).

Research on Children's Rights in the Developing World: A Canadian Initiative

To gain a better understanding of the lived realities of children internationally, in 2002 the Canadian International Development Agency (CIDA) introduced a 2-million-dollar research fund that supported research projects addressing children's rights and protections in developing countries. The Child Protection Research Fund (CPRF) sought to support initiatives that shed light on the conditions under which marginalized girls and boys are living, as well as the potential of research to influence policies and practices on their behalf.

Reflecting the goals of the CPRF, this edited collection of chapters highlights some of the many struggles and challenges related to the advancement of children's rights in developing countries. Eight of the twelve chapters in this collection are based on empirical research sponsored by the CPRF; the remaining four chapters[3] are supported by other funding organizations. All twelve chapters, however, provide accounts of field-based research projects in Africa, the Americas, and Asia that emphasize the primacy and challenges of recognizing and realizing children's rights. Importantly, while the data for many of the studies were collected between 2004 and 2008, the conditions that seriously undermined children's rights when these studies were conducted continue unabated in all of the noted contexts. This underscores the need for ongoing attention to the issues raised in this volume, ranging from those that are specific to local contexts to those that are inherently global and structural. Moreover, all of the research projects are multidimensional and field-based, and some have also identified sustainable and practical solutions to the problems faced by the children in need of special protections.

A number of features make this collection unique with respect to research design and implementation. Although the studies highlight the drastic conditions that many children face around the globe, rather than focusing solely on the vulnerabilities and victimization experiences of the children, the chapters provide accounts of projects that aim to enhance children's protection and their right to participation and empowerment. Each project attempted to facilitate or develop young people's capacity to exercise agency, by ensuring that to varying degrees their experiences and voices were represented and their participation encouraged. Indeed, the voices of children underscore not only their inherent capacities, but also the need for their greater involvement in planning and decisions that affect their well-being.

Some of the chapters also highlight the role of children in field research. In some cases, young people participated in aspects of research design, in data collection, in creative forms of reflection and analysis, and in the dissemination of research findings through media such as film, theater, music, and conference presentations. There were inevitably methodological and ethical challenges in conducting field-based research on children's rights issues in difficult situations, as well as ensuring meaningful participation in contexts where children's participation is rare or inconsistent with prevailing cultural mores. However, children's involvement highlights both their incipient capacities for field research (when these are developed and supported by experienced researchers) and the value of including children in research and in subsequent deliberations related to programs, policies, and advocacy.

Many of the children's life experiences as recounted in this collection convey profound tragedy, from the health risks involved in child mining in Bolivia, to the continued gender-based violence following abduction into war in Angola, to the deprivations experienced in institutional care in Viet Nam. These conditions are largely ecological in nature—rooted in historical, cultural, political, and economic factors. Although many of the children's stories are extremely disturbing, they convey hope, as revealed in the peer-support amongst AIDS orphans in Malawi, to the experiences of boys who are learning about human rights in Bolivia, to the benefits that accrue from involving children in decisions that affect them in Senegal. What all of these stories and experiences reveal is that in spite of great adversity, children have great resiliency and are able to foster constructive change and remain optimistic and positive. In the event that they have access to sustained assistance and support, they possess the inherent ability to act individually and collectively in the struggle for the realization of their rights. This underlines a singular purpose of this book—that despite children's vulnerability and all-too frequent victimization in a context of massive rights abuses, their innate resilience provides a firm basis for fostering improvements in their conditions and an enhancement of their fundamental rights.

This collection is also unique in terms of the North-South partnerships that characterized the research fieldwork described in each of the chapters. Each research project involved the collaboration between non-governmental organization (NGO) or community-based organization (CBO) staff from the South working with children and youth and Northern researchers and child rights advocates. A great strength of this type of collaboration is that the individuals directly involved in community engagement and data collection had a vested interest in documenting the realities of the children and adolescents with whom they worked and the community contexts where they had established trusting relationships. Likewise, the partner relations that were established between Southern practitioners and Northern researchers greatly facilitated the opportunity to elicit direct field-based knowledge from NGO workers and practitioners, and to gain an understanding of the diverse contexts "on the ground."

As the subtitle of this book indicates, these chapters are largely essays "from the field," providing unique snapshots of the lives of marginalized and underprivileged children on the basis of their own voices and the experiences of practitioners directly implicated in the promotion of children's rights. Inevitably, given the emphasis on research fieldwork and the voices of children, some of the chapters in this volume are largely descriptive and lack conceptual or analytic frameworks that are an integral norm of academic research. Nevertheless, what some of the chapters may lack in terms of broad generalizations and theory is counterbalanced by an empirical richness of the data concerning the children's lives. These empirical accounts greatly enhance our understanding of how children and youth experience, manage, and can potentially overcome extraordinary deprivations. Many of the chapters also present innovative, community-based initiatives designed to address these problems, and have engaged youth and local advocates for youth rights in the process. In addition, most of the chapters propose ways of improving the circumstances of children in need, which often entails increased participation of children themselves—both as a means to strengthen child rights programs and policies, and as a rights-based end in itself.

In an attempt to address a significant gap in much of the literature on children's rights, this collection of essays also draws attention to the experiences of marginalized young girls and in particular how they cope with gender-based violence. In a great deal of the research on children's rights, girls' experiences and voices often become subsumed under overall *children's* experiences, which invariably covers only boys' experiences. Unfortunately throughout much of the developing world, gender-based insecurity and sexual violence are widespread, and in times of political instability and war, girls are especially vulnerable to violent sexual assault.[4] While the accounts of many of the girls in this collection are highly disturbing, their stories and experiences nonetheless reveal a spirit of volition that counters a deterministic and commonly held depiction of girls as silent victims. As the chapters on girls within the contexts of Angola and Northern Uganda reveal, given their significant presence and multiple roles within the context of armed conflict, girls' experiences and perspectives should be considered as central and indispensable to understandings and analyses of war and political violence, and not regarded as peripheral or rendered invisible, however unwittingly.

Overview of the Book

This collection, which examines the lives of children in 10 developing countries and interventions that are designed to enhance their conditions and strengthen their rights, has been divided into four sections, each containing chapters that cover related topics. The first section focuses on the experiences of *children in institutional care*. This section demonstrates how institutional care in some developing countries has become a fallback option when political and economic changes, as well as poverty and despair, effectively "force" families to hand their children over to the state. The chapters in this part reveal a fundamental gap between the CRC's principles and the practices and environments of childcare institutions in these organizations. The chapter, entitled "Home Truths: Children's Rights in Institutional Care in Sri Lanka," by D. Seneviratne and F. Mariam describes the extensive negative psychological impact that institutionalization has on Sri Lankan children. Through participant observations and focus groups with children, the authors critically examine how children are relegated to institutionalized care and at the same time, assess the gaps in institutional childcare services. The authors conclude by arguing for the use of these findings in promoting evidence-based policy changes and involving both children and their families in finding alternatives to child institutionalization through more culturally relevant family care options.

The chapter entitled "Juvenile Justice in São Paulo, Brazil: Violence and Denied Opportunities" by J. McLennan, F. Rigato, and I. Bordin focuses on detention facilities in São Paulo and follows the circumstances of youth at the time of their incarceration, and one year after their release. The authors paint an exceedingly dismal picture of life in these facilities, one of overcrowding, understaffing, unsanitary conditions, and inappropriate transfers to adult jail. In an attempt to better understand the circumstances of these youth, through both quantitative and qualitative methods, this study underscores the urgent need to undertake interventions that are more effective in terms of prevention and rehabilitation, and are far more endowed with resources than are currently available, if rates of recidivism and premature death are to be reduced. The authors also recount the involvement of several children in dissemination of research findings, and the production of a documentary film coproduced by four of their youth participants describing their experiences and perspectives of incarceration and release. As the authors indicate, an abridged version was later disseminated to the Brazilian media. The results of this study demonstrate that it is only by expanding opportunities for education, employment, and recreation that the problems that incarcerated youth face can be redressed.

The chapter entitled "Children in Institutional and Alternative Care in Viet Nam: A Review of Current Policy and Practice," written by J. Bergeron and S. Tanaka, examines the quality of care for children placed in institutions and in community-based care centers in Viet Nam. In their review of a hundred institutions in three regions in the country, through interviews and focus groups with government workers, NGO staff, institutional care personnel, foster parents and children themselves, the authors learned that most children end up in those institutions due to poverty and a need for educational opportunities that families cannot afford. The results of their study emphasize the need to address the conditions of relative deprivation that exist in institutions (although less so in alternative care arrangements), and the need for more empirically grounded policy initiatives that address children's needs in institutional care settings in Viet Nam. The authors conclude by stressing the need for enhanced and continual staff training for the professionals who provide care to these children and their families.

The second section of this collection focuses on *child labor, violence, and exploitation*. Though the chapters in this section are written from differing contexts, they collectively reveal the urgent need for programs and policies that provide for the protection of children from exploitation that go above and beyond protective measures stipulated in the CRC.

The chapter entitled "Child Laborers in the Bolivian Mining Sector: Exploring Children's Experiences and Perspectives" by J. Albarracin-Jordan and T. Bouchard focuses on children working in the mines of Bolivia. Driven to mining largely as a result of endemic poverty, the child miners (or *baranquilleras*) are subjected to deplorable working conditions that expose them to great health risks. Despite the Bolivian government's ratification of the CRC and its passage of a national Children's Code of Law, these conditions remain a massive violation of the rights of impoverished children living in mining communities. Nonetheless, through the children's experiences, the authors demonstrate the extraordinary resilience of child mine workers and strongly advocate the necessity of social services and systems of support that will both protect working children and enhance the social development of mining communities. The second chapter in this section, entitled "Breaking the Silence: The Voices of Girls Forcibly Involved in Armed Conflict in Angola," by Vivi Stavrou examines the reality of young girls following Angola's civil war. This qualitative study recounts the experiences of these girls and reveals that in Angola's postconflict context, they are often stigmatized and ostracized by their families and communities. Girls are often vulnerable to continued abuse and exploitation, in ways that differ from that of young boys. The author argues strongly that Disarmament, Demobilization, and Reintegration (DDR) initiatives must overcome their tendency to ignore or neglect girls' experiences as former child soldiers. By considering the unique and devastating experiences of these girls during periods of conflict, DDR programs must accommodate their realities and facilitate the development of interventions that are specifically attuned to the enduring needs of girls and women in postconflict circumstances.

The following chapter, entitled "Addressing Youth Violence and Aggression in Colombia: Examining a Community-Wide Prevention Initiative" by L. Duque, M. Ungar, and B. Caicedo, provides an overview of the efficacy of a wide-scale violence prevention program in Colombia. Through the involvement of parents, teachers, government officials, and NGO staff, this multifaceted program focused on the prevention of violence among youth and encouraged simultaneous improvements in their education and long-term coping skills. While a number of methods were used to evaluate this program, the aspects of the program evaluation recounted in this chapter reveal that this ecological approach was most successful in diminishing the aggression of children whose families demonstrated effective child-rearing practices before the program began and who were more active during the program itself.

The third section in this collection focuses on *child rights, education, and participation* and underscores the value of engaging youth in pedagogical activities oriented toward their heightened awareness of their own rights and the rights of others. The first chapter, entitled "The Dynamics of Youth Participation: Insights from Research Fieldwork with Female Youth in Senegal" by R. Maclure, recounts a process of evolving youth participation in research fieldwork that began as an inquiry into their perspectives of daily life and their future prospects. The author demonstrates the symbiotic connection between the education and participation of young people, and the significance of sustained adult mentorship in this dual process. The author concludes by arguing that the symbiotic relationship between education and participation is suggestive of the need to alter the way these concepts are viewed in terms of mainstream child rights discourse. The chapter entitled "From Education to Equality? Bolivian Adolescent Males' Understanding of Gender Equality in the Wake of Sensitivity Workshops" by C. Gervais examines the evolving perceptions of a group of young Indigenous boys following their participation in community-based workshops in Bolivia. The workshops focused on human rights and gender equality among adolescents and through the voices of numerous former male workshop participants, the results reveal how the boys' attitudes changed regarding gender equity as well as the challenges that such attitude change entailed. The author concludes that ongoing proequality education is essential and that further research on the long-term effects of rights education among young people is needed.

The final section of the book, which examines *community-based approaches to child rights and protection*, comprises four chapters that describe alternative intervention approaches that rely on community-based actions for the protection of children's rights. Essentially, these chapters demonstrate attempts to work with the existing local resources and members of local communities, rather than relying on externally designed and administered programs for children. The chapter entitled "The Wayo Programme in Northern Uganda: Building on Traditional Assets in Supporting Acholi Young Women and Girls in the Context of War and HIV" by S. Patel, P. Spittal, H. Muyinda, G. Oyat, and N. Sewankambo examines the experiences of girls in three displacement camps in Northern Uganda. Using qualitative and quantitative methods, the authors examined girls' understanding of gender-based violence, their levels of sexual knowledge, their vulnerability to HIV/AIDS, and a traditional system long established for the combined socialization and protection of girls in Acholi society. The results of this study indicate that the inclusion of traditional teachings and contemporary approaches to health and sex education provide a "middle road" between tradition and modernity in the protection of girls at risk of violence in a period of conflict.

The chapter "Rethinking the Orphan Crisis: Community-based Responses to Orphan Care in Malawi" by L. Riley and E. Lupafya challenges the prevailing crisis narrative that depicts Malawian orphans as uniformly "helpless." By challenging this narrative and the corresponding propensity of outside agencies to "save" orphans, the authors present an alternative point of view regarding the need to support communities that are striving to provide for orphans and other vulnerable children. As the authors observe, the disadvantages confronting orphans in Malawi have less to do with their orphanhood per se than they do with the broader context of poverty and social inequality in Malawi. They emphasize the importance of policies and programs that focus on strengthening existing systems of community support for children and the expansion of social services such as education and health care that can strengthen children's existing reserves of resilience.

The chapter "The Fluctuations of Child Worker Support: A Study of Female Domestic Workers in Senegal" by D. Lavan and R. Maclure examines the working conditions of girls and young women as household domestics, and corresponding NGO efforts to mobilize domestic workers, along with other child workers, in defense of the rights of working children in Senegal. Yet as the chapter indicates, the advancement of the rights of female domestic workers appears to have waned in recent years, in large part because of the misplaced assumptions underlying child-centered strategies of assistance and the notion of "child protagonism" as a conceptual basis for such strategies. As the authors indicate, child protagonism should not be equated with child autonomy, nor can it discount the realities of the fluctuations of children's development and interest as they grow up. The authors conclude by arguing that in order to provide sustained support for working children, there is a need for the aid industry to focus less on the operational complexities of institutionalized aid partnerships, and to be more sensitive to local realities of working people.

The final chapter in this section, entitled "Circles of Care: Community-Based Child Protection in South Africa," by P. Cook and L. DuToit examines an attempt to provide support to children, families, and communities living with HIV/AIDS. The "Circles of Care" project was an effort to merge children's rights policy and practice, with special attention to mitigating the suffering and social pressures stemming from HIV/AIDS. By drawing on their cultural capital and inherent resilience, at-risk children, their families, neighbors, and local governments collaboratively developed a community-based child protection model, informed by a participatory research strategy. The project focused on examining support and protection strategies to assist vulnerable children, developing local human resources, by strengthening the resilience of community leaders, families, and children, and enhancing their capacities to contribute to both the development and implementation of child protection policies, as well as strengthening action research capacities. In this particular study, the methodology allowed for the identification and creation of local assets to support vulnerable children and youth and at the same time reinforced collective adult self-efficacy in support of vulnerable children. The authors found that participatory interventions can be an effective tool in supporting children living with HIV/AIDS and poverty.

While the essays in this collection have dealt with a number of significant topics concerning children's rights, it must be noted that other areas of serious concern have not been covered. Future research on children's rights is, therefore, essential in a number of noteworthy areas: child trafficking, the conditions of Indigenous youth and the impact of race and ethnicity on rights' recognition, the rights of children and young persons with disabilities or other health concerns, children and youth who are homeless or street-involved, and refugees or those who have been internally displaced. Finally, the significance of children's education in the developing world cannot be understated, and research regarding how to foster conditions to ensure this significant right beyond outmoded forms of pedantic, hierarchical school, particularly for millions of children who either have no access to school, or who are marginalized by their experience in schools, is sorely needed.

Although a number of chapters in this collection have underscored the importance of children's agency and participation in decisions that affect them, the difficulties in ensuring authentic children's participation are evident. Nonetheless, attention has been paid to what has been termed as a new "social studies of childhood," which repositions children as social actors, with viewpoints and distinct experiences that deserve as much scholarly attention as adults (Riley, this edition). Some of the chapters in this edition, through their participatory methodologies that involved children and youth, while valuing their perspectives and opinions, could likely fall under this categorization. This positioning reinforces the notion that young people are the vanguard of human rights activism, capable of exercising their agency in opposition to discriminatory attitudes and practices (Gervais, this edition; Quijada, 2008). Also noted is that when availed of adequate information and opportunities to participate, young people are often capable of making well-informed and responsible judgments (Maclure, this edition).

The clash between old and new worlds, so evident in the developing states in the Southern Hemisphere, also poses challenges for the acknowledgment and recognition of children's rights. While economic, social, and political realities dictate the roles and responsibilities for many children in the developing world, the media play a significant role in inundating children and youth with modern images that promote market-oriented consumerism and personal aspirations that are often beyond their reach. However, the research in Uganda by Patel et al. (this edition) is hopeful as it presents a "middle road" approach, one that includes both traditional and modern forms of support for children capable of generating positive and empowering results. Through the active engagement of community members, families, and children in finding solutions to the conditions that undermine their fundamental rights, efforts to combine community knowledge and experience with empirically effective external forms of assistance can, we believe, contribute significantly to the enhancement of children's rights.

The importance of realizing children's rights, despite the multitude of challenges in doing so, cannot be overstated. In the developing world, children tend to represent the largest portion of the population and children's overall engagement and their inclusion in socioeconomic and political spheres are key to involved citizenship. It is unacceptable that children, including those who were a part of the research in this collection, continue to suffer. It is also unacceptable that the nation states where these children reside are signatories to the CRC, where rights mentioned and acknowledged both on paper and in international forums are not recognized in practice, with devastating consequences. Children deserve to live in conditions of harmony and safety, where they can be assured of meaningful survival and access to health and education services, where they can be part of a safe family and community environment and accordingly be afforded the opportunity for nurture and healthy growth. Regardless of where a child is born or raised, all children around the world deserve these most basic of rights.

Notes

1. By children, this book refers to the definition set out in the United Nations Convention on the Rights of the Child. According to the Convention, a child is defined as "every human being below eighteen years" (Article 1). "Children" refers equally to both boys and girls.
2. The only two nation states that have not ratified the CRC are Somalia and the United States of America.
3. These include the chapters written by L. Riley, C. Gervais, D. Lavan, and R. Maclure.
4. Chapter 10, written by V. Stavrou, provides examples of girls' experiences as child soldiers.

References

Bisht, R. (2008). Who Is a Child? : The Adults' Perspective within Adult-Child Relationship in India. *Special Issue: Relationship Research in India and South Asia—Interpersona, 2*(2), 151–172.

Denov, M. (2005). Children's Rights, Juvenile Justice, and the UN *Convention on the Rights of the Child:* Implications for Canada. In K. Campbell (Ed.), *Understanding Youth Justice in Canada,* pp. 65–88. Toronto: Pearson Education Canada.

Denov, M. (2010). *Child Soldiers: Sierra Leone's Revolutionary United Front.* Cambridge: Cambridge University Press.

Guggenheim, M. (2005). *What's Wrong with Children's Rights.* Cambridge, MA: Harvard University Press.

Malone, D., & Hagman, L. (2002). The North-South Divide at the United Nations: Fading at Last? *Security Dialogue, 33*(4), 399–414.

Mawson, A. (2004). Children, Impunity and Justice: Some Dilemmas from Northern Uganda. In J. Boyden and J. de Berry (Eds.), *Children and Youth on the Front Line: Ethnography, Armed Conflict and Displacement.* New York: Berghahn Books.

United Nations Children's Fund (UNICEF). (2006). Convention on the Rights of the Child. Retrieved from www.unicef.org/crc/index_30229.html

Woodhouse, B. (2000). Children's Rights. *U of Penn. Law School,* Public Law Working Paper No. 06.

PART I

Children and Institutional Care

CHAPTER 1

Home Truths: Children's Rights in Institutional Care in Sri Lanka

*Dharshini Seneviratne and Fahmida Mariam**

Contextualizing Children's Institutionalization

According to the United Nations (UN), as many as 8 million children worldwide live in institutional care (UNICEF, 2009). Particularly in the developing world, institutional care is commonly imposed as a means of "rescuing" impoverished or otherwise disadvantaged youth (Fox-Harding, 1997). Although institutional care has generally been associated with caring for orphans who have lost both parents, Prisiazhnaia (2008) has recognized an increasing trend of institutionalizing children who would be considered "social orphans," that is, children who are "deprived . . . [of] parental care even though . . . [their] parents are alive" (p. 24). Indeed, Bilson and Cox (2007, p. 48) have argued that rather than parental death, "poverty is a major factor in the use of institutional care" in the developing world.

Institutional care, and its impact on young people, has been an often-studied field. In fact, academic research has repeatedly highlighted the various negative effects of institutionalization, including medical problems and widespread diseases (Frank, Klass, Earls, & Eisenberg, 1996), educational delays (Chitiyo, Changara, & Chitiyo, 2008; Frank et. al., 1996), stunted intellectual growth (Van-Ijzendoorn, Luijk, M. P. C. M., & Juffer, 2008), obstructed social and cognitive development (Johnson, 2000; Miller, 2005; Şimşek, Erol, Öztop, & Özer-Özcan, 2007) and behavioral and emotional problems among the children (Bilson and Cox, 2007; Şimşek et. al., 2008). For example, Frank et al. (1996) argue that institutions often fostered a deterioration in a child's health, particularly as they are fraught with diets of inadequate nutritional quantity and quality, offer children minimal recreational opportunities for physical activities, and given the large numbers of children housed together, often promotes the spread of infectious diseases.

Moreover, the psychological effects of institutionalization are vast. For example, the associated stigma, often experienced by children, may "decrease [their] self-confidence, [and] increase [their] feelings of loneliness and hopelessness, and... [their] psychological symptoms" (Rosen, Walter, Casey, & Hocking, 2000; cited in Şimşek et. al., 2008, p. 10). Also, institutional care greatly increases the prevalence of internalized problems, including "anxiety, depression and somatic disorders," and externalized problems, including "aggressive behaviors and rule-breaking," and "fatalistic thinking" among children (Şimşek et. al., 2008, pp. 9–10). This form of thinking involves a belief that "one's life belongs to an external power and neglect of one's own responsibility" and has a significantly negative effect on institutionalized youth's mental health as well as their future social integration (Şimşek et. al., 2008). Prisiazhnaia (2008, p. 26) likewise argues that institutional environments restrict children's "social experiences," leaving adolescents unable to "form an appropriate set of ideas about the life of society and the rules that govern functioning in society." In this way, institutional care lacks much of the educational, social, emotional, and cognitive challenges required by children for healthy development.

On the basis of these arguments, Bilson and Cox (2007) have observed that the notion of "rescuing" children may "devalue" the developmental benefits of parental involvement in a child's upbringing, and instead may focus on "the perceived inadequacies of parents." Studying the precarious and specific case of institutionalization in Sri Lanka, Bilson and Cox observed that a "key theme identified from the focus groups with children was that they wanted, above all, to be with their families" even when the physical conditions of the institution were "good" (pp. 41, 48). Given these challenges, we sought to provide a general overview of institutional care in Sri Lanka, and describe and explore the experiences of young people in such settings.

This chapter is based on a research study[1] conducted by Save the Children in Sri Lanka, funded by the Canadian International Development Agency. Stemming from the knowledge that institutional care for children was becoming the primary option for families in difficult financial circumstances (de Silva, 1981), we sought to provide basic information on children's institutions, both state-run and non–state run[2] in the Northern and Eastern, Southern, Western, and Central provinces, to highlight the quality of institutional services implicated in children's care, and to identify and assess gaps in existing policies and procedures relating to children's institutions. The research findings highlight the vast disparity between "official" and actual numbers associated with institutions, and address current practices, including a lack of material resources, privacy, and individuality for children within institutions. The chapter concludes by describing the implications of the study, and provides policy and programatic recommendations for Sri Lankan institutions in order to better adhere to standards of international children's rights.

Institutional Care in Sri Lanka

Since the early 1900s, economic and sociopolitical changes in Sri Lanka have increased the pressure on families to institutionalize their children. This shift has occurred as a result of economic and war-related hardships because of which families are less able to depend on extended family and traditional support structures[3] for childcare. While some parents struggle to balance (albeit minimally paid) employment with caring for their children, a vast number of the poorest families turn to institutionalization (de Silva, 1981). Supported by the Department of Probation and Childcare's probation officers, these placements often take on disadvantaged children without a thorough consideration of viable and more "child-friendly" alternatives.

In emergency situations, both natural and man-made, the risk of children being institutionalized further increases. For example, the protracted civil war between the government of Sri Lanka and the Liberation Tigers of Tamil Eelam (LTTE) increased the numbers of children in need of care and protection, especially in the Northeast. In this region, well-meaning philanthropists channeled funds to build and operate institutions for war-affected children.

Overall, according to the Department of Probation and Child Care Services (DPCC), which administers state institutions and regulates private institutions, there were 223 children's institutions and 11,495 children in institutional care in 2002 countrywide (Department of Probation, 2002). This represented a sharp increase in the number of institutions since 1991 when there were only 142 institutions registered with the DPCC (Wijethunge, 1991). However, most of the children's institutions in these areas were not registered at the time of the aforementioned study and, therefore, were not reflected in national statistics.

Delinquency and minor crimes among children have also prompted some parents to access the justice system when "they cannot control [their children] at home. Their concern for the child and fear that he [*sic*] will enter a life of crime make them seek court assistance" (de Silva, 1981). Moreover, many cases of juvenile delinquency referred to the DPCC have centered on instances of petty theft, mainly arising in significantly impoverished homes. De Silva (1981) found that "more than 93% [of remanded children] were from homes whose monthly incomes were less than Rs. 50 . . . (then about US $7)." Yet in offering an apparent blanket solution, institutionalization has failed to address the underlying causes of families' difficulties in supporting their children, and has thus further hindered the well-being of these children.

As such, there have been prolonged discussions by both government and nongovernmental agencies on the abuse of children's rights through institutionalization and the need to look for alternative care options within children's homes or in family-style settings. In practice, however, few positive steps have been taken by state or private bodies to address the issue.

Guidelines for Protection and Care

A key underlying reference point of this chapter is the UN Convention on the Rights of the Child (UNCRC) (1989), the treaty that most effectively articulates standards of international children's rights. By signing onto this Convention, countries have "accepted their responsibility towards their country's children . . . [including] the right to basic standards of living, education, health, social security and time to play, [as well as] . . . protection from abuse and neglect" (Guest, 2003, p. 11). In greater detail, the standards enshrined in the UNCRC (1989) include the right of a child

1. to obtain guidance from parents and family (Article 5), preserve his or her identity and the right to family relations (Article 8) and live among, or to maintain regular contact with his/her parents (Article 9).
2. to his/her opinions, and right to freedom of expression (Articles 12 and 13) and association (Article 15).
3. to privacy, family, home, and correspondence (Article 16).
4. to freedom from abuse, and the right to rehabilitative care (Article 19).

5. to specific judicial considerations; for example, children in conflict with the law ought to have the right to be waived judicial processes where possible (Article 40).

The UNCRC, therefore, recognizes the value of family and community in providing children with an environment conducive to their survival and development, and upholds their rights as citizens, warranting their input in relevant policy matters. The Sri Lankan government, having ratified the UNCRC, is thus responsible for ensuring the rights of children. Nongovernmental organizations (NGOs) such as Save the Children have likewise incorporated the principles of the UNCRC in their program policies and strategies.

Accordingly, Save the Children's position on children in institutional care is that they are often "discriminated [against] with regard to education, employment, privacy, identity and association" (Save the Children, 2003). Long-term residential care, in other words, has a tendency to either overlook or directly violate children's rights. Save the Children in Sri Lanka, therefore, advocates strengthening deinstitutionalization mechanisms by mentoring government social care workers and probation officers in individual case analysis. It also advocates the need to strengthen family care options, explore means of prevention and diversion from institutionalization, and realign policy and practice toward international children's rights standards. Save the Children has also collaborated with government and other stakeholders in the formulation of quality of care standards in cases where, at the exhaustion of all other options, institutionalization is sought.

This study sought to contribute to research on the protection and rights of children living in institutional care in Sri Lanka, and to use the subsequent findings to promote evidence-based policy changes. Specifically, we aimed to (1) map, describe, and quantify basic information on children's institutions in the Northeast, Southern, Western, and Central provinces; (2) identify the causal factors implicated in children's institutionalization, and care alternatives; (3) assess gaps in existing institutional policies and procedures; and (4) explore institutional services and their capacity to meet children's needs, and to highlight practices for quality care. As such, we assessed resource availability and funding, causes of institutionalization, children's needs and service-delivery, capacity of caregivers, nature of interaction between children and caregivers, families and communities, awareness of the UNCRC and the measures taken to implement its principles.

Methodology

This study's two-stage methodology consisted of (1) identifying and comparing all existing institutions in the Western, Southern, Central, and Northeastern provinces, and (2) providing contextual information on institutionalized children's experiences, via participant observation and focus group discussions. The first stage involved comparing and merging several sources of data on institutions, including data from provincial Departments of Probation and Childcare. An analysis of policy documents was conducted to explore and compare Sri Lanka's institutionalization policies and practices. Overall, the type of information collected included statistics on the types of institutions, the numbers of children in such institutions, information on the ethnicity, religion, gender and age of children, and facilities and assets of institutions.

Of the total of 329 institutions identified, a sample of 86 institutions was selected for the second portion of the study. The provincial breakdown for the sampled institutions included 13 out of the total 35 (35 percent) institutions in the Central province, 8 out of 31 in the Southern province (26 percent), 22 out of 89 (25 percent) in the Western province, and 43 out of 174 (24 percent) in the Northeastern province.

All of the selected institutions included state-run institutions, voluntary institutions, and institutions for children with disabilities.[4] A representative sample of the state-run institutions was selected, with a stratified random sample of the two other types of institutions. Not all categories were selected in each province due to the unavailability of certain categories in a few of the provinces. Three school hostels were also included in the in-depth study of the Northeast province, given that the role of boarding schools went beyond that of regular schools during the war. Moreover, two institutions that address counseling and training for children either in conflict with the law, or victims of abuse, were included in the study as they too provided an institutional context.

The researchers, who were specifically trained in conducting research with children, observed each of the selected institutions for a five-day period, studying 2,655 children in voluntary and 306 children in state-run institutions, all residents of the sampled facilities. Researchers explained the study to all of the institutional stakeholders, including the administrators, caregivers, and children, and obtained their consent to participate in the study. The researchers observed the caregiver-child interactions, the daily routines, the relationships among children, the level of parental involvement, and the services and facilities offered to the children. In addition, qualitative information was collected from children through participatory methods, including focus group discussions. Many other institutional-affiliates, including the state's Child Rights Promotion Officers (CRPOs), probation officers of the provincial Departments of Probation and Childcare, teachers, heads of institutions and schools, and religious leaders were interviewed using a semistructured interview schedule.

Consistent with a rights-based approach, the study centralizes the children's experiences of institutions. Children were involved in developing the research focus and participated in as many of the research stages as possible, including the initial consultation about their involvement. A Children's Research Advisory Group, comprising 10 children, participated in the training and sensitization of the research assistants, and commented on the research design and findings. Also, a range of child-friendly research techniques[5] was used throughout the study to enable optimum input from children. In fact, children's involvement both as research participants and members of the Advisory Group enabled a greater focus on issues of "child-friendliness" of institutions, such as their impacts on children's privacy, dignity, and individuality.

Research Findings

Overall, the research findings indicate that institutional care in Sri Lanka contravenes many of the rights set out in the UNCRC (1989). Institutions generally hinder, and often intentionally limit, contact and visitation with families, communities, and other children. Moreover, they commonly neglect children's individual and personal care, offer little stimulation, and rarely respond effectively to the medical and psychological needs of children. The widespread stigmatization and segregation of children was also noted, which appeared to compound the difficulties in adjusting to life outside institutional care. These issues are explored in greater detail below.

Policy Review

The care of children "needing support and protection" falls under the purview of several Sri Lankan ministries. These include the DPCC, the Department of Social Services, the Ministry of Labour, the police, the National Child Protection Authority (NCPA), and Child Rights Promotion Officers (CRPOs). For example, the NCPA, a division of the Ministry of Child Development, is mandated with "recommending appropriate steps for the safety and protection of children in conflict with the law and monitoring organizations which provide care for children" (Government of Sri Lanka, 2008). However, institutions for children with disabilities are registered and monitored by the Department of Social Services within the Ministry of Social Welfare. This fragmentation, in effect, fosters a situation in which no single agency assumes overall responsibility for the child's welfare throughout the entire process. Compounding the challenges to providing consistent care to institutionalized young people, there is no official coordination between these agencies.

Despite these constraints, a review of policy documents indicates that Sri Lanka has nonetheless officially recognized the negative impacts of institutionalization, and the importance of family-based care for children. The State Department of Probation and Childcare,[6] for example, has a long-standing official policy that emphasizes the importance of keeping children within their families and communities (Government of Sri Lanka, 1976). It mandates that probation officers, who are involved in all decisions regarding children's institutionalization, are not to admit a child to care facilities until all alternatives have been fully explored, should not place a child in an institution for economic reasons, and must limit all placements for three-year periods. In addition, when used as a last resort, children ought to be institutionalized in facilities within their own communities (Government of Sri Lanka, 1976). Nevertheless, as the following findings highlight, everyday practice often circumvents these official policies.

Overview of Sri Lankan Institutions and Their Child Residents

There is a vast disparity between the officially reported and actual numbers of institutions and their child residents. According to the Statistical Report of the Department of Probation and Childcare Services (2002), there were 11,495 children in 223 institutions throughout the country in that year. This study, however, uncovered evidence indicating that 15,558 children were living in 329 institutions in the 4 provinces. Of these, 8,622 (57.22 percent) children were in the Northeastern province, indicating a sizable trend of national underreporting, particularly of unregulated institutions that grew exponentially during the war. This was further exacerbated by the lack of comprehensive government monitoring and assessment mechanisms. In addition, there were no state-run homes in the Northeastern province, which often led children to being relocated to institutions that were geographically distant from their own familial, social, and cultural contexts.

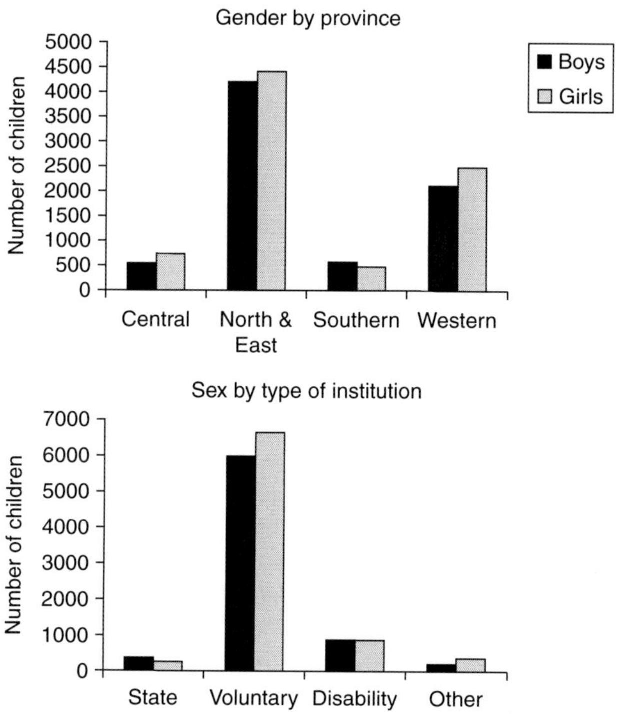

Figure 1.1 Gender and sex of gender by province and type of institution.

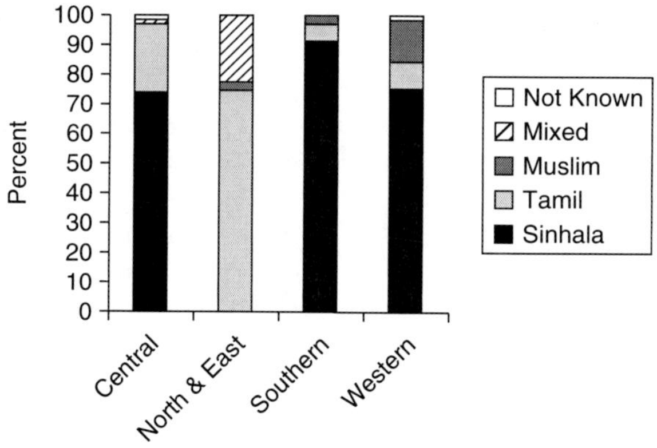

Figure 1.2 Ethnicity of children by province.

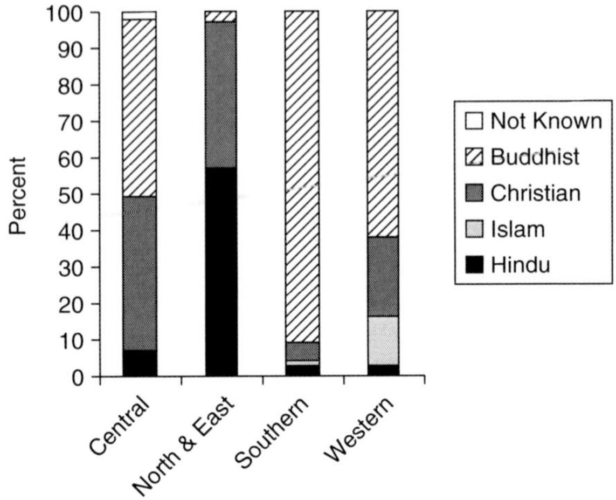

Figure 1.3 Religion of children by province.

In our sample, we identified the following statistics: 4,594 children institutionalized in the Western Province, 1,063 children in Southern Province, and 8,622 children in Northeastern Province. Data from the Southern and Western provinces indicate that a large proportion, 63 percent (n=262) and 31 percent (n=375) respectively, of the children were placed outside their provinces of origin.[7] In our subsequent focus group discussions, children who were placed outside their communities often noted that they were discouraged from speaking their own language and practicing their own religion, especially where the majority population's language and faith was different from their own. Moreover, children who were placed far from their families and communities experienced difficulties in maintaining familial contact, particularly as some institutions discouraged such contact, hindering the children's sense of connectedness.

The data also indicate a slight male/female imbalance among child residents, with the boys representing 47.8 percent (n=7442) and girls comprising 52.2 percent (n=8116) of children in care. The largest proportion of children in institutions was aged 11–18 years, followed by a large group of 5–10 year olds. The remainder consisted of a small group of children under 5 years old, most of whom had been abandoned at birth or handed to institutions by their families at a young age, and a another group over 18 years old who continued to reside in the institutions because of a lack of systematic societal reintegration mechanisms.

Table 1.1 Number of children by gender in children's institutions by province

Province	*Boys*	*Girls*	*Total*
Western	2111 (45.9%)	2483 (54%)	4594
Southern	580 (54.6%)	483 (45.4%)	1063
Northeast	4209 (48.8%)	4413 (51.2%)	8622
Central	542 (42.4%)	737 (57.6%)	1279
Total	7442 (47.8%)	8116 (52.2%)	15,558

The number of "adult" (over 18 years) residents was particularly high in the Northeast province, where 15 percent (n=284) of the males and 13percent (n=232) of the females in institutional care remained at the facilities following their eighteenth birthdays.

Despite DPCC policy that children not remain in an institution for over three years, of the 15,558 children identified in all institutions, 36.7 percent of children in voluntary institutions in the Southern province, 50.3 percent of children in the Western province, and 33.7 percent of the children in the Northeast had lived in the institutions for more than three years. Also, although official national policy dictates that state-run remand homes must limit the residency of children to a maximum of two weeks, in the Southern and Western provinces, an average of 8.5 percent of children had resided over a year in homes. Inevitably, these delayed "graduations" were straining the already-scarce resources available to these homes.

Causes of Entry to Institutions

> I receive everything here. But I value my parents and sisters' and brothers' love and affection. It may be because of sins committed in my previous birth that I do not get their love. (Child focus group participant)

Contrary to popular opinion that children entering voluntary institutions are mainly orphans, only 8 percent of the 2,655 children in such institutions were identified as having both parents deceased. Among the vast majority could be considered what was noted earlier as "social orphans" (Prisiazhnaia, 2008, p. 24). In fact, 50 percent (n=1328) had two living parents,[8] and 29 percent (n=770) had one living parent. A proportionately similar picture was found in the state institutions, where the sample included 306 children.

While poverty was the main factor mentioned in over half the state-run and voluntary institutions, the research uncovered a wide range of causal factors implicated in children's institutionalization. These included economic hardships, parents' marital disharmony, domestic abuse, parental struggles with addiction(s), death of a parent, and parents' migration to other regions in search of paid employment. Another reason for institutionalization, notably in the Northeast, was parents' desire to provide a good education for their children. In general, given their dire economic constraints and the prevailing armed conflict, most of these parents saw institutions as offering better material resources and educational opportunities than they themselves could provide. Other children in state institutions, specifically in remand homes, had been placed following conflict with the law. Many children were being held for lengthy periods despite having committed minor offenses, a practice that was exacerbated by delays in the criminal justice system.

Quality of Care

Standards of quality for children's homes are often judged by assessing the environmental conditions and the overall quality of life that they provide (Bilson and Gotestam, 2003). The study used the state-prescribed minimum standards for voluntary institutions as a basis for measuring the performance of all homes in the study.[9] The institutional environment was assessed by looking at institutions' physical conditions, including the facilities and resource availability. The institutional quality of life was also examined including caregiver-child relationships, familial contact, and the programmatic assistance offered to the children.

Institutional Environment

Overall, the quality of physical care in voluntary institutions varied from poor to satisfactory. In contrast, conditions for children in state-run institutions were extremely poor, including overcrowding, poor sanitation, inadequate supplies of basic necessities such as clothing, nutritious food, water, and hygiene materials, as well as inadequate sleeping arrangements. Some children spoke of sleeping on cement floors in the cold or damp corridors year-round. Upon further observation, we discovered that 38 percent (n=66) of the homes in the Northeast province did not have beds for children. Where beds were provided, only 49.5 percent (n=909) of the children thought they were adequate. According to the focus group discussions, the lack of proper sleeping facilities led some children to feel insecure and unsafe. These feelings were further exacerbated by the lack of individual storage for clothes and other possessions in state-run homes, resulting in instances of theft and invasions of privacy.

Children in state institutions frequently indicated that they did not receive prompt or proper medical care, but rather experienced scolding when they fell ill, particularly as the staff often assumed they were faking illness. When they were ill other children were sometimes expected to care for them. When they visited hospitals because of illness, they were often identified as being from an institution, a label that many found to be discriminatory and upsetting. Children with disabilities were usually assisted expeditiously, but they did not receive regular assessments of their specific conditions such as impaired hearing or vision. In the Northeast, where the effects of war increased the number of children with disabilities, there was a lack of appropriate facilities and equipment for their specialized treatment and a shortage of trained and qualified staff.

Other quality of care issues covered by the research included access to education, recreation, and leisure. Overall, in most institutions, education was not provided consistently. For example, although children in state-run homes had access to schooling, there was no provision of library facilities or an environment conducive to effective learning. In many instances, children were absent from school because they were being teased when placed with children younger than themselves, as they often were, or because they experienced neglect resulting from teachers' prejudice against institutionalized children. Children with disabilities likewise often had inadequate access to facilities and specialized equipment, and were confronted with teachers who were generally untrained to deal with their unique needs.

Children in voluntary homes generally fared better, with more institutional encouragement to attend local schools. Nevertheless, as expressed in numerous focus groups, children in both state-run and voluntary homes tended not to appreciate traditional vocational training, such as sewing and carpentry, and instead were more keen to be trained in information technology. Opportunities for sport and leisure were not consistently available in either state homes or voluntary institutions. The proportion of these institutions without recreational facilities was respectively 25 percent (n=6) in the Western Province, 58 percent (n=5) in Southern Province, 40 percent (n=5) in Central Province, and 54 percent (n=23) in Northeast Province.

Quality of Life

> My home is far away. So my mother cannot come to see me. Here we do not have any one to tell our sorrow [to]. Even at a time of sickness, when

> we tell [that we are at risk], they scold us. My father and mother are not like that. (Child focus group participant)

The children's quality of life was assessed by observing their relationships with institutional personnel, the maintenance of familial contact (or lack thereof), and the institutional services offered to assist with their healthy development. Most children had minimal or no contact with their parents. Many parents were simply unable to afford transportation fees to visit their children or lacked resources to stay overnight. For most children, therefore, caregivers in the institutions were seen as surrogate parents, yet few experienced consistent or close relationships with their caregivers. Children's timetables and daily regimes allowed little input into the decisions affecting them. Indeed, as borne out in focus groups and observations, institutionalized children were rarely consulted about matters affecting them. In addition, children who had been abused prior to institutionalization did not receive specialized care from staff. Findings indicated that although some institutions housed a vast number of girls who had been victims of abuse, counseling services were available in only 49 percent (n=11) of institutions in the Western province, 26 percent (n=2) in the Southern province, 64 percent (n=8) in the Central province, and 62 percent (n=27) in the Northeastern province.

Few institutions showed any systematic propensity to monitor or evaluate children's progress or well-being throughout their state or nonstate residency, nor to plan for children's reintegration to their communities. This resulted in many children languishing in institutional facilities into adulthood. Not surprisingly, the absence of reintegration planning left many children feeling apprehensive about their future prospects for eventual familial and societal integration. Largely this was due to a paucity of methodical documentation and record-keeping among institutions and probation officers, and a lack of coordination among state and nonstate agencies responsible for institutionalized children.

Institutional Staff

> If we had the good fortune to stay with our parents we would not have to face scolding. (Child focus group participant)

Overall, at the time of this study, the vast majority of child agency staff was female, although in the Northeastern province there was relatively equal parity between male and female staff. Interviews with, and observations of, staff members revealed that many felt unqualified to care for institutionalized children, especially as they had received little or no training upon being hired. Complaints of insufficient numbers of institutional personnel and no regular external supervision or support were common. Staff members were unhappy with their salaries that were generally low: 55 percent of the staff in institutions in the Western province and 44 percent in the Southern province received a monthly salary of only Rs. 1,001– 3,000 (approx. US$10–28), and only 8 percent and 10 percent of the staff in the same institutions received a monthly salary of more than Rs. 6,000 (approx. US$58). Low salaries were a general trend in both state and nonstate institutions, and this fostered an environment in which caregivers often felt overworked, unappreciated, and unmotivated. Some spoke of the resulting frustration as a factor compounding resource-scarcity, and thus hindering the ability of institutions to care for children. Given these difficulties, staff turnover rates were consequently high.

Alternatives to Institutionalization

Despite considerable problems associated with the institutionalization of children in Sri Lanka, alternatives to institutional placement are minimal and underutilized. The fostering of children is a possibility through the Fit Persons Scheme whereby, following a court report and hearing, a child is placed under the supervision of a responsible "fit person."[10] However, given that institutional placement is far less complex, there is relatively little administrative and bureaucratic incentive to encourage fostering. Adoption can also provide a placement option. At the time of the research, national adoptions were on the rise and international adoptions declining (Department of Probation, 2002). Yet there is evidence of informal discrimination among prospective parents. During interviews, probation officers who are responsible for national adoption processes noted that adoptive parents were often highly particular about their child's physical appearance, and commonly preferred attractive, fair, and healthy babies, thus creating a backlog of children who fell outside these desired parameters. Such discrimination coupled with bureaucratic hurdles exacerbates the long waiting times for national adoption. Paradoxically, therefore, while there is a demand for adoptive children, and certainly a need for alternatives to discriminatory selection and institutionalization of children, bureaucratic constraints too often cause delays in the process.

Apart from the institutionalization of children, the government of Sri Lanka has undertaken a number of initiatives to provide support for impoverished families. These include the Kepakaru Mapiya Scheme and the Sevana Sarana Fund (both child sponsorship programs), and the Sisu Nena Kirana educational support program for families with twins and triplets. There are also social welfare programs that focus on poverty alleviation, nutrition, and medical support for vulnerable families. Children with disabilities are likewise entitled to hearing aids and wheelchairs and a state-sponsored monthly grant. Yet there is no public notification system or formal application process to promote these assistance options. Discretion remains with probation officers to identify children in "need" and refer them to the DPCC for grant consideration. This ambiguous procedure explains why so few children receive essential support services.

Other difficulties concerning community alternatives include the scarcity of social services in some regions, bureaucratic and time-related obstacles that hinder probation officers' ability to adequately assess available options, and a lack of awareness regarding alternatives and social welfare mechanisms among the community and service providers. According to the probation officers interviewed, these obstacles detract from the proper assessment of individual cases and the development of locally based family-centered services. There is also a specific problem in the Northeastern province, where many of the alternatives managed by the national government were not implemented because CRPOs and probation officers were not provided with translated documents and forms for Tamil-speaking populations. In such circumstances, institutionalization is often implicitly accepted as the only alternative available to families, implemented as a "first resort" for children rather than as a "last resort" as stipulated by government policy.

Good Practices

Although much of the findings of this study highlighted practices and environments that are detrimental to children's rights, health, and development, our observations nonetheless yielded a few "child-friendly" practices in a handful of institutions. These good practices were observed primarily in nonstate institutions and were often initiated by individual staff members. Notable among these practices were the following:

1. The provision of overnight accommodations for visiting parents, and permission to take their children outside the institutional environment to nearby shops.

2. The implementation of child-friendly routines, such as informal visits to the kitchen after school if children are hungry.
3. The inclusion of caregivers' own children in their work with institutionalized children, thus fostering wider peer networks.
4. Efforts to ensure quality education through the provision of extra classes and time set aside for homework.
5. The provision of vocational opportunities such as job training and placements with employers so that children can have secure incomes upon leaving institutions.

These innovative, yet rare practices that prioritize children's psychosocial well-being help bridge institutional care and children's rights standards and serve as a basis for the following discussion and recommendations.

Discussion

The most salient lesson of this research centered on the fundamental gap between the UNCRC's (1989) principles and the practices and environments of childcare institutions in Sri Lanka. Through the isolation associated with institutionalization, children experience obstructions to their "harmonious development." They are unable to "preserve" their "familial relations"; they are deprived of regular contact with their parents; and they cannot "freely express their views in all matters affecting" them (UNCRC, 1989, preamble; Article 8, 9, 12). As this study has shown, institutional care in Sri Lanka has too often failed to safeguard "the best interests of the child" (UNCRC, 1989, Article 3). There is a singular lack of congruence between government policies espousing the need for family-based care, and the widespread practices of child institutionalization. This divergence derives from official as well as popular perceptions of children at risk as implicitly "less deserving" of the emotional and material care considered to be essential for a child's healthy development.

In an effort to promote child-friendly priorities, we conclude this chapter by proposing recommendations to align children's institutionalization in Sri Lanka with the country's international commitment to the UNCRC.

Focusing on Root Causes

Any interventions designed to address concerns raised in this study should first of all consider root causes, such as economic policies and social welfare cuts, which have put both families and childcare services in considerable hardship, and have thus limited the provision of effective child welfare services. Interventions must prioritize support for family and community as the social bases of children's well-being and incorporate the involvement of family and community in childcare to the greatest degree possible. Thorough evaluations that assess root causes of problems confronting individual children and their families must be undertaken to ensure that institutionalization is implemented only when it is in the children's best interests.

Quality of Care

Where institutionalization is deemed to be in children's best interests, young people's views regarding (1) their care plan, (2) their day-to-day care, and (3) their concerns and complaints should be regularly gathered and compiled. Children and their parents should be involved in formulating the care plan detailing their needs, arrangements for familial contact, and a strategy for eventual reunification or long-term placement options. Care plans should reflect and address children's individual health, psychosocial, and educational needs, and prioritize family reunification and social reintegration. Above all, children's feelings and familial input must be the principal underlying factors of this needs assessment and care planning.

In light of the children's descriptions of strictly regimented routines and inadequate living environments, it is imperative that "quality of care" in institutional practices be broadened to reflect concepts of integrity, privacy, individuality, and participation (seeking children's input regarding their daily activities and the services provided to them). Child participants in the study consistently expressed these desires. We share this perspective and accordingly sought to ensure that this study served as a vehicle for children to be "heard." In our view, children should be able to participate fully in the life of the local community and be encouraged to access community resources and activities, including playgrounds and community halls, as though they were permanent residents. To facilitate this process, staff should be in contact with local residents, develop progressive plans for the children's involvement, and oversee their access to such local education. Children should likewise be allowed to see their care plans and records when they wish, and their views must be sought in all matters, as is set out in UNCRC Articles 9 and 12. In addition, they should be permitted to contribute input and provide feedback to the staff on their experiences in the institutions.

In each institution, such feedback should be overseen by a representative group of all institutional stakeholders, and include a children's advisory group. CRPOs could monitor the documented feedback and complaints, as well as the subsequent remedial actions taken. In order to improve the accountability toward children, records ought to be kept both at each institution and with the DPCC. Equally critical to this process is the necessity of an attitudinal shift among childcare workers. This will require additional training regarding the developmental benefits of consulting children, and promoting the maximum allowable familial and social contacts is essential.

Children in Conflict with the Law

The particular treatment of children in conflict with the law should likewise be subject to substantive reforms. Given inadequate staff training, resource scarcity, and bureaucratic barriers that prioritize the least complex means of channelling children's cases, children in conflict with the law may end up in institutions without a proper assessment of their cases, and an in-depth exploration of institutional alternatives. Too often, therefore, they may be sent to state remand homes for minor crimes that could be addressed through rehabilitation programs or probation. Thus, there is also a need for attitudinal change among legal decision makers such as magistrates, lawyers, and probation officers in assessing each case individually. This would be in line with Article 40 of the UNCRC (1989), which states that, wherever possible, children in conflict with the law should be diverted from judicial proceedings. Instead, they should be provided with care, guidance, and supervision.

Registration, Monitoring, and Coordination

Provincial DPCCs should systematically monitor institutions, evaluate the competencies of their caregivers, and review the registration of institutions every couple of years. Failure to comply with the aforementioned childcare standards should have clear and direct consequences, including the potential removal of an institution's formal registration, and thus its legal status. This sanction would deprive the institution of nominal state-sponsored, per-child funding, and would subsequently threaten facility closure.

Moreover, all institutions, probation offices, and services working with children should have staff development plans that cover the necessary professional skills, with a corresponding system of training, supervision, and support. When hired, each staff member should be provided with such a plan, and this should be regularly reviewed as part of an ongoing self-improvement process. Training should continue throughout their careers, and staff should be encouraged to enroll in additional training opportunities wherever possible.

Expansion of Alternatives to Child Institutionalization

Above all, it is imperative to reduce institutional care incentives and options. To achieve this, police, courts, and childcare agencies should be coordinated centrally under the DPCC. Each provincial DPCC should develop a plan that includes a range of family and community-based services, and short-term temporary placements for some children, that will serve as alternatives to long-term institutionalized care. Likewise, each province should devise its own culturally relevant alternatives in consultation with educational and health practitioners, *grama niladharis* (village officials), community leaders, parents, and children themselves. Additional funding and material support should be provided for alternative services. This undoubtedly would help to motivate officials in seeking out these alternative options, as the "money would follow the client" (Fox & Gotestam, 2003).

Conclusion

In keeping with Save the Children's advocacy-related objectives, this study has promoted dialogue on institutional care issues in Sri Lanka. Since the completion of the study, Save the Children has collaborated closely with the Sri Lankan government's Ministry of Social Welfare and Social Services, and the Department of Probation and Childcare to disseminate the study's recommendations, and draft new minimum standards for all institutions. The findings have also been a strong basis for the design of formal admission criteria, care and reunification plans, community-based care and life skills development. Save the Children hopes that the positive momentum will be maintained within the Ministry of Child Development and Women's Empowerment that was created in November 2005. Fittingly, the aim of this department is to create real change in the lives of institutionalized children and bring their experiences into alignment with international children's rights standards.

Notes

* We would like to acknowledge Harini Amarasuriya and Ramani Jayathilake who contributed to the original report.

1. In September 2003, Save the Children in Sri Lanka, supported by Save the Children Canada, commissioned three centers of research to conduct the study: the University of Colombo to study the Western and Southern provinces.
2. The types of institutions that came under the purview of the study included *state homes*, which fall under the responsibility of the Department of Probation and Childcare (DPCC), and *nonstate homes*. State homes included *remand homes* for children in conflict with the law, *certified/approved schools* for the rehabilitation of children who are convicted of crimes, or victims of abuse, *detention homes*, for street children and children in other difficult circumstances, *national training centers* for the rehabilitation of victims of child abuse, and *receiving homes* for children up to the age of five years. Homes for children with disabilities were also run by the state and are either administered through or assessed by the Department of Social Services. All nonstate homes, by regulation, should be registered with and monitored by the probation officers of the DPCC.
3. Religious institutions have historically offered impoverished families support through education, food, and accommodation. Moreover, some landowners have provided informal foster care to poorer families by providing food and accommodation to their servants' families. However, these support structures are gradually eroding, particularly given both economic and political shifts, which make resources scarce.
4. Approximately 8 percent of institutions in Sri Lanka were state-run; these largely catered to children convicted of crimes, and victims of abuse. Private homes are set up independently, but require registration with the Provincial Departments of Probation and Childcare or the Department of Social Services. However, this compulsory registration is often unmonitored and thus frequently not implemented in practice.
5. These child-friendly research techniques included Venn diagrams, pairwise ranking, diamond ranking, and the barometer.
6. The State Department of Probation and Childcare falls within the jurisdiction of the new Ministry of Child Development and Women's Empowerment. This is the key agency responsible for ensuring the welfare of children in institutions.
7. Unfortunately, no data was available from government or other sources on the numbers of "out of province" child institutional residents in either the Northeastern or Central provinces.
8. However, 18 percent (n=239) of these children had been living in a home where the parents had separated.

9. At the study's commencement, these were the only available standards by which the researchers could assess institutional environments and practices. As a result of the advocacy around institutional care issues, partially based on this study (and in participation with Save the Children, Sri Lanka), a common set of minimum standards for both state and nonstate institutions have since been formulated. The findings on children's perceptions of care in institutions were integral to the formation of these new minimum standards.
10. Section 17 of the Children's and Young Person's Ordinance (CYPO) of Sri Lanka defines a "fit person" as one who is of the same religion as the child to be fostered, or one who undertakes to bring up the child according to these religious values. The "fit person" has the same rights, powers, and liabilities as a parent. There are no further criteria for the selection of a fit person, which is at the discretion of the case's probation officer.

References

Bilson, A., & Cox, P. (2007). Caring about Poverty: Alternatives to Institutional Care for Children in Poverty. *Journal of Children & Poverty, 13*(1), 37–55.

Bilson, A., & Gotestam, R. (2003). Improving Standards of Child Protection Services. *Changing Minds, Policies and Lives.* United Nations Children's Fund (UNICEF)/ World Bank Series. Florence, Italy: UNICEF Innocenti Research Centre.

Child Protection from Violence, Exploitation and Abuse. (2009). *UNICEF.* Retrieved from http://www.unicef.org/media/media_45451.html.

Chitiyo, M., Changara, D. M., & Chitiyo, G. (2008). Providing Psychosocial Support to Special Needs Children: A Case of Orphans and Vulnerable Children in Zimbabwe. *International Journal of Educational Development, 28,* 384–392.

Death by Default: A Policy of Fatal Neglect in China's Orphanages. (1996). *Human Rights Watch: Asia.* New York: Human Rights Watch-Asia.

Department of Probation and Childcare Services. (2002). *Statistical Report 2002.* Colombo, Sri Lanka: Department of Probation and Childcare Services.

De Silva, K. M. (1981). *A History of Sri Lanka*. London: C. Hurst.

Dias, M. (2001). *Study on State Receiving Homes, Remand Homes and Detention Centres for Children*. Colombo: CENWOR.

Fox-Harding, L. (1997). *Perspectives in Child Care Policy* (2nd ed.). New York: Longman.

Frank, D. A., Klass, P. E., Earls, F., & Eisenberg, L. (1996). Infants and Young Children in Orphanages: One View from Pediatrics and Child Psychiatry (Special Article). *Pediatrics, 97*(4), 569–578.

Galappatti, A. (2002). *Caring for Separated Children: An Approach from Eastern Sri Lanka.* Save the Children. Norway.

Government of Sri Lanka. (1976). Circular. 12/76.

Government of Sri Lanka. (2008). *National Child Protection Authority.* Retrieved from http://www.childprotection.gov.lk/home.html.

Guest, E. (2003). *Children of AIDS: Africa's Orphan Crisis* (2nd ed.). Sterling, VA: Pluto Press.

Johnson, D. E. (2000). Medical and Developmental Sequelae of Early Childhood Institutionalization in Eastern European Adoptees. In C. A. Nelson (Ed.), *The Effects of Early Adversity on Neurobehavioral Development* (pp. 113–162). Minnesota Symposia on Child Psychology, 31.

Miller, L. C. (2005). *The Handbook of International Adoption Medicine: A Guide for Physicians, Parents and Providers.* New York: Oxford University Press.

Prisiazhnaia, N. V. (2008). Orphan Children: Adjusting to Life after the Boarding Institution. *Russian Education and Society, 50*(12), 23–39.

Rosen, A., Walter, G., Casey, D., & Hocking, B. (2000). Combating Psychiatric Stigma: An Overview of Contemporary Initiatives. *Australasian Psychiatry, 8*(1), 19–26.

Samaraweera, V.(1997). *Report on the Abused Child and the Legal Process of Sri Lanka.* National Monitoring Committee on the Children's Charter.

Save the Children. (2003). A Last Resort: The Growing Concern about Children in Residential Care. Save the Children. London. Retrieved from http://www.scslat.org/search/publieng.php?_cod_19_lang_e.

Şimşek, Z., Erol, N., Öztop, D., & Münir, K. (2007). Prevalence and Predictors of Emotional and Behavioural Problems Reported by Teachers among Institutionally Reared Children and Adolescents in Turkish Orphanages Compared with Community Controls. *Children and Youth Services Review, 29,* 883–899.

Şimşek, Z., Erol, N., Öztop, D., & Özer-Özcan, Ö. (2008). Epidemology of Emotional and Behavioural Problems in Children and Adolescents Reared in Orphanages: A National Comparative Study. *Turkish Journal of Psychiatry, 19*(3), 1–13.

Social and economic policy. (n.d.). *UNICEF.* Retrieved from http://www.unicef.org/socialpolicy/index_48560.html.

Tolfree, D. (1995). *Roofs and Roots: The Care of Separated Children in the Development World.* Surrey: UK. Ashgate.

UNICEF. (2009). Child Protection from Violence, Exploitation and Abuse. Retrieved from http://www.unicef.org/media/media_45451.html.

Van-Ijzendoorn, M. H., Luijk, M. P. C. M., & Juffer, F. (2008). IQ of Children Growing Up in Children's Homes: A Meta-analysis on IQ Delays in Orphanages. *Merrill-Palmer Quarterly, 54*(3), 341–366.

Wijethunge, S. (1991). *A study on Children's Homes to Investigate the Needs of Children in Institutional Settings.* Colombo, Sri Lanka: Save the Children Norway, Redd Barna.

Woodhead, M. (2001). Psychology and the Cultural Construction of Children's Needs: Postscripts. A. James, & A. Prout (Eds.), *In Constructing and Reconstructing Childhood: Contemporary Issues in Sociological Study of Childhood* (pp. 63–76). London, UK: Falmer Press.

CHAPTER 2

Juvenile Justice in São Paulo, Brazil: Violence and Denied Opportunities

*John D. McLennan, Fatima D. Rigato, and Isabel A. S. Bordin**

Introduction

Brazil is the fifth largest country in the world and the largest in the southern hemisphere. With a current population of about 186 million, of whom 33 percent are under 18 years of age (Instituto Brasileiro de Geografia e Estatística [IBGE], 2006b), it is the fifth most populated country in the world (IBGE, 2006a). Despite being a regional economic giant, Brazil is an extremely inequitable society, with the richest 10 percent of the population having a mean monthly income 16 times greater than the poorest 40 percent segment of the population (IBGE, 2006b). An estimated 54 million Brazilians live on less than US$2.00 a day, of whom 17 million subsist on less than US$1.00 a day (CIDA, 2005). These realities situate Brazil in fourth place among countries with the greatest inequality (Pearson Education Inc., 2006a).

Paradoxically, however, Brazil has been a leader in children's rights legislation and policy. One of the first countries to ratify the United Nations Convention of the Rights of the Child (UNCRC), Brazil has also enacted some of the most progressive legislation on child rights. With the passage of the Estatuto da Criança e do Adolescente (ECA) (the Statute of the Child and Adolescent) into law in 1990, the government of Brazil recognized the rights of children and adolescents as a major policy priority (Ribeiro & Trench, 2001; UNICEF, 2001). In keeping with this legislation, the state was expected to vigorously protect and promote these rights and to rectify practices harmful to the development of children and adolescents. Two decades on, however, it has become evident that there continue to be gaps in the realization of child rights, particularly with regard to youth in conflict with the law. Within the youth justice system, reliance on strategies of repression and social isolation, rather than education and rehabilitation, has characterized institutionalized treatment of youth (Diversi, Moraes, & Morelli, 1999; Scanlon, Tomkins, Lynch, & Scanlon, 1998).

In Brazil, children and youth aged 12–18 years can be held responsible for delinquent and criminal acts. Special youth courts, the Vara Especial da Infância e Adolescência, are mandated to judge these cases. As outlined in the ECA, in order to ensure that restrictive and harsh measures directed at young offenders be used as a last resort, six levels of response to youth in conflict with the law are mandated. The six levels are as follows:

1. reprimands and warnings from judicial officials to youth and their caregivers;
2. reparations for damages;
3. community services as assigned by the municipal authorities;
4. "assisted liberty" in which youth must regularly attend a state agency office or a contracted nongovernmental organization office;
5. "semiliberty" in which youth must stay in a state facility each night but are allowed to attend school and/or to work outside during the day; and
6. "lack of liberty" in which youth are held full time within a locked state facility.

In addition to these national stipulations, local boards for children and adolescents' rights (Conselho Municipal de Direitos da Criança e Adolescente e Conselho Estadual de Direitos da Criança e Adolescente) are mandated to develop policies related to youth in conflict with the law.

In São Paulo state, the largest and most urbanized region of Brazil, Fundação do Bem-Estar do Menor (FEBEM) (Foundation for the Well-Being of Minors), is the agency commissioned by the state government to administer key components of the youth justice system, including the management of juvenile detention centers.[1] In 2003, there were 56 locked units for youth throughout São Paulo State, with 36 located within the greater metropolitan area of São Paulo city. While the locked units and semiliberty units of detention are under state jurisdiction, administration of the assisted liberty program has increasingly become a municipal responsibility. This in turn has led to the subcontracting of NGOs for some aspects of the system.

In January of 2000, 3,794 youth were reported to be incarcerated in FEBEM within São Paulo State (Secretaria de Assistência e Desenvolvimento Social, 2000). This represented an estimated 50 percent of all youth incarcerated in Brazil despite the fact that São Paulo State comprises only a quarter of Brazil's overall population. Conditions of detention have long been criticized as grossly inadequate and harsh. Several studies have revealed the youth detention system in São Paulo, and in other parts of Brazil, to be in violation of youth rights as outlined in the ECA. Human Rights Watch (2005) and Amnesty International (2000) have reported on a litany of problems confronting youth in detention: overcrowding, unsanitary conditions, physical abuse, understaffing and lack of staff training and inappropriate transfers of youth to adult prison facilities. A more recent study highlighted similar violations of the rights of incarcerated youth despite apparent attempts to improve the juvenile justice system in Brazil. These included overcrowding, lack of basic health and hygiene standards, physical trauma from use of corporal punishment and beatings, lack of educational opportunities, and the inappropriate use of incarceration rather than community alternatives (Bochenek & Delgado, 2006).

In light of these realities, this chapter provides an account of the life courses of youth who are incarcerated and subsequently discharged in São Paulo and proposes strategies for improving treatment of youth in conflict with the law. Following a brief discussion of the UNCRC as it relates to children's rights and youth justice in Brazil, and an overview of the methodology for this study, we examine the characteristics of youth incarcerated in detention facilities in São Paulo and the circumstances of these youth one year following their release from detention. We then consider policy measures for improving the lives of Brazilian youth discharged from incarceration.

Child Rights and Juvenile Justice: Realities in Brazil

The UNCRC is of particular relevance for youth in conflict with the law (Howe & Covell, 2001). Certain articles of the UNCRC, notably Articles 37 and 40, speak specifically to protection issues relevant to detention and immediate conflict with the law. The UNCRC prohibits arbitrary deprivation of liberty, the use of torture, and other cruel treatment. It stipulates that incarceration of youth should be implemented as a last resort and that it should be used for the shortest appropriate period of time. In addition, the UNCRC states that youth should not to be detained with adults, that they should have access to legal assistance, and, barring exceptional circumstances, they should have access to family members. Given that youth in conflict with the law are also disproportionately exposed to the effects of poverty, violence, sexual exploitation, and organized crime (Bagley & Young, 1987; Benda, Corwyn, & Toombs, 2001b; Farrington, 1995; Jarjoura, Triplett, & Brinker, 2002; McCarthy & Hagan, 1992; Veneziano, Veneziano, & LeGrand, 2000), other Articles of the UNCRC have direct relevance for systems of youth justice. These include Article 6 that identifies the "inherent right to life....and survival"; Article 19 that underscores the need for protection from a range of abuses; Article 28 that describes the need to "make primary education compulsory and available free to all"; and Article 33 that requires "State Parties to take all appropriate measures... to protect children from the illicit use of narcotic drugs... and to prevent the use of children in the illicit production and trafficking of such substances." These Articles are all highly relevant in light of widespread evidence that incarcerated youth may be at risk of premature death (Teplin, McClelland, Abram, & Mileusnic, 2005), and that children and youth in conflict with the law often have histories of exposure to domestic violence (Herrera & McCloskey, 2001; Kim & Kim, 2008), tend to have lower educational attainment are more likely to have dropped out of school (Oliveira & Assis, 1999), and are at increased risk of being involved with drug use and drug trafficking (McLennan, Bordin, Bennett, Rigato, & Brinkerhoff, 2008; Sheley, 1994).

Article 40 (1) of the UNCRC highlights the need for children in conflict with the law to be "treated in a manner consistent with the promotion of the child's dignity and self worth... promoting the child's reintegration and the child's assuming a constructive role in society." Nonetheless, there are growing concerns about the plight of youth who are discharged from detention facilities and who are expected to be reintegrated into society. In Northern countries, particularly in the United States, there is a significant body of research on youth discharged that points to high levels of recidivism, subsequent violence, and disproportionately high rates of death (Telpin, McClelland, Abram, & Mileusnic, 2005). Underlying factors include early age of first conviction, repeat offenses, conduct disorder, low cognitive abilities, gang membership or delinquent peer group association, drug and alcohol use, ineffective use of leisure time, parental substance use and/or criminality, history of abuse, and family problems (Benda, Corwyn, & Toombs, 2001a, 2001b; Cottle, Lee, & Heilbrun, 2001; Dembo, Turner, Chin Sue, Borden, & Manning, 1995; Heilburn et al., 2000; Stinchcomb & Terry, 2001; Langstroem, 2002; Vermeiren, Schwab-Stone, Ruchkin, De Clippele, & Deboutte, 2002).

Similar research on reintegration and recidivism is still relatively scarce in middle and low-income countries. Nevertheless, in Brazil there is some evidence to show that problems leading up to incarceration and recidivism are even more acute than in most Northern countries. A 1994 study conducted in three detention facilities in Greater Metropolitan Rio de Janeiro identified the following proportionate reasons for incarceration: petty theft (34 percent), armed robbery (27 percent), drug trafficking (8 percent), and drug use (1 percent) (Oliveira & Assis, 1999). Of the youth who were in detention at the time of the study, 32 percent had been incarcerated at least twice and 73 percent were not attending school when they were apprehended. Other studies have examined additional problems faced by these youth. For example, high rates of substance use were cited in self-reports of literate youth incarcerated in detention institutions in Porto Alegre in Southern Brazil (Ferigolo et al., 2004). In a convenience sample of youth on parole in the State of Rio de Janeiro, the majority screened positive for mental health problems, though only a small fraction, had ever received any treatment (Andrade, Silva, & Assumpcao, 2004). A small pilot study conducted by Lescher focusing on a small group of first-time offenders who had been incarcerated and subsequently discharged from a detention unit in São Paulo City indicated that of the two-thirds of discharged youth who were located by the researcher a year after being discharged, over 40 percent had suffered adverse outcomes, including death, reincarceration, or drug use (personal communication with A. Lescher). Since a third of the original group of respondents could not be found, the incidence of tragic outcomes was likely higher.

In light of the limited Brazilian findings in relation to incarceration, reintegration, children's rights, and juvenile justice, there is a compelling need for further research on youth in conflict with the law. In response, this project sought to provide information about the life courses of youth who are incarcerated and subsequently discharged in São Paulo, Brazil, in order to propose measures to improve their life trajectories. More specifically, we sought to examine

1. the characteristics of youth incarcerated in detention facilities in São Paulo, Brazil;

2. the circumstances of these youth one year after release from detention; and
3. the measures that may help to improve the life outcomes of these youth.

In addition, we hope to contribute to the existing literature on children's rights and juvenile justice in Brazil.

Research Design and Methodology

This project was realized through an interdisciplinary partnership involving researchers from five institutions. In Canada these included the University of Calgary and McMaster University, and in Brazil, Universidade Federal de São Paulo (UNIFESP), Projeto Quixote, a non-governmental organization working with marginalized youth (linked with UNIFESP), and the Instituto Latino Americano das Nações Unidas para a Prevenção do Delito e Tratamento do Delinqüente (ILANUD) (Latin American Institute of the United Nations for Crime Prevention and Treatment of Delinquents). In addition to the core research team,[2] six young people who themselves had been in conflict with the law participated in the study by helping to produce a documentary film.

The study itself was conducted in São Paulo City, the capital of São Paulo state. With a population of over 19 million, the greater area of São Paulo City is one of the largest urban regions in the world. As noted in the introduction to this chapter, although there are pockets of great wealth in São Paulo, the vast majority of the city's population lives in varying degrees of poverty and exclusion from good quality social services such as daycare centers, schools, and hospitals (Sposati, 2001). São Paulo is also marked by extreme levels of violence. In 2004, for example, for every group of 100,000 inhabitants, 32 died during robberies or intentional homicides (Fundação SEADE, 2005). Among youth, the proportion has been higher: in 1999, 185 out of every 100,000 inhabitants between the ages of 14 and 24 years died (Calil, 2000). It is in this context that we sought to examine the realities of youth in conflict with the law.

The research, which was undertaken between April 2003 and June 2006, consisted of four components. First, using a structured, quantitative interview schedule, the researchers collected baseline information on a sample of youth awaiting discharge from juvenile detention centers (FEBEM) in São Paulo. The second component entailed qualitative interviews with youth who had been incarcerated or with caregivers of these youth. The third component consisted of a second round of structured interviews with a subsample of the youth (or their caregivers) who had participated in the first component. The final component involved the production of a video with youth who had been incarcerated to capture aspects of their lives from their own perspectives.

Ethical Considerations

The study was reviewed and approved by the ethics committee of the Universidade Federal de São Paulo. The study was also reviewed and approved by a judge responsible for FEBEM youth. In addition, verbal assent was obtained from the youth after the voluntary nature of the study was explained to them. During the interviews, youth were reminded that they also had the choice to skip any questions they did not want to answer, that they could withdraw at any time, and that FEBEM would not have access to any of the raw data obtained within the study. An important challenge faced by the research staff was coming to know of youth experiences of maltreatment and not being able to offer direct services. However, all youth who participated in the study were invited by the research team to attend the Projeto Quixote program. Quixote is a free program that has a variety of professionals on staff (psychiatrists, psychologists, paediatricians, and educators) who support marginalized youth with a range of programs. In addition, all research staff had access to these professionals during the study and could seek consultation as needed.

An additional concern was exposure of the youth who participated in the video component. The youth revealed important information about their lives within the video clips. Several discussions were carried out with the youth to review what would be retained in the final version of the video. The youth had the final say in what would be included and some clips were edited out that might have been compromising for them. There were also several discussions with youth as to what would be the proper venues for subsequently showing the video. For presentation purposes, the youth agreed that the video could be shown at academic and educational events. In contrast, however, those involved in producing the video were cautious about presentations through popular media outlets. Eventually, in respecting the instructions by the researchers and youth to refrain from showing certain segments of the video, an abridged version was shown on Brazilian television.

Component One: Baseline Assessment

Sampling

Youth were recruited between April and October 2004 from locked detention units of FEBEM in São Paulo city. At the time of the research fieldwork, there were 36 units for boys in FEBEM's locked detention system in the greater São Paulo area: 5 were free-standing units and 31 were clustered within 5 large compounds. Participants for the study were recruited from two free-standing units and seven units within two of the compounds. An eighth unit was later added to include a sample of the youngest incarcerated children. All incarcerated girls were housed in two free-standing units, which were both included in this study.[3]

All youth within the selected units were eligible to participate in the research if they met the following inclusion criteria: (1) they were aged 12–17 years; (2) their last home address, prior to incarceration, was in the greater metropolitan area of São Paulo City; (3) they held the status of *Privação de Liberdade* (full time locked status in one of the detention centers); and (4) they held the status of *Aguardando Decisão Judicial* (being considered for a release date by the youth court).

Measures/Procedures

The survey instrument for component one comprised a series of questions, some drawn from preexisting standardized instruments used in Brazil and elsewhere, and a series of questions developed specifically for this study. Youth were interviewed face-to-face by trained Brazilian research assistants in as private a space as was available within the incarceration facilities.

Overview of the Participants

A total of 36 girls and 289 boys participated in the baseline survey. A brief description of the sociodemographic features of the youth participating in the baseline survey is found in table 2.1. The majority of the youth were from lower income backgrounds—the third (C) and fourth (D) social class. Though C class is not deemed to be in a circumstance of abject poverty, those in this category generally do experience substantial economic strain. The mean age of the youth was just under 16 years and ranged from 12 to 17, with the largest group being 17 years (37 percent). Mean years of education was just over six years with a range from 1 to 11 years.

Of the offenses that led to their incarceration, robbery was the most common among boys and girls (table 2.1). Over half the girls and just

Table 2.1 Characteristics of youth incarcerated in FEBEM who participated in the study

Characteristics	*Girls (n=36)*	*Boys (n=289)*
	Mean (S.D.)	*Mean (S.D.)*
Age (years)	15.8 (1.0)	15.9 (1.1)
Last grade attended (years)	6.1 (1.8)	6.1 (2.1)
Number of people in the home	6.2 (2.0)	5.5 (2.0)
	% (n)	% (n)
Index crime type*		
Violent crime	63.9 (23)	82.0 (237)
Robbery	55.6 (20)	74.0 (214)
Other	11.1 (4)	10.7 (31)
Property crime	13.9 (5)	10.0 (29)
Drug related crime	11.1 (4)	8.0 (23)
Other crime	27.8 (10)	6.9 (20)
Access to a lawyer	66.7 (24)	69.9 (202)
Youth reports being hit by the police	63.9 (23)	74.7 (216)
Had a previous correctional measure	58.3 (21)	44.3 (128)
Social Class**		
A	0.0 (0)	1.0 (3)
B	11.1 (4)	15.9 (46)
C	47.2 (17)	52.2 (151)
D	38.9 (14)	28.4 (82)
E	0.0 (0)	2.1 (6)
Unknown	2.8 (1)	0.3 (1)

*Youth could indicate more than one type of crime.
** Social class based on the Brazilian Economic Classification Criteria (Associação Brasileira de Empresas de Pesquisa, 2003). Based on a series of SES indicators such as the educational level of head of household and acquired consumer goods, families are classified into five categories of economic class with A the highest and E the lowest levels.

under half the boys had previously had a correctional measure applied to their cases from earlier conflicts with the law. More than half the youth reported that they had been assaulted by police at the time of their arrest, and approximately two-thirds reported having had access to a lawyer when they were charged with the crime that led to their incarceration, a right that should be available to all charged youth. Prior to their arrest and incarceration, most of these youth had experienced a broad array of adverse life experiences (table 2.2). The most frequent included having slept on the street, not attending school during a six-month period prior to incarceration, separation from either one or both of their parents, death of a parent, and physical abuse by one or more

Table 2.2 Adverse life exposures prior to incarceration for participating youth

Characteristics	*Girls (n=36)* % (n)	*Boys (n=289)* % (n)
Family and home		
Has slept on the street	50.0 (18)	27.0 (78)
Lack of food in the home	8.3 (3)	5.9 (17)
Biological parents living together	22.8 (8)	30.8 (89)
Mother dead	19.4 (7)	6.2 (18)
Father dead	27.8 (10)	21.5 (62)
Physical violence in the home	13.9 (5)	9.0 (26)
Physical abuse		
Adult has kicked you	38.9 (14)	32.9(95)
Adult has choked you	13.9 (5)	6.6 (19)
Adult has tried to suffocate you	5.6 (2)	3.8 (11)
Adult has burnt you	5.6 (2)	3.5 (10)
Adult has beat you	22.2 (8)	29.1 (84)
Experienced any of the above abuses	47.2 (17)	48.1 (139)
Sexual abuse		
Adult has touched your private parts	13.9 (5)	2.4 (7)
Threatened sexual relationship	13.9 (5)	1.0 (3)
Forced sexual experience	16.7 (6)	0.3 (1)
Attacked sexually	13.9 (5)	0.7 (2)
Experienced any of the above abuses	19.4 (7)	3.5 (10)
Experienced community violence in the last 12 months		
Chased by gang/individuals	5.5 (2)	15.9 (46)
Threatened with serious physical harm	27.8(10)	34.3 (99)
Beaten up or mugged	41.7 (15)	30.8 (89)
Attacked/wounded with knife	13.9 (5)	5.5 (16)
Seriously wounded in violent incidence	8.3 (3)	15.6 (45)
Shot or shot at with a gun	8.3 (3)	24.2 (70)
Other		
Involved in drug trafficking	52.8 (19)	43.9 (127)
Not attending school prior to incarceration	63.9 (23)	38.1 (110)
Ever "marked for death" (*jurado de morte*)	8.3 (3)	21.5 (62)

adults. Approximately half were involved in drug trafficking and many had experienced violence, including attacks from assailants with guns or knives, in their community. A number of youth, particularly boys, had experienced the threat of physical harm, or *jurado de morte* (marked for death), a belief that a youth in question is targeted to be killed.

Description of Gender Differences

Though girls and boys within this sample demonstrated many similar characteristics and experiences, there were a number of significant differences, particularly in relation to the offenses committed. A greater proportion of boys than girls had been engaged in robbery, while a higher proportion of girls were incarcerated for having violated conditions of probation orders related to an earlier offense. Similarly, more girls than boys had experienced sexual abuse, had slept on the street, had lost a mother due to death, and had not been attending school prior to their incarceration (table 2.2).

Components Two and Three: Qualitative Interviews and Follow-Up Interviews with Discharged Youth

A subsample of youth and caregivers of other youth who participated in component one were purposefully selected to participate in in-depth interviews. These interviews sought to obtain additional contextual information, as well as participants' perspectives on youth life course experiences not captured in the first round of structured interviewing. In total, seven girls, seven boys, and six mothers participated in these interviews.

Attempts were made to reinterview all youth (and/or their caregivers) following the youths' discharge from the FEBEM facilities. This was a challenge for several reasons. Information from FEBEM on discharged youth was inconsistent and incomplete, thus making it difficult to identify when individual youth had been discharged and where they currently resided. A number lived in homes where there was no active phone, and others had relocated following their discharge, and their whereabouts were unknown.

The research team was nonetheless able to locate and reinterview 103 youth approximately 12 months following their release from custody. Of those youth not interviewed, we were able to find and interview an additional 69 caregivers or associates of the youth, in most instances their mothers. Furthermore, another 25 of our original cohort who had reoffended soon after being discharged, and who were once again incarcerated, were identified though not interviewed. In total, therefore, we obtained some follow-up information on 197 (61 percent) of the original sample of youth. Issues explored with previously incarcerated youth during this second round of interviews included the challenges and difficulties the youth had confronted following their release from custody. These included reincarceration, substance abuse, drug

Table 2.3 Sociodemographic differences between those interviewed and not-interviewed at 12-month postrelease*

Characteristic	*Follow-up*	*Not-followed up*
	(n=172)	*(n=128)*
	Mean (S.D.)	*Mean (S.D.)*
Age (years)	16.0 (1.0)	15.8 (1.2)
Last grade attended (years)	6.5 (1.9)	5.7 (2.2)
Number of people in the home	5.4 (2.0)	5.8 (2.0)
% (n)	% (n)	
Social Class**		
A	1.2 (2)	0.7 (1)
B	15.7 (27)	15.0 (23)
C	52.9 (91)	50.3 (77)
D	28.5 (49)	30.7 (47)
E	1.7 (3)	2.0 (3)
Unknown	0.0 (0)	1.3 (2)

* The follow-up sample does not include those reincarcerated for whom we did not perform an interview (n=25).

** Social class based on the Brazilian Economic Classification Criteria (Associação Brasileira de Empresas de Pesquisa, 2003). Based on a series of SES indicators such as the educational level of head of household and acquired consumer goods, families are classified into five categories of economic class with A the highest and E the lowest levels.

trafficking, school attendance, and opportunities for employment and/or skills training.

Incidence of Recidivism

Among the youth interviewed a year after being discharged from incarceration, 38 percent had reoffended. Of this group, 66 percent had committed criminal acts and 34 percent had violated probation orders; 30 percent of the sample had been incarcerated again, of whom 20 percent were in custody at the time of the interviews. An additional 9 percent reported that they had engaged in delinquent or criminal acts for which they had not been caught. On a more positive note, 62 percent denied having been in conflict with the law during the year following their release.

Education

Fifty-nine percent of the participating youth reported attending school within six months *prior* to incarceration. Of this group, there was a substantial gender difference, with 62 percent of boys attending school in contrast to only 36 percent of the sample of girls, a statistically significant difference ($\chi^2 = 7.7$, $p<0.01$). Educational attainment of these youth ranged from 1 to 11 years, with a mean level of 6.1 years (SD = 2.1). Considering their mean age was 15.9 years (SD = 1.1), this group is substantially behind in their expected grade level attainment; 16-year-old children in Brazil are normally at a tenth or eleventh grade level.

Approximately one-third (35 percent) of these participants reported having problems in school related to behavior and learning difficulties. Girls demonstrated a similar level of problems to that of the boys. Surprisingly, the youths' perceptions of problems in school were not related to their levels of attendance or to grade attainment. This may suggest that the manner of eliciting this information was inadequate, and that information derived from other sources, such as a parent or the school, would have allowed us to identify more nuanced indicators of youth difficulty in school.

Among those youth interviewed 12 months following discharge from custody, only 41 percent reported that they were attending school. This was a substantial drop in school participation from preincarceration levels, and represented a marked failure to reintegrate these youth back into the school system. This decrease occurred despite efforts to provide some educational opportunities within FEBEM's incarceration facilities and a typical requirement that youth be enrolled in school during the approximately six-month probation period following their release from custody unless they were old enough to work.

Among those not attending school, the most common reason reported in the survey was lack of motivation to continue studying. As one youth said, "In FEBEM you stay there wanting to go to school, everyday, but once you are out and on the streets... then you don't have a wish to study anymore." A second common reason for not returning to school was lack of openings in the school system. As one of the caregivers of a youth indicated, "We couldn't get a place for him at that time.... I think the waiting time is too long."

Other comments from the qualitative interviews provide additional reasons why many of the youth did not attend school in the postdischarge period. Several youth feared exposure to violence:

> I don't want to go back. Even the school gate has bullet holes in it.
>
> I used to study in the evening... there were a lot of people... people involved in crime... it was very difficult... it is hard to be studying and then sometimes a fight breaks out...

These sentiments reflect the sometimes hazardous environments of some public schools in Brazil where violence and drug activity are occasional, and sometimes frequent, occurrences on school grounds.

The age of the youth is also an important factor in considering whether to carry on with school. As several youth indicated, while a focus on school may be critical for those under 16 years of age, for older youth the focus needs to be on attaining jobs. Sixteen is the age at which youth are legally allowed to seek employment in Brazil.

Girls experienced additional barriers to returning and staying in school. In explaining why she was no longer attending school, one girl recalled, "I was studying when I got pregnant, but then my belly started growing a lot and I left." Girls who already have babies or small children are generally unable to continue their schooling because of a lack of schools with daycare programs.

Employment

Among the youth who were interviewed during their period of incarceration, 69 percent said that they had been working prior to their incarceration. Most of the work consisted of sporadic low paying jobs such as ticket taking in small buses, attending to parked cars, cleaning windshields, selling candies, delivering goods such as pamphlets and pizzas, and helping at car washes. Twenty-seven percent indicated that they had been involved in some form of vocational training, the most common being basic computer skills acquisition.

At the time of the 12 month-follow-up, 39 percent of the located sample reported that they had been employed soon after their release from custody, a substantial drop from preincarceration levels. The types of jobs were similar to those of the preincarceration period, and many also consisted of irregular, sporadic work. Several of these youth indicated that they had either been fired or quit their jobs. Of this postdischarge group, 22 percent indicated that they were in vocational training activities, most involving computer skills.

The need for work opportunities emerged repeatedly in the qualitative interviews. Obtaining work was often framed as a critical factor preventing recidivism. Three comments highlight the trade-off of employment versus crime as a basis for economic survival:

> There was a time when I stopped stealing because I managed to get a job. I looked after cars at the university. I was earning good money you know? I could live on that. I could buy clothes without having to depend on my mother or father.

> When I left there (FEBEM) I said to myself: "Bro' if I get a job, if I get a job, I won't steal, bro'. For why would I steal? But if I don't find a job . . . to go around naked without money . . ."
>
> You know . . . I couldn't get a job, everything was difficult, I had no money for anything. So I chose to steal, man. It was the easiest and the fastest way to get a few bucks.

Indeed, youth leaving FEBEM detention centers must struggle against both high rates of youth unemployment and the added stigma of their incarceration that may further hinder their chances of gaining employment. On occasion, however, exceptions do occur. One employer, who was interviewed in the video (discussed below), explained why he had hired a recently discharged youth:

> The person has to have a chance to show his values, to show that it was just a slip . . . He just happened to do something that the law does not allow . . . we are going to give him a chance, he's a good boy . . . and he really is. That's how you do your part. We're going to have him back here the moment he comes out.

Recreation

Among the incarcerated youth who participated in the first round of interviews, 43 percent indicated that they had had access to recreational activities before they were arrested. Yet this group consisted almost entirely of boys who were referring to activities like playing soccer in the street. In contrast, very few of those postincarcerated youth who were interviewed indicated being engaged in organized recreational activities. This low rate is indicative of the lack of activities and structures designed to prevent recidivism among formerly incarcerated youth. The most common barriers cited for this paucity of recreational resources are distance and cost. As one youth observed, "For them to go (to the recreational activities), it is far away, I would have to give them money for the ride and sometimes we don't even have this money, you know?" Another youth caregiver explained, "I don't have the means to pay R$80.00 (about $30 US) for a computer course. (But) we will register him in a theater workshop, it's all paid for."

Violence Exposure and Death

Many of these youth had significant exposure to violence prior to their incarceration (table 2.2). In addition to experiencing violence directly, many youth witnessed violent events, such as someone being beaten, shot, or badly hurt. During the third component of the research—12 months after the first round of interviews with incarcerated youth—the research team learned that 7 boys among the initial respondents had been killed—3 in shoot-outs with the police, 2 in execution style hits, 2 in brawls, and 1 in unknown circumstances. Five of these deaths occurred within the first four months of release from incarceration. There may have been other deaths amongst those youth who were not located for component three of the research. Accounts of violence and violent death were vivid:

> We tried to escape [from the detention unit], but the officers caught us and beat the stuffing out of us. And it was during Christmas. We got beaten up the whole night long with the fireworks popping out there and they beat the shit out of us.
>
> So, they killed [my father]. In front of our house. They stopped the car, they called, he answered. He saw who was there, he knew them so he came out.(...) Then I only heard- Pa! pa! pa! pa! pa! I heard it six times, you know? Then it stopped. Then I ran, opened the kitchen door(...) and I saw the crazy man shooting my father three more times. Pa! Pa! Pa!

Component Four: The Video

The fourth component of the research provided an opportunity for some direct youth engagement in the study. In an effort to ensure that the research would capture youth voices and perspectives as fully as possible, this fourth component involved the participation of six youth in the production of a video. Five boys and one girl were engaged by Projeto Quixote (led by A. Lescher) to work with a documentary maker, Daniel Rubio, from the Instituto Imagem Viva, and several staff members of TV UNIFESP. The goal was to engage youth in the production of a video that would highlight their own experiences, and particularly their perspectives of incarceration and subsequent release from FEBEM institutions. The youth came to this aspect of the project through differing routes. One of the boys had participated in the baseline survey while he was incarcerated. He had demonstrated a keen interest in the study, and upon his release he had sought out Projeto Quixote and had asked to join the project. Four additional youth had participated in the qualitative interviews and were recruited by one of the research staff. All four had been incarcerated in a FEBEM detention unit and had expressed a desire to join the video project. A sixth youth, also previously incarcerated, was recruited by one of the initial participating youth.

For several months, these six youth met with staff on multiple occasions. Over time they combined learning of filming technique with group discussions concerning their own experiences prior to, during, and after their incarceration. Some of these group sessions were captured on the video itself. The main purpose of the video, however, was to enable the youth to film aspects of their home and community life that were regarded as important in providing insights into their experiences and struggles. Through this participatory process, the six youth gradually shifted from a state of marginalization and dependency, to a state of increased reflection, analysis, and confidence in articulating their perspectives and feelings. As Daniel Rubio observed, this was a process of two worlds meeting in the production of a video, a process captured in the final version of the video itself. Through collaboration on the video, the youth were "willing to make a change meeting with a society which is ready to help." In so doing, the youth reported that they began to see themselves "differently," particularly as they were both producers and subjects of the video. One of the participating youth initially described being intimidated by the process and cautious with these new adults in his life. However, little by little he and others in the group gained confidence. Another youth noted that he initially did not expect anything to come of his involvement with the research. Yet after initial apprehension, he described his "interest growing day-by-day and with every meeting new ideas coming forth." Still another youth recalled the process as follows: "I thought it was great, the behavior of the people of the project.... the trust that they gave us... it was a great experience... those eight months were important for me and we are seeing the results."

Exilados do Mundão (Exiles from the World) is the title of the 45-minute film produced by the team of youth with the NGO and television staff. It captures the critical variables that shaped the lives of the six youth participants, including the process of video production itself. Images in the video of the youth's neighborhoods in the *favelas* (slums) depict the lack of recreational space. With homes crowded close together in the *favelas*, the video opens with youth playing soccer in the streets and the narrator explaining, "Kids stay playing till late, there's no field, there's no court... It's been a long time since we've been asking for a field here in our neighborhood, right man? But we never got anywhere..." Themes captured in the video include experiences of conflict with the law, family, friends, and neighborhoods, loss of freedom, incarceration, and the challenges of release and reintegration.

Discussion: Improving the Lives of Youth Discharged from Incarceration

We are hopeful that the findings from this study will be helpful for researchers, program planners, policymakers and child advocates alike. However, this is a single study of a very complex problem. Clearly, further work is required to better understand the plight of youth in conflict with the law in Brazil, and to determine effective strategies to improve the outcomes of this population and help them more fully realize their rights. In particular, there is a need for a longer period of follow-up so the trajectories of these youth are more fully understood. Given the limited time allowed for this study, we were only able to follow our cohort of youth for one year. Future studies will require longitudinal designs to ensure that the experiences of youth are better traced over time.

In conjunction with efforts to better understand the circumstances of these high-risk youth, there is a need to undertake interventions that aim specifically to improve the life chances of young offenders. Several interventions are proposed for this population. These include the provision of increased opportunities for employment, education, recreation, and prevention interventions to reduce exposure to violence. Employment is a core component that all youth must navigate as they move into adulthood. Youth leaving FEBEM detention units have many disadvantages, most notably the stigma of being "ex-cons" and having little education. This is further complicated by the context of high unemployment and underemployment in Brazil. This situation leaves youth at high risk of recidivism and a life of crime. Expanded efforts to provide high quality apprenticeship programs and meaningful employment are essential if these youth are to have increased opportunities for a better future.

One such example is a pilot employment project cosponsored by Projeto Quixote and Price Water House Coopers (PWHC) that is designed to integrate high-risk youth, including those who have been incarcerated, into a positive and meaningful work environment. Typically youth first enter a preparatory period with Quixote to help address health, family, and school problems, and to provide initial job training. PWHC then hires a cohort of youth for a one-year period. The contract includes mandatory school attendance and ongoing monitoring and support from Projeto Quixote. Twenty-one youth from Projeto Quixote have already participated in this program with nine obtaining permanent employment with PWHC and only three having not finished the one-year program. Further evaluation of this employment project may guide the optimal development of similar interventions.

Education, of course, is a fundamental right of children and youth. Unfortunately, for multiple reasons, some youth leave FEBEM detention centers without an adequate primary school education. Special efforts need to be attempted to improve current school enrolment rates for this high-risk population. Potential strategies include developing a preparatory prerelease FEBEM-school liaison effort, expanding the probation period of educational monitoring, and providing more special education opportunities to address the substantial learning needs among this population.

Organized youth recreation is also a right, one that may result in decreased delinquency and conflict with the law (Jones and Offord, 1989). A potential for development in this regard are the Casa da Juventude (Youth Houses) that involve community buildings in various Brazilian neighborhoods where free recreational activities for youth and families are offered by local governments and NGOs.

Many youth in conflict with the law have been victims of violence or even killed. Strategies that reduce their exposure to violence are sorely needed, especially for youth who are "marked for death." Strategies that relocate these individuals to safe areas on release should be considered. Ideally more systemic efforts to prevent abuses from occurring in the first place would also be a top priority.

Limited information exists on the unique needs of girls in conflict with the law. We suggest that all the above areas of proposed foci are equally applicable to girls, but additional special support programs should be considered for girls. In particular, there is a need for increased protection from sexual violence among girls, as well as treatment interventions for those victimized. Girls who have young children or who are pregnant face additional challenges related to employment and educational opportunities. The example of "Lua Nova" (New Moon), a Brazilian NGO program specifically for girls at high risk (e.g., sleeping on the street or having been sexual exploited), who are pregnant or who have young children, demonstrates what can be possible. Here girls are provided a residential placement and are offered a combination of education and childcare. Programs such as this should be expanded and further studied to determine how they may best help these girls toward a healthier life trajectory.

Youth in conflict with the law are a population whose rights are often not fully realized and who are at high risk of recidivism and early death. In our study we attempted to shed light on the circumstances facing youth incarcerated in São Paulo, Brazil, before, during, and after their period of custody. There is much to be done to improve the life trajectories of high-risk children and youth in Brazil. Key foci should include attention to employment, educational and recreational opportunities, and violence prevention. Though a substantial struggle lies ahead, there is reason to be optimistic. As one of the video youth explained, his participation gave him "the opportunity to show that for everything there is hope."

Notes

* We dedicate this chapter to the struggling boys and girls of FEBEM and to the memory of Dr. D. R. (Dan) Offord. Dan was one of the coinvestigators of this project who sadly passed away during the course of this study. Dan, a recipient of the Order of Canada, was a champion for creating opportunities for underprivileged children and was an inspiration and mentor to many. Thanks to the many youth and their parents who participated in this study and shared their personal experiences with us. Thanks also to the staff at Projeto Quixote to realize this study. Special thanks to the Canadian International Development Agency for funding this research.

1. The Foundation has been renamed Fundação Centro de Atendimento Sócio-Educativo ao Adolescente (Fundação CASA SP) (Foundation for the Social and Educational Care of the Adolescent) to better express the concept of socioeducational support.
2. The Canadian team comprised a child psychiatrist, a sociologist, and an epidemiologist, and the Brazilian team comprised a child psychiatrist, a paediatrician, and a lawyer.
3. Sampling was constrained somewhat due to the fact that two compounds were inaccessible because of unrest and periodical riots. As these compounds tended to house older and more recidivistic youth who had engaged in more serious crimes, there may have been under representation of these subgroups.

References

Amnesty International. (2000). Brazil A Waste of Lives: FEBEM Juvenile Detention Centres, São Paulo. A Human Rights Crisis, Not a Public Security Issue. AI Index: AMR Retrieved February 8, 2007 from http://web.amnesty.org/library/Index/ENGAMR190142000?open&of=ENG-BRA/

Andrade R. C., Silva V. A., & Assumpcao, F. B., Jr. (2004). Preliminary Data on the Prevalence of Psychiatric Disorders in Brazilian Male and Female Juvenile Delinquents. *Brazilian Journal of Medical and Biological Research, 37*(8), 1155–1160.

Bagley, C., &Young, L. (1987). Juvenile Prostitution and Child Sexual Abuse: A Controlled Study. *Canadian Journal of Community Mental Health, 6,* 5–26.

Benda, B., Corwyn, R., & Toombs, N. (2001a). Recidivism among Adolescent Serious Offenders: Prediction of Entry into the Correctional System for Adults. *Criminal Justice & Behavior, 28,* 588–613.

Benda, B., Corwyn, R., & Toombs, N. (2001b). From Adolescent "Serious Offender" to Adult Felon: A Predictive Study of Offensive Progression. *Journal of Offender Rehabilitation, 32,* 79–108.

Bochenek, M., & Delgado, F. (2006). Children in Custody in Brazil. *Lancet, 367,* 696–697.

Calil, M. I. (2000). *Da rua para a cidadania: 5 anos de Travessia.* São Paulo: Publisher Brasil.

Canadian International Development Agency (CIDA). (2005). A Synthesis of Canada's Cooperation Strategy in Brazil 2005–2010. Retrieved March 28, 2007 from http://www.acdi-cida.gc.ca/INET/IMAGES.NSF/vLUImages /Brazil/$file/Brazil-country-strategy-FINAL.pdf

Cottle, C., Lee, R., & Heilbrun, K. (2001). The Prediction of Criminal Recidivism in Juveniles: A Meta-analysis. *Criminal Justice & Behavior, 28*, 367–394.

Dembo, R., Turner, G., Chin Sue, C., Schmeidler, J., Borden, P., & Manning, D. (1995). Predictors of Recidivism to a Juvenile Assessment Center. *The International Journal of Addictions, 30*(11), 1425–1452.

Diversi, M., Moraes filho, N., & Morelli, M. (1999). Daily Reality on the Streets of Campinas, Brazil. *New Directions for Child and Adolescent Development, 85,* 19–34.

Farrington, D. (1995). The Development of Offending and Antisocial Behaviour from Childhood: Key Findings from the Cambridge Study in Delinquent Development. *Journal of Psychology and Psychiatry and Allied Disciplines, 36,* 929–964.

Ferigolo, M., Barbosa, F. S., Arbo, E., Malysz, A. S., Stein, A. T., & Barros, H. M. (2004). Drug Use Prevalence at FEBEM, Porto Alegre. *Revista Brasileira de Psiquiatria, 26*(1), 10–16.

Fundação SEADE. (2005). Mortes por agressões e ocorrências de homicídios dolosos e latrocínios (Death by aggression and occurrences of intentional homicides and robberies). Retrieved March 19, 2006 from http://www.seade.gov.br /produtos/spdemog/nov2005/Sao_Paulo/Sao_Paulo.pdf

Heilburn, K., Brock, W., Waite, D., Lanier, A., Schmid, M., & Witte, G. (2000). Risk Factors for Juvenile Criminal Recidivism: The Postrelease Community Adjustment of Juvenile Offenders. *Criminal Justice & Behavior, 27,* 275–291.

Herrera V., & McCloskey, L. (2001). Gender Differences in the Risk for Delinquency among Youth Exposed to Family Violence. *Child Abuse & Neglect, 25,* 1037–1051.

Howe, R. B., & Covell, K. (2001). Youth Justice Reform and the Rights of the Child: A Step Forward or Backward. *Canadian Journal of Community Mental Health, 20*(2), 91–106.

Human Rights Watch. (2005). In the Dark: Hidden Abuses Against Detained Youth in Rio de Janeiro. New York: Human Rights Watch, 2005.

Inciardi, J., & Pottieger, A. (1991). Kids, Crack, and Crime. *The Journal of Drug Issues, 21*(2), 257–270.

Instituto Brasileiro de Geografia e Estatística (IBGE). (2006a). Estimativas da populaçáo. Retrieved April 24, 2006 from http://www.ibge.gov.br/home/disseminacao/online/popclock/popclock.php

IBGE. (2006b). Síntese de Indicadores Sociais 2005—Estudos e Pesquisas: Informaçáo Demográfica e Socioeconômica, número 17 (ISSN 1532-1696). Retrieved April 24, 2006 from http://www.ibge.gov.br/home/estatistica/populacao/condicaodevida/indicadoresminimos/sinteseindicsociais2005/indic_sociais2005.pdf

Jarjoura, R., Triplett, G., & Brinker, G. (2002). Growing Up Poor: Examining the Link between Persistent Childhood Poverty and Delinquency. *Journal of Quantitative Criminology, 18,* 159–187.

Jones, M. B., & Offord, D. R. (1989). Reduction of Antisocial Behavior in Poor Children by Nonschool Skill-Development. *Journal of Child Psychology & Psychiatry & Allied Disciplines, 30*(5),737–750.

Kim HS., & Kim HS. (2008). The Impact of Family Violence, Family Functioning, and Parental Partner Dynamics on Korean Juvenile Delinquency. *Child Psychiatry Human Development, 39,* 439–453.

Langstroem, N. (2002). Long-Term Follow-Up of Criminal Recidivism in Young Sex Offenders: Temporal Patterns and Risk Factors. *Psychology, Crime & Law, 8,* 41–58.

McCarthy, B., & Hagan, J. (1992). Mean Streets: The Theoretical Significance of Situational Delinquency among Homeless Youths. *American Journal of Sociology, 98,* 597–627.

McLennan, J., Bordin, I., Bennett, K., Rigato, F., & Brinkerhoff, M. (2008). Trafficking among Youth in Conflict with the Law in São Paulo, Brazil. *Social Psychiatry and Psychiatric Epidemiology 43,* 816–823.

Oliveira, M. B., & Assis, S. G. (1999). Teenage Law Offenders in Rio de Janeiro and Institutions that "Rehabilitate" Them: The Perpetuation of Negligence. *Cad. Saúde Pública,15*(4), 831–844.

Pearson Education Inc. (2006a). Gap Between Rich and Poor: World Income Inequality. Retrieved April 24, 2006 from http://www.infoplease.com/ipa/A0908770.html

Riberiro, M., & Campone, M. (2001). Homeless Children: The Lives of a Group of Brazilian Street Children. *Journal of Advanced Nursing, 35,* 42–49.

Scanlon, T., Tomkins, A., Lynch, M., & Scanlon, F. (1998). Street Children in Latin America. *British Medical Journal, 316,* 1596–1600.

Secretaria de Assistência e Desenvolvimento Social. (2000). Adolescentes em Conflito Como a Lei (27/10/99-27/02/00). Governado do Estado de São Paulo.

Sheley, J. (1994). Drug Activity and Firearms Possession and Use by Juveniles. *Journal of Drug Issues, 24*(3), 363–382.

Sposati, A. (2001). *Cidade en Pedaços*. São Paulo: Editora Brasiliense.

Stinchcomb, J., & Terry, W. C. (2001). Predicting the Likelihood of Rearrest among Shock Incarceration Graduates: Moving beyond Another Nail in the Boot Camp Coffin. *Crime & Delinquency, 47*(2), 221–224.

Teplin, L. A., McClelland, G. M., Abram, K. M., & Mileusnic, D. (2005). Early Violent Death among Delinquent Youth: A Prospective Longitudinal Study. *Pediatrics, 115,* 1586–1593.

UNICEF. (2001). Making Child Rights Constitutional in Brazil. Retrieved March 18, 2007 from www.unicef.org/sowc96/lbrzil.htm

Veneziano, C., Veneziano, L., & LeGrand, S. (2000). The Relationship between Adolescent Sex Offender Behaviors and Victim Characteristics with Prior Victimization. *Journal of Interpersonal Violence, 15,* 363–374.

Vermeiren, R., Schwab-Stone, M., Ruchkin, V., De Clippele, A., & Deboutte, D. (2002). Predicting Recidivism in Delinquent Adolescents from Psychological and Psychiatric Assessment. *Comprehensive Psychiatry, 43,* 142–149.

Yeager, C., & Lewis, D. (1990). Mortality in a Group of Formerly Incarcerated Juvenile Delinquents. *American Journal of Psychiatry, 147*(5), 612–614.

CHAPTER 3

Children in Institutional and Alternative Care in Viet Nam: A Review of Current Policy and Practice

*Julie Bergeron and Sakiko Tanaka**

Introduction

Children in need of special protection, including those who have suffered abuse or neglect, those who are orphaned or abandoned, those living with HIV/AIDS, those in conflict with the law, and those with mental or physical disabilities represent a particularly vulnerable group. Often, as wards of the state, their future depends on the care and support they receive from governments and benevolent others. Historically, governments around the world have responded to the needs of these children by placing them in institutional care, based on the notion that institutionalization would protect them from harm (Browne, 2009). However, studies dating back more than 50 years (Bowlby, 1951; Goldfarb, 1944) have shown the negative impact of prolonged placement in institutional settings. In particular, the lack of a consistent primary caregiver and denial of a family-based upbringing, typical in institutional settings, is linked to problems associated with the emotional, cognitive, and behavioral development and social functioning of institutionalized children (Browne, 2009; Johnson, Browne, & Hamilton-Giachritsis, 2006; Smyke, Dumitrescu, & Zeanah, 2002). The United Nations Convention on the Rights of the Child (UNCRC) echoes these concerns regarding the damaging effects of institutionalization, emphasizing the importance of family-based care for children (Article 9). Furthermore, it stresses the responsibility of governments to take all legislative, administrative, social, and educative measures to ensure the protection of children from abuse, neglect, or maltreatment (Article 19).

Yet despite consensus over the harmful effects of institutionalization among childcare specialists and the near universal ratification of the CRC among governments around the world, institutionalization continues to be the preferred method of response to children in need of special protection (Browne, 2009; Johnson, Browne, & Hamilton-Giachritsis, 2006). Moreover, the absence of appropriate alternative avenues of care in the community has left millions of children to spend the formative years of their development in institutional care centers (Browne, 2009).

In Viet Nam, there are more than 2.5 million children considered in need of special protection, including 1 million children with disabilities, over 100,000 without parental care, over 150,000 orphans, and nearly 300,000 affected by HIV/AIDS (SITAN, 2004). The remaining children represent street children, children in conflict with the law, child laborers, and sex workers. Despite marked improvements in many social and economic sectors in the country in recent decades,[1] these children have grown increasingly vulnerable. The economic reforms of the 1980s in Viet Nam known as *doi-moi* (renewal) deepened the poverty of many communities, resulting in a higher number of abandoned, abused, neglected, and exploited children. In addition, the transition to a market-led economy in the 1990s led to rapid urbanization and industrialization, heavy rural to urban migration, and often the breakdown of families (Browne, 2009).

Under the stewardship of the Ministry of Labor, Invalids, and Social Affairs (MOLISA), the government has attempted to respond to the needs of these children through two types of interventions: placement in institutional care and support for alternative community-based care. This chapter offers a discussion of the quality of care in these two settings, and draws primarily on the findings of a national study called the Situation Analysis of Institutional and Alternative Care Programmes in Vietnam (SITAN) conducted by UNICEF Viet Nam and MOLISA in 2004. This study was based on a review of 100 institutions in 3 regions of the country: Hanoi (Hanoi), Ho Chi Minh City (south), and Quang Tri (central). The SITAN study relied upon qualitative and quantitative questionnaires, in-depth interviews, focus groups, field visits, and observation. Interviews were conducted with 5 individuals working in various government agencies, as well as 10 focus groups with institutional staff from 10 institutions.[2] Interviews were also conducted with children living in institutional care. A total of 100 children (10 children from 10 different institutions) between the ages of 8 and 18 were interviewed for the study and all discussions were tape-recorded and later translated into English. Interviews were also conducted with 12 foster children and 14 foster parents. Questionnaire results were obtained from a total of 85 government officials and government and nongovernment institutional staff and representatives. Finally, field observations were used to observe the situation of the institutions and to collect data from directors, staff, and children. This chapter highlights the main findings of SITAN and concludes with some recommendations for improving the situation for children in care in Viet Nam.

The State of Institutional Care

Institutional care is commonly defined as a living arrangement for more than 10 children, in which a much smaller number of adults provide remunerated care (Browne, 2009). In these settings, children lack the one-on-one attention and nurturing of a primary caregiver that is commonly associated with healthy growth and social development. The institutions that were surveyed for the SITAN in Viet Nam included social protection centers catering to the needs of abandoned or orphaned children, children affected by HIV/AIDS, children with disabilities, and street children under 16, rehabilitation and vocational centers for sex workers and drug users, and detention centers and reformatory schools for juveniles in conflict with the law. These facilities vary considerably in terms of their specific mandate, size, and quality of the services they provide for children. As a case-by-case assessment of each center is beyond the scope of this chapter, the overarching findings from the institutions are provided.

Factors Influencing Placement

The majority of children placed in institutional care in Viet Nam has at least one living parent. These parents are often willing to care for their children but are constrained by poverty. In the wake of the economic reforms that occurred throughout the 1980s, the situation for the country's poorest families worsened, and their ability to provide care for their children diminished. The SITAN revealed several cases in which parents made the decision to send their children away because they could not afford to feed them. A 15-year-old boy interviewed for the SITAN explained, "I know why I am here, my family is miserable and they sent me here because I am an economic burden for them." A 10-year-old girl recounted a similar story, "My mother couldn't afford both of us, so she kept my elder brother and sent me here." Poverty also forces many children to find work on the streets. In fact, some families reportedly encourage their children to earn money by begging, selling drugs, or prostituting themselves, while other children run away from home and attempt to survive on their own. Many of these children are at serious risk of abuse, exploitation, injury, or developing health problems and are eventually taken in by institutional facilities.

A lack of educational opportunities was also found to be a strong factor behind the institutionalization of children. The testimonies of children and parents suggested that the lack of access to quality education at the primary level led many parents to perceive institutional care as the best means to educate their children. Although there are no tuition fees for primary schools, the so-called voluntary charges that are requested to enlarge the schools' budgets prevent many families from being able to send their children to school. The tuition fees for secondary and tertiary levels limit access even further. In institutional settings, these excluded children are given the opportunity to receive an education that they may not otherwise have received. The testimony of an 18-year-old living in a rehabilitation center offers support for this claim, "When I entered the social protection center, I started school and now I am in Grade 1. Before I did not go to school as my mother did not have money for my school."

In a small number of cases (less than 30 percent), children in care have been orphaned or abandoned, the product of a divorce, unwanted pregnancy, or have parents affected by HIV/AIDS. Institutionalization is also a common response for children with serious mental or physical illness, as many parents are overwhelmed by the burden of extra care required for these children. Moreover, children who are in conflict with the law, abuse drugs, are homeless, or engage in prostitution are often institutionalized. Overall, the findings from the SITAN indicate that institutionalization is not used as a measure of last resort. In fact, it is frequently used to address wider social problems, relating to poverty and lack of education.

The Quality of Institutional Care

In reviewing the state of institutional care in Viet Nam, a number of special areas of concern were identified, including the overall welfare of the children in terms of having their basic needs met, the presence of abuse, neglect or discrimination, the duration of stay in the institutions, the participation of the children in decision making, the quality of services, and the existence of consistent standards and protocols of care. The quality of care in these settings was assessed using a rights-based framework in reference to the principles of the UNCRC. As a consequence, principles of participation, nondiscrimination, and promoting the best interests of the child were especially influential.

Meeting the Basic Needs of Children

Overall, it appears that the basic needs of the children are being met in the surveyed institutions with respect to the provision of adequate food, shelter, clothing, and access to clean water and sanitation. While the children surveyed in the SITAN expressed an appreciation for the care and support they received in the centers, many also conveyed the desire to live at home with their parents or relatives, or to be adopted by a family. Many children seemed to recognize that poverty is the likely reason for their institutionalization and believed that they were lucky to have some material support if they could not remain with their families. A 12-year-old boy explained, "I am lucky because I am fed and taught at the center. Street children like me don't always have such luck." However, interviews with employees working at the institutions frequently voiced their dissatisfaction with the lack of funding available to meet the children's needs and respect their rights and entitlements, suggesting that the level of care is somewhat deficient.

Presence of Abuse and Discrimination

Studies have shown that children in institutions are more vulnerable to abuse and neglect than children living with their families (Browne, 2009). Given that these children are isolated from the community and the fact that they lack a primary caregiver, their risk of being victimized is increased. Therefore, attention to the presence of abuse, neglect, and discrimination was an important point of focus in the SITAN. While no evidence of systematic abuse was found in the institutions, the testimonies of a few brave children raised concern over cases of maltreatment of certain groups. Children with mental disabilities and children previously involved in commercial sex work were reportedly punished more severely than other groups. There was also evidence that children affected by HIV/AIDS were treated poorly compared to other children.

Some were isolated from other children and denied acceptance into certain public schools. A 16-year-old boy with HIV/AIDS confessed that he was locked in a room with four others, and that he was not permitted to dine or watch television with other children. He also said that he was allowed to leave the center only to visit his family once a year.

While Viet Nam's laws and regulations do not consistently establish a child's right to maintain regular contact with their parents while in institutional care, in practice, contact with parents is not made easy. There tend to be restrictions on the frequency and duration of the visits. Often, parental visits with institutionalized children will only occur once or twice a year, if at all. This may be the result of a number of other factors outside the control of the institution as in some cases the children's parents cannot afford the transportation costs to make the trip, or simply choose not to visit their child. In some rare but unfortunate cases, parents are not notified about their child's whereabouts for a long period of time.

There was no evidence of sexual abuse within the surveyed institutions. At the same time, this is not necessarily indicative that it is not occurring, but may rather be a consequence of children's lack of willingness to speak about the abuse, for fear of the repercussions. However, physical abuse and humiliation was not uncommon, according to interviews with some children. Some reported that they were beaten both in the centers and at communal schools, for being "naughty," "disobedient," or "stubborn." Others reported being forced to kneel before caregivers for extended periods of time, being locked in rooms, and being forced to clean toilets as punishment. One nine-year-old girl stated, "I hate aunt Mai (*caregiver at the center*). I hate people who beat small children." While physical discipline for educative purposes is to some extent part of Vietnamese culture, it was found that this treatment of institutionalized children was severe and unnecessary, and greatly affects the disposition and well-being of these children. Despite the testimonies of the children, staff members at the centers insisted that physical abuse was not tolerated and that it occurred only in a few isolated instances.

Few centers had neither procedures in place to help facilitate disclosure of abuse nor policies in place that require staff members to report abuse. Nonetheless, some centers have begun to take steps to allow children to speak out about abuse or mistreatment. For example, one center placed a locked box in a common room, to allow children to submit reports of abuse that would then be directed to higher authorities. However, children in this center seemed suspicious of their ability to lodge anonymous complaints that would be taken seriously. Similarly, when asked about the possibility of children's voices being heard regarding testimonies of caregiver abuse, most interviewed staff members replied with complete denial that such abuse occurs at all.

Duration of Stay

Studies have shown that the prolonged institutionalization of children leads to higher incidents of intellectual and behavioral problems, particularly in cases of social interactions. The UNCRC states that children should not be arbitrarily deprived of their liberty (Article 37, 40), and thus placement in institutional care should be seen as a temporary arrangement, not a long-term solution. Browne (2009) explains that many countries in transition view institutionalization as a quick fix to the problem. In Viet Nam, the majority of institutionalized children stay an average of 8 years; the longest reported stay is 16 years. These figures are unacceptably high, in light of the many adverse consequences prolonged placements can have on the children. Many children are placed as infants and leave the institution as adults. A 17-year-old boy stated, "I have been living in the center all my life. I don't know what a family means."

Excessively long stays at the centers occur in part through weak monitoring and evaluation procedures, which results in many children staying for indeterminate amounts of time. While the law[3] prioritizes and encourages the use of community-based care for abandoned children who are infected with HIV/AIDS, the National Strategy on HIV/AIDS Prevention and Control in Viet Nam for 2004–2010 nevertheless places a heavy emphasis on the institutionalization of these children, and calls for the establishment of more institutions rather than promoting family-based care.

Children's Participation

Children have the right to participate in decisions and matters that affect their lives; this right is protected under the UNCRC (Article 12) and as signatories, governments have a duty to uphold these rights. In most institutions in Viet Nam, however, there is a lack of involvement of children in decision making. The administrators and caregivers take it upon themselves to determine for the children how their needs and interests should be met. This is particularly apparent with regard to decisions around the children's education, vocational training, and future occupations. The children interviewed for the SITAN expressed a strong willingness to participate in these decisions, wishing to have a say in the direction of their own lives. In the majority of institutions, there were no formal or informal policies in place to allow the children to exercise any meaningful degree of influence over the course of their lives. While in a small number of facilities, the staff members reported that the children's participation in decision making was encouraged, however, the extent to which such channels of communication are open remains unclear.

Quality of Services Provided

The quality of service in institutional care was measured based on three main pillars: the working qualifications of caregivers, the extent to which the environment is stimulating, and standards and protocols of care. In Viet Nam, there are neither laws that specify minimum standards or qualifications for workers in institutions, nor is there a specified minimum ratio of staff to children. Of the mainly publicly run institutions surveyed, 35 percent reported having their own minimum standards for the selection of staff members; nonetheless these appeared limited in scope and rigor. With respect to minimal educational requirements, nearly 95 percent of the workers surveyed held a college or university level degree in a variety of disciplines. However, at several of the institutions, candidates are required to demonstrate enthusiasm for the work, love for children, and high moral standards. These are highly subjective, nontechnical requirements that cannot be reliably measured or verified and that ultimately lead to a wide range of talent and qualifications.

About half of the centers reported requiring in-house training in general social work practices and childcare, and 68 percent reported offering educational workshops to staff members on children's rights. However, when caregivers were asked to describe the type of training they received on childcare or children's rights, many were unable to describe the programs with any clarity, making it difficult to assess their efficacy. There was wide discrepancy in the ratios of staff to children in the surveyed institutions. The majority was understaffed, with some exceptions. The SITAN study reported that there was an average of 1 childcare worker to every 3.15 children. Centers catering to the needs of disabled children tended to have better ratios. However, in some centers 1 childcare worker was responsible for nearly 30 children under the age of 10 years.

Some staff developed positive relations with the children. Many interviewed children spoke with affection of their caregivers in the various centers, and even reported "loving" them. Many referred to them as "mothers" and "aunties." At the same time, others had a completely different view. One 17-year-old child stated, "I love no one among the caregivers and also hate no one. They are strangers to us and pay little attention to us." The divergence in views among the children speaks to a lack of consistency in the style and quality of care provided to the children in institutions. It is apparent that some children are nurtured during their experience in the institutions while others are left feeling isolated and alone.

The level of stimulation offered to children in these settings is also of great concern. Most children receive education outside of the institutions in public schools in the community, as well as obligatory vocational training in tailoring, motorbike repair, electrical work, and carpentry is provided for children 15 years and over. In addition, children spend a large amount of their spare time, four hours/day on average, helping with the daily upkeep of the facilities, including cleaning yards, sweeping floors, and working in the kitchen. Although these are recognized rights under the UNCRC (Article 31), other aspects of the children's holistic development, their need to play, to have fun and socialize, are neglected. Moreover, there is a general lack of importance attached to incorporating cultural traditions and activities into institutional curriculums, which only further isolates the children from their roots and home communities.

Standards and Protocols of Care

The standards and protocols of care in place in most institutional facilities govern preplacement eligibility assessments rather than post-placement affairs. The absence of these standards of care for existing institutional operations has serious implications for the quality of the children's experience.[4] For example, regulated periodic assessments to track the children's progress do not exist in many institutions. Moreover, it is not uncommon to have children with vastly different needs placed together in the same center with few or no measures taken to adapt the type of care provided to individual children's needs. In another instance, children with hearing impairments were placed in centers that were not equipped with hearing aids or specialized services. In a few exceptional cases, children were found in the same facilities as adults with severe mental illnesses. Furthermore, the lack of systematic follow-up mechanisms in most institutions means that children are not tracked or supported during their transition to the community or to other care arrangements.

The State of Alternative Community-Based Care

Forms of Alternative Care

In Viet Nam, thousands of children in need of special protection receive alternative or community-based care. Alternative care refers to care that is provided in a family-based setting. In 2006, more than 63,900 children were the recipients of government subsidies for alternative care and were reared in communities by their relatives and sponsors (The Third and Fourth, 2008). In Viet Nam, several forms of alternative care exist including informal foster care, kinship care, adoption or care through social organizations. Informal foster care involves a child being placed in a family unrelated to him or her in the absence of any legal agreement and is the prevailing form of alternative care in the country. A child may also receive kinship care, which involves placement with a member of the child's extended family, be it a grandparent, aunt, uncle, or another relative. The majority of children, who have been orphaned or abandoned, are adopted or taken into care by blood relatives. Most commonly, grandparents assume the role of caregivers for their grandchildren. This form of care also occurs in the absence of any formal agreement or documentation. Social organizations, including pagodas and churches, can also assume guardianship for abandoned or orphaned children. Adoption is also a form of alternative care for children in need and occurs within country or internationally. For international adoption from Viet Nam, a new Law on Adoption was passed in 2010 that ensures procedural compliance with international standards, including clarity on the role of a central coordination agency responsible for both domestic and international adoption.

Children may also be placed in social houses or group homes and by definition, these facilities are small-scale, typically involving the care of less than 10 children at one time. Currently there are six social houses set up across the country, which are administered and run by government agencies. In the absence of clear guidelines and mandates, these centers vary considerably from one another. Some receive former street children and children from reform schools aged 14 and above, while others receive orphans, disabled children or former sex workers. There appears to be a lack of clarity about the purpose and objectives of group and social homes, in terms of the nature and services offered by them and the inability of these homes to meet the multifarious needs of these children. In addition, there is little formal regulation or monitoring of alternative care in Viet Nam.

Quality of Alternative Care

Few studies have examined the experiences of children receiving care in the community and as there is no central coordinating body to regulate this form of care, many of these children slip through the cracks. Not only does this make it difficult to assess the quality of care, but their invisibility renders them more vulnerable to mistreatment. Guidelines and procedures for selecting caregivers for guardianship, kinship, and foster care do not exist. Foster care and adoption arrangements are viewed by many people and officials as an agreement between the adoptive or foster parents and the child, and, therefore, they believe that there is no need for state or legal intervention. The current framework assigns different agencies and ministries jurisdiction over stated areas of child protection, often causing confusion over roles and responsibilities.

At the community level, the People's Committees[5] also assist in child welfare issues, helping families and caregivers care for children in need of special protection in the community. However, the law does not provide any detailed criteria or principles to guide the People's Committee in its provision of services. Also, members of the Committees are not required to have any special training or expertise in child protection issues or children's rights. This may be due in part to an overall lack of national guidelines on alternative care with respect to specific criteria or minimum requirements for the selection of families for alternative care. Nor does the law require officials to take into account the views of the child when considering alternative care options or decisions on guardianship.

Under the current legal framework, many families caring for these children are eligible for public funding, totaling approximately US$5–6 per week, a minimal amount that scarcely covers the cost of food for the children. Families who choose to care for children who are not their own are often living in difficult conditions themselves and without the additional income, struggle to make ends meet. Given that many forms of care in the community are informal arrangements, families are often not identified or compensated for their work. More than 78 percent of caregivers in the community receive no financial or social support from the government (SITAN, 2004).

Support for Alternative Care

Promoting alternative forms of care in the community hinges on the availability of a sufficient number of trained social workers and childcare workers to offer support to care-giving families on the ground. The expertise of these professionals is needed to help monitor the quality of care provided to children in family and group home settings, and to ensure that their rights and best interests are safeguarded. In lieu of the limited number of trained professionals, there is a well-established network of volunteers at the grassroots level with the potential to support the care of children in the community, although their numbers are few. The primary responsibility of the volunteers is to provide regular visits to families in difficult circumstances, collect relevant statistical information, and provide advice and information in light of the challenges that families may be facing. The number of families on the caseloads of one volunteer is often as high as 300 (the average is 100–150). This makes it almost impossible for the volunteers to have regular or more than superficial contacts with these families, or to provide follow-up services to children and young people who return to the community after a stay in an institution. In addition, very few of these volunteers possess formal training in social work, case management skills and intervention methods for families and children, and knowledge of the system necessary to respond to the multifaceted needs of these children and families. Social work, as a legitimately recognized profession and integral part of an effective child protection system, is only beginning to take root in Viet Nam. In 2009, the first group of 1,500 students graduated with Bachelors of Social Work degree, and the curriculum for the Bachelor's degree has been further improved to be in line with international standards. A pilot Masters level training program is being carried out to train 70 university faculty officers from key government ministries. The professionalization of the field is likely to improve the situation and provide increased support for children and families in need of care. Yet the diffusion of social workers into communities, with the proper training to navigate the child protection system and improve the quality of care given to children, remains an issue of concern, and is needed to minimize the risk of abuse and exploitation that many children placed in alternative care settings currently face. According to UNICEF,

> Viet Nam has [a] limited number of professional social workers who are able to conduct risk assessments on child abuse and maltreatment. This impacts [on] the quality of services that are provided to each child, which are often not tailored to their specific needs. The monitoring and data collection system is also not comprehensive enough to provide reliable data on the magnitude and nature of violence against children in Viet Nam. (UNICEF, 2007)

Unregulated and unmonitored alternative care is not necessarily superior to institutional care. To ensure that children are properly cared for and protected from harm while in the community, checks and balances must be in place.

A Review of State Responses

To correct some of the existing flaws of the current child protection system, the government of Viet Nam, through MOLISA, has begun a series of initiatives aimed at restructuring policy and practice in this regard. In 2003, the Committee on the UNCRC provided the government of Viet Nam with a list of recommendations, emphasizing the need to improve care for children in need of special protection in adherence to the UNCRC. In particular, the government was advised to substantially reduce the rate of institutionalization and make improvements in the availability and regulation of alternative care in the community. As a result, the government developed a Draft National Social Protection Strategy for 2011–2020 with the support of UNICEF. This initiative emphasized the need to build a protective environment for children in their communities, prioritizing the prevention of abuse and maltreatment. The initiative also called for a total restructuring of the administration of the governance of children in care, shifting from a vertical approach, which operates by responding to the needs of children on the basis of the category to which they belong (whether the child has disabilities, is affected by HIV/AIDS, or is living on the streets), to a horizontal approach that prioritizes individual assessments of needs. A horizontal system involves the provision of care along a continuum, in which placement in social protection centers and institutions is a measure of last resort, and placement back to the child's community and/or family is the ultimate goal. For this system to be effective, there needs to be coordination of the different streams of care in the community and institutional settings with improved monitoring and regulation.

In fostering the new Strategy, the government and UNICEF identified and subsequently implemented several interventions. First, a thorough review of all national policies and laws relating to child protection has been completed, in order to ensure that community-based care is prioritized. Second, in 2004, a Code of Professional Practice for Social Work was approved, and as noted earlier, newly developed social work programs and courses at several Vietnamese universities have emerged. In addition, members of relevant government ministries and departments are increasingly receiving social work training. While this is an area of significant improvement, community sensitization in relation to professional social workers in the field remains an issue of concern. Viet Nam has a long history and tradition of people giving and receiving support and assistance through family and community networks. As such, the idea that unknown professionals "intrude" on the personal affairs and circumstances of the home to provide "help" and "assistance" challenges traditional social norms (Hugman, Thai Lan, & Thuy Hong, 2007). Third, Guidelines for a Community-Based Child Protection Network (CBCPN), establishing a framework for Common Care Needs, a Continuum of Care,[6] and a Continuum of Service Response[7] have been drafted. The main goals of the Guidelines are to assist in identifying children who are being harmed or are at risk of being harmed, to prevent harm to a child through the provision of professional services and to support the resources and capacities of families and communities to care for children. These Guidelines also focus on strengthening primary, secondary, and tertiary child protection services to provide a "standard" community-based service response to the care needs of all children. This includes improving the quality of social health care, hygiene, and education services, training for families and caregivers on parenting and child protection, specialized services in response to the children's special needs and services for individual children and their families.

Finally, the availability of funding for community-based care providers has been identified as an important issue of concern. In response, in 2005, financial support for families and individuals caring for children in need of special protection was increased, granting qualified caregivers 200,000 VND per child per month (about US$10). Unfortunately, these funds have not been made available to all communities, and consequently, caregivers continue to lack the support they need to provide optimal care. Moreover, given the conditions placed on caregivers and the categories of children they care for, many do not meet the requirements for funding, suggesting once again that the criteria are overly narrow and exclude deserving caregivers and children. Those who do not qualify for this funding receive 65,000 VND per month (approximately US$4) instead of the full amount. Nevertheless, in 2007, additional funds were made available for the care of orphans, children with HIV/AIDS, children and adults with disabilities and the elderly, benefiting both those living in the community in social protection centers and in social houses.

The government also launched the National Plan of Action on Community-Based Care in 2005, which further reflected the government's commitment to developing an effective formalized structure of community-based care. The plan calls for the reduction of long-term institutional care, the piloting of a small-scale family care model in social housing units with less than 10 children in each household, a strengthening of existing alternative care models and developing new models based on the guidelines. It also calls for the transfer of children from institutional care to community-based care where possible, but neglects to specifically address the needs of children who were sexually exploited and abused.

Alongside the push to improve community-based care, the government is also working to improve the quality of institutional facilities. Recent and ongoing policy reforms are expected to streamline current activities, establishing higher standards of quality and promoting greater integration of the centers in the national childcare system.[8] Noteworthy reforms include requiring greater numbers of formally trained staff and more rigorous case management processes, including needs assessment reviews prior to admission to institutions and follow-up assessments. In 2004, of the 373 centers providing care to children, nearly half of which were government run, all were at full capacity and evidently underresourced. It is hoped that the current reforms, as yet unevaluated, will address the severe deficiencies in the provision of both institutional and community care for these at risk children and youth. A further benefit of these reforms would be greater adherence to the mandate of the UNCRC in terms of addressing and protecting children's rights.

Conclusion: Strategies for Moving Forward

The Social Protection Strategy, while not yet fully adopted or implemented, reflects the government's acknowledgment of the current system's failures and its attempts at change. Given that the systemic flaws are great, further issues require attention. First, more accurate data on the status of vulnerable children and youth in the country, including migrant youth, homeless youth and orphans, is urgently needed. Existing facts and figures on these children are scarce and unreliable. A national inquiry into the scope and severity of the problems of children at risk is essential in developing a system that is better equipped to respond to their needs.

Second, the government should continue to enhance the legitimacy of the social work profession in Viet Nam. Qualified and trained professionals, with knowledge of human and child rights, social justice, and the intricacies of the child protection system are needed to help support children in care, whether in institutions or in the community. The development of a national network of community centers in which individuals and families can obtain assistance from a social worker at the grassroots level is needed. One way social workers could also be enlisted would be to help facilitate the dialogue around sensitive, often taboo issues. In Viet Nam, child protection issues are often confined to the privacy of the home and not openly discussed. Greater openness would ultimately facilitate the development of more protective environments for children.

Third, more focused and ongoing training should be made available to caregivers and caseworkers in the community. UNICEF Viet Nam is currently planning to support two training sessions of four weeks each at two project sites, with the intention that the government will duplicate the exercise at other project sites. Moreover, specialized training is needed for directors and caregivers on strategies to make more meaningful spaces for the involvement of children in decision making. Children who are given the opportunity to actively participate in decision making may be better equipped for the transition to independent living when they leave the centers and return to the community. As stated in the SITAN (2004), "A participatory approach to care not only equips children with skills to make independent decisions when they grow up but also increases their feelings of belonging, significance and solidarity" (p. 44). In order for this to materialize in institutional policy and practice, this will require a conceptualization of the child as a subject engaged in a dialogue with his/her surroundings instead of as merely an object and a helpless victim.

Finally, the government should continue to develop policies that address the prevention of child abuse and neglect.[9] The link between children in care and poverty has been clearly demonstrated, and, therefore, steps must be taken to help alleviate the burden on the country's poorest families. The availability of greater resources to families to allow them to meet their children's needs and provide greater access to education will likely go a long way to addressing these issues.

Children in need of special protection deserve a system that seeks first and foremost to promote their best interests and their rights. An overreliance on institutional care has threatened the emotional and social development of thousands of children across the country and should be the last, rather than the first, resort. Investment in community-based care, in both capital and human resources, and improvements in its regulation will allow for the creation of more protective environments in order for children to develop and thrive. The restructuring of the system is no small undertaking. The government must stay the course of its current reform and strive to offer children in need of special protection the highest possible quality of care.

Notes

* We wish to acknowledge the contribution of the Vietnamese and international researchers as well as the Vietnamese government and agencies, in particular the Ministry of Labor, Invalids, and Social Affairs (MOLISA) for their involvement in conducting and drafting reports and studies related to child protection and children without primary caregivers. In particular, we extend a special thanks to the authors of the 2004 "Situation Analysis on Institutional and Alternative Care Programs in Viet Nam," a project funded by the Canadian International Development Agency. It is worth noting that these have been used as key tools in drafting this chapter. The contribution of Dr. Yvon Dandurand and Ms. Vivienne Chin is acknowledged with deep appreciation. Their extensive knowledge and experience with child protection issues have enhanced the depth of this chapter. Finally, special thanks should also be addressed to the UNICEF Viet Nam Child Protection Team, in particular, Dr. Pauline Meemeduma, Child Protection Consultant for UNICEF Viet Nam, Ms. Nguyen Thanh Truc, Child Protection Officer for UNICEF Viet Nam, and Ms. Siobhan King, Child Protection Officer for UNICEF Viet Nam, for their continuous support and insights.

1. Examples of these improvements include a sharp decrease in poverty rates; reductions in infant and child mortality; and significant progress toward its goal of universal primary education.
2. Institutions included in the study were run by government, nongovernment organizations, and by private and religious organizations. The institutions included mental health institutions, social protection centers, drop-in centers, rehabilitation centers, and institutions that provide occasional care for children such as special schools for children with disabilities.
3. Neither the Law on Protection, Care, and Education of Children (2004) nor the Law on HIV/AIDS Prevention and Control (2006) clearly prioritize community-based care for abandoned children infected with HIV/AIDS. However, the government enacted several regulations, including Decree No. 38/2004/QD-TTg, Decree No. 67/2007/ND-CP (revised by Decree No. 13/2010/ND-CP) stipulating financial supports for families who take care of orphans and abandoned children, and children infected with HIV/AIDS. These Decrees may be viewed as encouragements for community-based family care for such children.
4. On May 30, 2008, however, the government enacted Decree No. 68/2008/NĐ-CP on conditions and procedures of social protection institutions'

establishment, operation, and dissolution. It is hoped that directives will help to improve the quality and consistency of care offered to children in these institutions.

5. People's Committees comprise members appointed by an elected People's Council. They are an executive arm of provincial governments and are responsible for formulating and implementing policy.
6. It is believed that the standard of care in response to children's needs can best be met through a range of responses, along a continuum of care (UNICEF, 2007).
7. This requires that professional interventions be offered at various points along a continuum including prevention, intervention, and reintegration to ensure that the children's care needs are met as they arise (UNICEF).
8. For example, in 2009, support was provided to MOLISA to introduce new care functions and operational procedures for Social Protection Centers. In addition, national child protection standards and guidelines, including minimum standards of care for institutions are being finalized.
9. Toward this end, a Circular on Interventions in cases of Child Maltreatment and Sexual Abuse and a new Decree to guide the Implementation of the Law on Protection, Care, and Education of Children are currently being developed toward protection of children from abuse, violence, and exploitation.

References

Bowlby, J. (1951). *Maternal Care and Mental Health.* Geneva, Switzerland: World Health Organisation.

Browne, K. (2009). *The Risk of Harm to Young Children in Institutional Care.* The Save the Children Fund.

Goldfarb, W. (1944). The Effects of Early Institutional Care on Adolescent Personality. *Journal of Experimental Education, 12,* 106–129.

Hugman, R., Thai Lan, N. T., & Thuy Hong, N. (2007). Developing Social Work in Viet Nam. *International Social Work, 50*(2), 197–211.

Johnson, R., Browne, K., & Hamilton-Giachritsis, C. (2006). Young Children in Institutional Care at Risk of Harm. *Trauma, Violence and Abuse, 7,* 34–60.

Situation Analysis of Institutional and Alternative Care Programs in Vietnam. (2004). UNICEF: Hanoi.

Smyke, A. T., Dumitrescu, B. A., & Zeanah, C. H. (2002). Attachment Disturbances in Young Children. I: The Continuum of Caretaking Casualty. *Journal of American Academy of Child & Adolescent Psychiatry, 41*(8), 972–982.

The Third and Fourth Country Report on Viet Nam's Implementation of the United Nations Convention on the Rights of the Child in the 2002–2007 Period. (2008). Hanoi: Office of High Commissioner for Human Rights. Retrieved August 29, 2010 from http://www2.ohchr.org/english/bodies/crc/docs/AdvanceVersions/CRC.C.VNM.3-4.pdf

UNICEF. (2007). The State of the World's Children. Retrieved from http://www.unicef.org/sowc07/docs/sowc07.pdf

United Nations. (1989). Convention on the Rights of the Child. Adopted and Opened for Signature, Ratification and Accession by General Assembly Resolution 44/25 of November 20, 1989. Entry into Force September 2, 1990, in accordance with Article 49.

PART II

Child Labor, Violence, and Exploitation

CHAPTER 4

Child Laborers in the Bolivian Mining Sector: Exploring Children's Experiences and Perspectives

*Juan Albarracin-Jordan and Thérèse Bouchard**

Introduction

Child labor constitutes a major problem faced by developing countries in Latin America. Child employment rates are highest in the Andean region, notably in Peru, Ecuador, and Bolivia (Sedlacek, Duryea, Ilahi, & Sasaki, 2005). Some 50 percent of child employment occurs in the rural areas and approximately 90 percent of the labor performed by children is carried out in the informal sector (Oficina Internacional del Trabajo [OIT], 2005). In Bolivia, informal mining activities are among the most hazardous types of work and they often involve children. Unsafe mining related tasks are often carried out under precarious conditions, with high levels of risk to health and life. In Bolivia, a country with 8.5 million people, of whom 36.4 percent live in extreme poverty, there are some 120,000 mining children (IPEC & MINERÍA, 2001).

Despite numerous studies related to the risks of mining and a range of assistance programs that have provided for mining communities, viable long-term solutions have been few and far between. Despite the sizeable population of children who work in the mining sector, few efforts have focused on garnering children's perspectives. Too often mining children have been perceived as objects of assistance whose experiences and opinions count for little, thus minimizing their involvement in the search for improvements in their living and working conditions. In response, our study sought to explore two mining regions in Bolivia—Chima-Chuquini and Huanuni—where children are frequently involved in mining activities. Conducted by researchers from the Canadian Centre for International Studies and Cooperation (CECI) and Medioambiente, Minería e Industria (MEDMIN), the study aimed to provide an "emic" view of mining children's daily lives. Their perceptions and testimonies, therefore, constitute the main source of the study's data and analysis.

A Historical Perspective on Child Labor in Bolivia

The term "child labor" commonly refers to all work performed by young people aged 14 years and younger who generate income (as opposed to unpaid domestic chores, for example) and is deemed to be dangerous to the health, security, and psychosocial well-being of children (International Labor Organization, 2004). Although abolitionist and critical perspectives on child labor differ in their philosophical and political bases, both agree with the need to defend and promote the rights of children (Domic Ruiz, 1999). Historically, although domestic and productive tasks in peasant societies involving young children have varied according from one cultural and geographic context to another, children's work was generally a function of socialization processes that encouraged them to develop the capacities necessary to assume their eventual productive roles and responsibilities as adults. Yet in more recent times, with the legacy of colonialism and the advent of industrialization, unregulated capitalism, and weak systems of governance, extreme poverty has left whole populations destitute and forced children into low paying jobs that are frequently dangerous and exploitative. For these children, the fulfillment of fundamental rights such as access to education and health care is little more than a pipedream.

The antecedents of current child labor practices in Bolivia are rooted in a colonial system dating back to the mid-1500s when Native populations, including children, were press-ganged into extracting minerals, mainly silver and gold, for colonial authorities. Under this system of "obligatory servitude," working conditions were harsh and remuneration was highly inadequate (Arce, 1990; Capriles, 1977). Moreover, despite Bolivia's independence from Spain in 1825, conscripted child labor, especially in the mining sector, has continued up to the present time. For more than a century and a half following independence, the mining sector constituted the main pillar of Bolivia's economy, with tin and silver as the main extracts (Albarracin-Millan, 1993). In the latter part of the 1980s, however, the mining sector in Bolivia lost its economic preeminence. As international prices for silver and tin dropped, many mining families who had long worked in the traditional mining regions of Oruro and Potosi migrated to the northern subtropical Department of La Paz where gold mining became the main source of subsistence. Yet conditions of miners and mining families, many of whom are indigenous people, have remained dismal. The main difficulties encountered by these families are low pay, poor nutrition, and limited access to health services and education. Parental alcoholism—generally among fathers—and violence against women and children appear to be widespread and undermine family stability. In mining communities, therefore, children of low-income families tend to drop out of school and work in the mines (Oficina Internacional del Trabajo [OIT], 2001). In part, the employment of children as mine workers is a means to supplement needed family income, but it also reflects the vestiges of indigenous and peasant values concerning work as a form of socialization for adulthood (OIT, 2005). Yet the conditions of most child mine workers in Bolivia continue to be detrimental to their biological and psychological development (UNICEF, 2004). In addition, because of their status as minors, they remain largely an invisible work force. Their voices are unheard, and we know little about their needs, aspirations, and creative potential.

These conditions of child mine workers have continued largely unabated despite the promulgation of Bolivia's Child and Youth Rights Code (*Código Niño, Niña, Adolescente)* promulgated in 1999. Many of the provisions of the *Código* are consistent with the UN Convention on the Rights of the Child (UNCRC). Among the rights stipulated by the *Código* are (1) access to health services, including the healthcare of the mother; (2) secure family life; (3) access to education, cultural activities, and recreation; (4) protection and safety; and (5) treatment with dignity and respect. Specifically, Article 134 of the *Código* officially prohibits any kind of work that puts children's physical and/or mental integrity at risk. This includes work in quarries and mines, as well as work that involves explosives and toxic substances. Unfortunately, however, most of the rights stipulated in the *Código* are largely rhetorical and are not adhered to in Bolivia's mining industry.

Research Problem and Objectives

The study aimed to increase our understanding of child mining from the emic side, that is, from the individuals' description of cultural behaviors and beliefs as they are meaningful to him or her. It also aimed to support the active engagement of mining children in the transformation of their sociocultural surroundings. At the same time, since the implementation of child rights approaches and child participation are rare in social interventions in Bolivia, the research sought to sensitize program developers and policy makers on child rights and engage them in the project implementation process.

Other objectives of the study were to

- implement multidimensional and qualitative analyzes that increase our knowledge of the cultural factors that contribute to child labor in the mining sector;
- expand our understanding of the capacity of children to contribute to the analysis of the problem, as well as to its possible solutions;
- promote future policies, and the development of programs concerning the protection of working children, highlighting their experiences and perspectives; and
- provide recommendations for decision makers, including state officials and organizations that promote the development of mining communities.

A Methodological Approach Based on the Children's Perceptions and Participation

This study focused on how mining children perceived their world—a first step in attempting to understand their culture and reality from their point of view. This approach enabled us to analyze the obstacles that they encountered, as well as the opportunities. The study took into consideration the participation of the children, as well as a gendered approach in order to establish differences and similarities between and among both sexes.[1] As a result, this study hoped to reinforce the idea that children themselves are entitled to claim the rights and responsibilities awarded to them as citizens. In Articles 12, 13, 14 of the UNCRC, it is stated that children have the right to express their views, to organize themselves, and to participate in decision making that affects their lives. In accordance with these Articles, the methodology employed in the study, based on earlier investigations promoting social change and development (e.g., Cook, Blanchet-Cohen, & Hart, 2004), sought to promote children's participation in the discussions and recognized and acknowledged their capacity to contribute to integral solutions.

While the study aimed to be participatory in its approach, children did not take part in the planning stage—mainly because it would have demanded a large amount of time and effort from them. Nevertheless, a group of children contributed to the collection of data, the preparation of questionnaires, and verification of the data. Moreover, some children took part in formal presentations of the study results, providing accounts of their personal experiences and acting as spokespersons for their peers. Throughout the research process, special attention was paid to suggestions and comments made by the children. Local customs and views were also taken into consideration. Adults in the area often do not believe mining children have a right to express themselves, let alone discuss their needs or make decisions. Despite these constraints, the study proceeded in a manner that sought to promote children's capacity to speak about their reality, and to address their concerns to government authorities. Hart (1992) has developed a scale or ladder of young people's participation in decisions that affect them and their life situations, ranging from nonparticipation at the low end of the scale, up to shared decision making with adults at the highest end of the scale. This project, aiming to promote child participation, focused upon the fifth level, whereby children are questioned and informed; and on the sixth level, whereby decisions are taken by adults, but shared with the children.

The study included children who work in the mines and those at risk of becoming informal mining workers. Child participants came from three communities: Chima, Chuquini, and Huanuni. Two social workers were hired six months prior to the commencement of the study. In order to gain the children's and family's trust, as well as to communicate the purpose and methodology of the study, they lived alongside the participants in the villages. These social workers and other members of the research team were trained in issues surrounding child rights, as well as in participatory methodology.

In their work, the research team relied upon open communication, exchange, and feedback. This was done in such a way as to avoid overburdening the children, who already had great pressures on their lives and their time. In particular, the team attempted to avoid interrupting school, family, and social life. Thus, children's limited time availability, level of education and illiteracy, age group, girl/boy dynamics, and their relationships with nonworking children were all taken into account. The goal was to build a cordial and motivating ambiance in order to facilitate communication. Moreover, we hoped that the children would view the study as an interesting activity and not as additional work.

Ethical issues were of serious concern throughout the research process. Before the beginning of any research activity, the team made sure that confidentiality was openly and clearly discussed with the participants in order to protect the children's safety. In some instances, a lack of confidentiality could put them in danger of violent reactions from their families, other community members, and employers. To avoid this and to gain the children's and families' trust, necessary precautions to protect their identities were taken. More importance was placed on protecting the children than on any other research objective.

One way of collecting a plethora of sociocultural data was through Rapid Assessment (RA), a research methodology outlined in the Methodological Guidelines of the ILO[2] and UNICEF (Harris, Jerome, & Fawcett, 1997). Its main strength rests in allowing for the collection of a "detailed analysis of workers' lives and everyday contingencies in different types of labor." RA was specifically designed for small samples obtained within the context of local communities. This method facilitates the gathering of qualitative data and also allows for the discovery of "hidden" or "invisible" forms of child labor, as well as taking into account high-risk situations (hazardous or unhealthy). In this study, RA was used to

- explore the lives of working children, their families and communities, migration, work history, and the factors that lead them to enter mining activities;
- examine the relationship between school and work; the attitude of children and parents toward education, the powers and pressures that force children in one direction or another;
- identify hazardous, psychologically harmful, or illegal circumstances, the number of children involved in mining activities, possibilities for improvement, opportunities that mining children have to leave their current working conditions, and their hopes for change;
- establish foundations for the future work of NGOs, governments, and other organizations.

The children interviewed explained that there were approximately 200 *barranquillero* families in Chuquini and 240 in Chima. Taking the number of children into account, per family, in both towns, there were 678 children in Chuquini and 720 in Chima. Consequently, there were 1,398 children, both boys and girls, under 18 years of age, who worked, or will work prematurely, in the mining sector.[3]

In-depth interviews with the child participants were conducted in August of 2005, and lasted several months; 30 children were interviewed from the Chima and Chuquini area, while a further 50 were interviewed from the Huanuni area. In addition, a questionnaire was used to obtain information from 63 children who were currently working as *barranquillero* (open pit panners).[4] This questionnaire gathered data on the children's (1) sex and age; (2) education; (3) the tasks carried out and amount of time spent on them; (4) income; (5) family situation; (6) free time; (7) feelings regarding their work and family, and (8) opinion regarding the banning of child labor. In total, 45 boys and 18 girls from Huanuni, Chima, and Chuquini participated in the questionnaires and interviews.

Other means of data collection included the identification and mapping of the locations where children worked, participant observation, focus groups with children, discussions with key Bolivian organizations holding advanced knowledge of the mining sector, and the review of secondary data.

Research Findings

Child Labor in the Barranquillas (Open Pit Mines) of Chima, Chuquini, and Huanuni

A total of 30 children were interviewed in Chima and Chuquini. Table 4.1 shows the distribution of the sample. The age of children working as *barranquilleros* ranged between 5 and 16 years; boys and girls worked in equal numbers. Because of the impoverished conditions of the mine workers, whole families—husbands, wives, and children—worked in the *barranquilla* in order to contribute to the family's economy. Children of *barranquillero* families did not work directly in mines per se. Rather their labor focused on searching for the spoils and run off from the ore of the mines. When boys become teenagers they are allowed to carry out other tasks. Girls, however, tend to have no other option but to continue working as *barranquilleras*. Later in life, of they become mothers, there is a strong likelihood that their children will be employed as *barranquilleros* as well. Before the economic crisis of the 1980s, *barranquillero* children came mainly from families where the mother or guardian (widow, single mother, or a mother who had been abandoned) was a *barranquillera*.

The work of child *barranquilleros* is arduous. Within Chima and Chuquini, children worked primarily in river-banks, where they screened soils, mainly in search of gold particles and occasionally cobalt fragments. Although sometimes children worked near the mines, generally

Table 4.1 Number of children interviewed in Chima, Chuquini, and Huanuni

	Chima	*Chuquini*	*Huanuni*	*TOTAL*
Boys	8	9	37	54
Girls	7	6	13	26
Total	15	15	50	80

they preferred the river-banks, despite the fact that they were contaminated by waste from neighboring towns. To get to the riverbanks, the children had to walk between 15 and 20 minutes, carrying their tools through narrow pathways. Their tools generally consist of shovels, picks, metal sticks, *chajrañas* (hard branched bushes used to remove soil), and pans. Children between five and seven years old usually work with a pan, *chajraña,* and *pallalla* (small shovel). The older children use heavier tools. Children who work as *barranquilleros* often are often abused by other gold miners, particularly when they stray near areas mined by adults. Children are also prone to abuse from adult *barranquilleros* who work and compete with the children for the same areas. Children likewise are exposed to dangerous chemicals. The rivers where they work are contaminated with mercury, sulfur, and other mineral residues, the result of up-stream waste produced in the mining camps. Some of the children amalgamate mercury with gold, but they almost never know how to handle the mix appropriately and know nothing about the health risks involved. At the time of fieldwork for this study, although adults were in charge of the amalgamation process, the *barranquilleros* were exposed to contaminated soil and water, as well as to the mercury gases generated by the burning of the amalgamation of mercury and gold. Under these conditions, it is likely that both adults and children suffered from chronic mercury intoxication through constant exposure.

Children worked in the mines because their parents could not adequately support their families. Both boys and girls were involved in this work, and girls, in addition to this, carried out household chores without being acknowledged for the extra work. Because work in the *barranquilla* meant screening residue soils from primary mining activities carried out by the cooperatives, not a great deal of gold was ever obtained. Children normally worked until a *palo*[5] of gold is obtained. The money was used to help the family buy food and pay for other needs. In some cases, children kept their money to buy clothes, school materials, or something to eat at recess.

Almost all children who worked also went to school. Nevertheless, they had very little time left to do their homework and, consequently, ended up doing poorly or failing some of their classes. Mining children tended to lag behind their age grade in school and were consequently much older than their classmates. At the same time, their work colleagues were much older adults.

The work carried out by the *barranquilleros* was done in unsafe and unhealthy conditions. All of the 30 children interviewed in Chima and Chuquini had dark skin due to their exposure to the sun. The children also had scarred feet and worn out fingernails. Their typical outfit consisted of shorts and t-shirts. While the children were conscious of the diverse risks they faced at work, they believed that working was the best option they had to survive. Working in the riverbeds, most children suffered from colds, flu, fungus, chilblain (a sore or inflamed swelling caused by exposure to cold), stomach aches, diarrhea, sun stroke and bone pain, which often leads to rheumatism later in life. Although there was a health center in both Chima and Chuquini, the children who were ill did not go to see the doctor because they could not pay for the services or for prescriptions. In general, they reported using home remedies, such as herbal teas, while in many cases, they let the illness heal itself.

At the time of research fieldwork, some 90 percent of all mining children in Chima and Chuquini earned a salary of Bs. 4 (approx. US$50 cents, per day). In some cases, a few children earned up to Bs. 15 (US$1.90), but these were the children who had the most experience and skill. Importantly, they used their income to cover their basic needs and that of their families, thus confirming that one of the main reasons why children work is because of insufficient family income.

The combination of work and school did not allow these children to have much rest or recreation. Their parents' exhaustion and, in many cases, their alcoholism and involvement in violence forced these children to work. In some cases, children provided for their parents, which undoubtedly affect their psychological and social development and overall well-being.

As far as their aspirations were concerned, many children stated that their greatest wish was to finish school, begin a career, becoming doctors, teachers, or police officers. They hoped that in the future they could make enough money to be able to buy all the food they wanted and to stop working.

Chima

In Chima, working boys who were interviewed were aged 10–12 years, while girls' ages were distributed more widely, from 7 to 17 years. Sixty-seven percent of them had already worked from three to five

Table 4.2 Child residence, working experience, work days per week, and education level, in Chima (in percentages).

	Residency			*Years of experience*							*Work days per week*			*Education*						
														Elementary (Grade)					*High School (Grade)*	
	M	*F*	*B*	*1*	*2*	*3*	*4*	*5*	*6*	*7*	*1*	*2*	*7*	*3rd*	*4th*	*5th*	*6th*	*7th*	*1st*	*4th*
Boys			53		13		7	20		13	13	33	7			20	26	7		
Girls	7		40	7		20	7	13			13	34		7	13			7	13	7
Total		100					100					100					100			

M=Mother
F=Father
B=Both

years. Most of them worked from 4 to 8 hours per day for two days a week, with a 30- to 60-minute break each day. The majority (73 percent) of the children reported that their job was difficult and that it demanded great effort. As shown in table 4.2, 93 percent of the children lived with both parents, most of whom were miners and worked for more than eight hours a day. In fact, as reported by the children, 60 percent of the mothers were *barranquilleras* and 33 percent were full-time housewives.

The Story of Andrea

The following verbatim account by "Andrea" exemplifies the experiences and conditions of mining children in Chima:

> I am 12 years old. I don't know my father; my mother says that he made a trip one day and never came back. I have four younger siblings—a girl and three boys. Now, I have a new dad because my mom remarried another man and my younger siblings are his children. He's good to me, but he is always sick, and he can't work all the time. He's very thin. I help my mother at work, taking care of my brothers and sister. She works a lot in the riverbanks. I feel sorry for her because she is always tired and she falls asleep sitting down. She gets up very early to cook our food for the day: rice, potatoes, banana, eggs, and coffee. Sometimes, when we find more "sparks,"[6] she buys meat; it's delicious. I go to school with my two brothers, and my mom goes to work

> in the river with the two younger ones. I like school a lot, but sometimes I'd like to have all the things some of my classmates have. They get new notebooks, picture books, toys, and new clothes. Their parents are members of the mining cooperative and they have a lot of money. We don't have a television, or electricity, because we have to pay the cooperative, and my mom says it's very expensive. With my siblings, I watch television in the stores; there we can watch movies. After school, we all go and help my mother in the riverbanks. My brother Moses is lucky because he always finds "sparks" and he buys soda and chocolate for himself. At dusk we go home. On the way, we gather wood for the kitchen. My mom keeps the "sparks" in a little bottle that hangs from her neck. When we find nothing, she cries and is very sad because she can only buy rice and other things. There is a lady who is very nice. She gives us food and we can pay her later. My mom says that one day we will go to La Paz to buy a house. I want to be a doctor to help my mom, and heal my step-dad and my siblings. My step-dad fights with my mom sometimes and disappears for a few days, but he always returns. He doesn't drink because he's ill; but he smokes a lot. He smells bad. I want to visit the city. My friends went there and they told me that it's really nice and that there are many things you can buy. When I ask my mom when we'll go, she always says "one day," and that's it. When we go, we'll take our dog, called Blackie, even if he is afraid of cars.

Chuquini

In Chuquini, most children who worked in the *barranquilla* were 7–12 years old and they worked from 3 to 4 hours per day. These children reported they only had between 15 minutes and a half an hour break in their work day. As shown in table 4.3, 80 percent of the children in this area lived with both parents. More than half of them had been working from three to four years, and 27 percent had five to six years work experience. Similar to children in Chima, those in Chuquini had begun working at a very young age (around age seven), and a great majority indicated that their work involved heavy and difficult tasks. Contrary to what occurs in Chima, approximately half the children in Chuquini claimed that they did not eat at work. Similarly, half the children's parents were miners and the other half were *barranquilleros.* Sixty percent of the mothers were *barranquilleras* and thirty-three percent were full-time housewives. Most fathers worked eight hours a day, but the children indicated that generally their mothers worked longer hours per day.

Table 4.3 Child residence, working experience, work days per week, and education level, in Chuquini (in percentages)

	Residency			*Years of experience*							*Work days per week*			*Education*						
														Elementary (Grade)					*High School (Grade)*	
	M	*F*	*B*	*1*	*2*	*3*	*4*	*5*	*6*	*7*	*1*	*2*	*3*	*3rd*	*4th*	*5th*	*6th*	*7th*	*1st*	*4th*
Boys			40			20	13	7			13	27			20	7		13		
Girls	20		40		20	20		7	13		33	27		20	7	7	13	7	6	
Total		**100**					**100**					**100**					**100**			

M=Mother
F=Father
B=Both

The Story of Joel

The story of Joel is a reflection of the lives of many children in Chuquini:

> I live with my grandfather and my younger brother. I am 14 years old. My parents and little sister died in the landslide that happened two years ago. My house was destroyed by the mudslide. My parents and other people's bodies were never found. I don't go to school any more. I work at the *barranquilla* all day. My brother stays with my grandfather in his *pahuichi* (rustic cabin). He's very old and can't work because he can't walk or move his hands and fingers. I have my own tools because I bought them myself. Before, I worked for someone else, and I had to pay for using the tools.
>
> I learned to chew coca leafs, which help me fight hunger and sleep. One day my friends gave me alcohol mixed with coca-cola. They told me that all men have to learn how to drink alcoholic beverages. I felt as if things were spinning around me; I was really happy, but, later on, my head hurt and I felt like vomiting. My grandfather got mad at me.
>
> I want to work at the cooperative; you can make a lot of money there and I want to be one of the partners; but you need a lot of money to become a partner. I was told that a share in the cooperative costs 10,000 dollars. My friends have girlfriends, but it's expensive because you have to take them out to eat and buy them things. It's really difficult to have friends. I have two friends who are my age and they already have babies. They hide because they don't want to raise their children.

> When my grandfather, or brother, gets sick, I need to find the doctor and buy medicines. Sometimes I have no money and they have to get better with herbal teas. When insects bite you, you can also get sick; when you drink water from the river, the same thing. I have an uncle in the city, but he never comes to visit. He didn't even show up when my parents died.
>
> Gold is very pretty. It is yellow when it appears on the trough; this is when one finds a good spot in the riverbank. It is better to work alone. If you find a good place, and others see you, the place gets full quickly. So, the gold vanishes rapidly. My dream is to become a partner of the cooperative and I will work a lot to save money and buy stocks.

Child Laborers in the Highlands: The Case of Huanuni

Huanuni is historically a mining community. Most of the population is made up of immigrants and there are over 500 children involved in the mining sector. Fifty children from Huanuni participated in the study—13 were girls and 37 were boys, ranging in age from 10 to 17 years. They all indicated that their work was dangerous. Sixty-eight percent had two to four years mining experience. Half said that they worked on average between seven and eight hours per day, and most indicated that they had between 15 minutes and half an hour break during their work day. Contrary to the situation in Chima and Chuquini, only 48 percent of the children lived with both parents, indicative of greater family fragmentation. In this community, the father was often no longer the sole provider because women tended to work outside their homes to supplement the economic needs of the family. Children also worked and contributed to the upkeep of the family and to satisfy their own needs. Compositions of families were varied. Many included mother and children, or grandparents, parents, and children. In some instances families were made up of children without parents who lived with uncles, aunts, nieces, and nephews. In other situations, orphans lived with their tutors or godparents. Some families had up to 10 members, but in other circumstances children lived entirely alone. Still others, ranging from 16 to 18 years of age, started their own families.

Within this community there was a distinction between children who worked for the cooperatives and those who mined clandestinely. The monthly income earned by children who worked in the cooperatives ranged approximately from Bs. 700 to Bs. 900 (approx. between US$88 and 113). Generally these were the children of the

Table 4.4 Child residence, working experience, work days per week, and education level, in Huanuni (in percentages)

	Residency			*Years of experience*							*Work days per week*			*Education*						
														Elementary (Grade)					*High School (Grade)*	
	M	*F*	*B*	*1*	*2*	*3*	*4*	*5*	*6*	*7*	*1*	*2*	*7*	*3rd*	*4th*	*5th*	*6th*	*7th*	*1st*	*4th*
Boys	8	6	42	18	18	32	6					28	16	4		8	12	4	14	4
Girls	6	6	6		6	4	2		8	6		8	4			6			4	2
Total		100					100					100					100			

M=Mother
F=Father
B=Both

miners who worked in the cooperatives and received preferential treatment in the mining organization. The income of the parents ranged from Bs. 900 to Bs. 1200 (between US$113 and 150), which was not enough to sustain the family, forcing children to work to supplement that income.

In contrast, the earnings of child clandestine miners varied according to the amount of minerals they found. Usually, they mined in groups of six and if they found a large amount of minerals, they distributed it equally among themselves. Nevertheless, sometimes they were unable to find sufficient quantities and worked in vain for 15 hours or more a day. As they were in constant fear of being caught by the miners of the cooperative (adults), the children often worked in dangerous places and sold their labor to older youth who organized them into work parties. If they were caught, the adults took away the minerals that the children collected.

In Huanuni, most children who worked inside the mine dropped out of school because they had no time to continue studying. Interviews conducted with teachers found that some mining children were perceived as "rebellious," while others were extremely introverted, with low academic achievement levels.

The health of mining children in Huanuni was constantly at risk. Continuous exposure to dust caused silicosis, as well as nose and eye irritation, and poisonous gases affected their respiratory and nervous systems. The high levels of noises produced by the drills and explosions were also likely to produce hearing impairment. Exposure of their feet to mud and water may later cause rheumatism and bone pain. The children reported trying to reduce the pain and exhaustion by chewing on coca leafs. None of those who were interviewed visited the doctor, either because they had no money, or because they decided to ignore the pain. As in the case of Chima and Chuquini, many reported using home remedies.

The children who worked inside the mine clandestinely reported that they had no safety equipment—they wore ski masks, bandanas, and old clothes. They frequently carried backpacks, chisels, drills, and heavy sledgehammers, tools that were a risk to their safety. The guards who controlled the mine entrance checked the young workers and their equipment (helmet, boots, and masks), but once inside the mine, children reportedly dropped their security equipment in order to slide down the narrow galleries more easily. The working hours were long, and the work was hazardous, which affected the children's break time and recreation during the day.

The Story of Karen

The following interview, depicting at length the life and perceptions of "Karen," typifies the lives of mining children in Huanuni. Interestingly, in sharing her life story, Karen referred to herself in the third person.

> Karen is a nine year old girl. Her family consists of nine people: mother, father, and siblings. She has two sisters and four older brothers. Her father and the brothers are miners. Karen began working informally with her mother and her elder brothers when she was 7 years old. She is not scared of entering the mine, because her brothers take care of her. She helps to pick up pieces of rock that contain tin. The brothers carry loads of mineral. Karen doesn't think she's ready to do this type of work, but she has a lot of knowledge about how to handle raw minerals. She is not the only one who performs these tasks; her friend also works with her.
>
> Karen gets up at 6 o'clock in the morning with her mother and helps her with breakfast and lunch so that her brothers can take it to the mine. Lunch is made up of rice, *chuño* (dehydrated potatoes), beef jerky and half a liter of cinnamon water. Those who come home for lunch eat what is left for them. After breakfast, which includes tea and bread (sometimes cornbread toast), Karen goes to school. She is in fifth grade. She does her homework during recess, when she has the time. Nevertheless, she always tries to comply with her school duties. Karen is sensitive yet tough. Her teachers say that she is a hyperactive person, who gets mad easily and who

fights with the boys. The other children's influence and the environment of the mine shaped Karen's personality. She is rebellious but, at the same time, tender. She gets out of school at 1:00 pm, and she goes home for lunch. She shares lunch with whoever is at home, generally her mother and younger sisters. Her brothers work at the mine with her father. In the afternoon she helps her mother wash clothes and cook dinner.

During the week, her father and brother work at the quarry inside the mines. Karen and her mother work there on weekends. Sometimes she works inside the mines during the week with her two brothers. Karen wants to show that she is fearless and strong. She defends herself from other children and is a very hard worker. She is the one who contributes most to her family; yet, she is ignored by her brothers. She helps her mother wash clothes from Monday to Sunday and with the sewing of her brothers' and father's clothes. Her brothers have time to play football or go to parties in town, but she has almost no time to play. She only plays when she is at school.

Her brothers don't help around the house. They don't cook, or wash their clothes. The only time they do so is when she, or her mother, is not at home. Her father is always tired and comes home from work to eat and sleep. Karen has the most responsibilities, as she is the eldest of the girls. She does housework and contributes to her family with her earnings from working in the mine. Her brothers don't help at home because they say they work at the mine. With so many things to take care of, she would like to have more spare time to play. School is the place where she can play and learn.

She is happy with her family, although she would like to change her brothers. She wants to finish school, graduate, and become a mining businesswoman to give her friends a place to work. She also wants to be a teacher. If her father brought money to eat, paid for school, and bought her clothes, she would stop working. Then, she would study and play. She and her brothers work because they don't have enough money to pay for the family's basic needs. At home they don't have electricity; they use candles.

Dissemination of the Study Results

A key objective of our study was to disseminate our findings to mining children and their families, and to those responsible for their welfare, including teachers, government officials, adult miners, and mining sector businessmen. Toward the end of the research fieldwork, therefore, we organized the following dissemination activities in Chima, Chuquini, and Huanuni:

1. Information sessions and workshops with children, families, employers, and miners. Our principal aim in these sessions was to

foster awareness among the participants, particularly the children, regarding the situation of children in mining communities.
2. Production and distribution of brochures explaining the rights of children.
3. Production and broadcast of radio and television spots on local stations, providing reflective information on children's rights.
4. Organization of public events where panels, newspapers, photos, videos, and other dissemination materials were made available. Among these materials, drawings made by the children about their situation were also exhibited.
5. Activities organized with schools and other organizations that sought to create public awareness concerning child labor. As an example of this, school children were encouraged to send letters to several government ministers addressing their wishes and suggestions to improve their living conditions as child workers.
6. In one instance, the children who participated in the research presented a play to share their findings, dreams, and suggestions.

Once the study was concluded, the results were shared in activities that involved the children. The first activity was coordinated with the Ombudsman of Bolivia, who participated in a breakfast meeting with the children, along with representatives of the Ministries of Labor, of Education, of Health and others from international organizations working with children, such as UNICEF. At this meeting, held in the capital city of La Paz, 12 of the child participants presented the key findings of the research. Two journalists, a national television reporter and a newspaper columnist, attended the meeting as observers. During the meeting, the Ombudsman stated that as long as the economic situation compels children from poor families to work, "this should be done in the absolute respect of their constitutional, social and human rights. These rights should be guaranteed by the employers and by the State". The Ombudsman committed himself to promoting and coordinating the efforts of the many institutions that are striving to ameliorate the rights of working children.

Four months after this official meeting with representatives of the government, the minister of labor referred publicly to what the children had said emphasizing that any action should pay particular attention to the children's needs. Unfortunately, the electoral process and the changes that occurred in the Bolivian government did not allow for an immediate follow up of this commitment.

Finally, a CD-Rom with the findings of the research, including drawings made by the children and copies of the letters sent to the ministers, was distributed in English and in Spanish to local NGOs, schools, and government ministries. This allowed for massive dissemination of the results of the study to different ministries of government, NGOs, and people who were not necessarily part of the social context in which the study was carried out, but who promote children's rights.

The Challenges of Understanding and Changing the Conditions of Child Labor in Bolivia

While children in mining communities ought to be afforded the rights to good quality education, health, and recreation, and satisfactory conditions of work, it is clear that the rules and principles outlined in the UNCRC and in the Bolivian Child and Youth Rights Code are neither respected nor reinforced. In part, this is due to a poorly developed system of values and priorities in relation to children as a whole. Children are generally not perceived as valued members of society and their rights to health and education are frequently violated. The difficult economic situation of the country and the widespread poverty that has ensued have further exacerbated the difficulties of children, especially those in the mining sector. The money that children can make in mining contributes to family earnings, and, therefore, is a great impetus for families to send children into the workforce at an early age despite the risks and hardships.

Child labor in the mining sector not only contributes to increased family incomes, but also becomes a way of life for children. Yet as they are forced to support their families, their fundamental rights are consistently ignored. As our research revealed, most children are aware of the adverse social conditions in which they live and work. Yet their occupational roles are essentially determined by structural factors, both global and local, that are extraordinarily difficult to reverse.

Though children can learn about their rights, little change will occur unless there is a concerted effort to redress predominant economic, political, and cultural barriers. Moreover, as children were encouraged to participate in this research, particularly in the dissemination of findings and in discussions concerning the need for specific changes in the social conditions of the mining sector, so too should dispossessed children be enabled to exercise their rights to articulate their voices publicly and be engaged in decisions and actions for improving their lives, and more specifically the conditions of their work. While this study is not the impetus for a burgeoning child rights movement in Bolivia, through the dissemination process it has nonetheless demonstrated how children can be mobilized to enhance awareness of adults and government officials about their plight. With regard to our own findings and dissemination in Bolivia, it is our fervent hope that the Ombudsman will follow through on a commitment to coordinate efforts, including those of UNICEF and NGOs, to improve the conditions of the working children in Bolivia

Conclusion: Listening to Children's Voices in Chima and Chuquini

The children in Chima wanted to express the following publicly:

> We request that children stop being abused, because they have a soul. Parents, you must think before you abuse your children. It is better when the parent talks to his/her child.
>
> We want to ask other people not to reprimand children because they work to help their families and because fathers don't get money. That is why children work here. There is nowhere else to work.
>
> Tell our parents and mothers to send their children to school so they can become someone in the future.
>
> Regarding the right to health services, we ask everyone's cooperation; we ask the government and its officials to bring us medicine to cure our illnesses.

The children in Chuquini stated the following:

> There are several rights that are not complied with here in Chuquini. There is one we will mention: the right to not be abused. For example, when a child has done something and he or she is beaten for that. [Also], all children should not just work, they [parents] have to make an effort to allow them to study so that they become somebody in life.
>
> They should give support to teachers so they can teach the children well.
>
> They should work on the parents' awareness regarding child protection.
>
> Authorities should be aware of the reality of child labor in the mines.
>
> Children should be allowed to exercise their rights and be supported when they want to get ahead with their lives.

Although it is difficult to break traditional structures and relationships that poverty has generated in the mining sector, these statements represent a plea for change and support for children's basic rights. It is imperative, therefore, to continue to work for change. It is especially important to involve children, their families, and other interested stakeholders in promoting changes in the economic and cultural underpinnings of child labor. In this process, children should be encouraged to put forth their own suggestions for the resolution of their problems and the reinforcement of their fundamental rights. In the long run, the realization of the rights of working children will enhance their overall well-being and that of the society as a whole.

Notes

* Financial support for this project was provided by the Canadian International Development Agency (CIDA). The CECI and MEDMIN were the grant recipients. Primary data for the study was collected by Máxima Flores, Yvette Guzmán, and Yovana Nina. Carola Soruco and Félix Carrillo participated actively in the research. We thank them all for their contribution to the success of the project. We also thank Norman MacIsaac (Regional Director of CECI-Andes) for his valuable comments and insights on earlier versions of the chapter. We are grateful to the communities of Chima, Chuquini, and Huanuni, especially the children who participated in the study. Any mistakes remain our own.

1. Although the study attempted to maintain a balance in terms of the information obtained from young boys and girls, it paid special attention to girls' needs.
2. See http://www.ilo.org/global/lang--en/index.htm.
3. This study does not include children from the nearby towns of Guanay, Mapiri, and Teoponte.
4. *Barranquilla* refers to the riverbanks where people (*barranquilleros*) wash soils in search for gold particles. The term *barranquillero* is used to describe a person who uses a pan to screen soil in riverbanks, searching for gold particles that may run off from larger mining operations upstream. Children are frequently employed to perform this task.
5. *Palo* refers to the weight of a match (a tenth of a gram), which is valued, approximately, at one U.S. dollar.
6. "Sparks" is slang and describes the small gold particles found by the *barranquilleros*.

References

Albarracin-Millan, J. (1993). *El desentrañamiento del estaño. Los republicanos en la historia de Bolivia*. La Paz: Publicidad Arte Producciones.

Arce, R. (1990). *Pasado y futuro de la minería boliviana*. Oruro: Editorial Universitaria.

Capriles, O. (1977). *Historia de la minería boliviana*. La Paz: Bamin.

CARE. (2004). *Progresiva y Prevención del Trabajo Infantil Minero. Boletín II*. La Paz.

Cook, P., Blanchet-Cohen, N., & Hart, S. (2004). *Children as Partners: Child Participation Promoting Social Change.* International Institute for Child Rights and Development. Paper prepared for the Canadian International Development Agency (CIDA), Child Protection Unit.

Costa Du Rels, Adolfo. (1942). *Félix Avelino Aramayo y su época.* Buenos Aires: Domingo Viau y Cia.

Domic Ruiz, J. (1999). *Niños trabajadores: la emergencia de nuevos actores sociales.* La Paz: Programa de Investigación Estratégica en Bolivia (PIEB).

Harris, K. J., Jerome, N. W., & Fawcett, S. B. (1997). Rapid Assessment Procedures: A Review and Critique. *Human Organization, 56*(3), 375–378.

Hart, R. (1992). *Children's Participation from Tokenism to Citizenship.* Florence: UNICEF, Innocenti Research Centre.

Hart, R. (1997). *Children's Participation: The Theory And Practice of Involving Young Citizens In Community Development And Environmental Care.* UNICEF.

International Labour Organization. (2004). IPEC Action Against Child Labour 2003–2003 Progress and Future Priorities. Retrieved from http://www.ilo.org/public/english/standards/relm/gb/docs/gb289/pdf/tc-4-ax1.pdf

Oficina Internacional del Trabajo. (2001). Estudio Nacional sobre Trabajo Infantil en Ecuador.

Oficina Internacional del Trabajo. (2005). *Qué hacer para liberar a los niños del trabajo infantil minero. Guía para la acción institucional.* Programa para la Prevención y Eliminación Progresiva del Trabajo Infantil en la Minería Artesanal en Sudamérica. Lima.

Programa Internacional para la Erradicacion del Trabajo Infantil (IPEC) & MINERÍA. (2001). Documento resumen presentado en el Seminario Nacional sobre la Erradicación del Trabajo Infantil en la Minería Artesanal. La Paz: Julio.

Sedlacek, G., Duryea, S., Ilahi, N., & Sasaki, M. (2005). *Child Labour, Schooling, and Poverty in Latin America.* Social Protection Unit, Human Development Network, The World Bank.

United Nations Children's Fund (UNICEF). (2004). *Buscando la luz al final del túnel. Niños, niñas y adolescentes en la minería artesanal en Bolivia.* La Paz.

United Nations General Assembly. (1986). Declaration on the Right to Development. Retrieved from http://www.un.org/documents/ga/res/41/a41r128.htm

CHAPTER 5

Breaking the Silence: The Voices of Girls Forcibly Involved in Armed Conflict in Angola

Vivi Stavrou[*]

Introduction

This study examines the roles of young women and girls in Angola's lengthy civil war and in the recent aftermath. Based primarily on in-depth interviews with 40 formerly abducted girl soldiers, the research examined the significant stages of these girls' lives—before their abduction, at the time of their abduction, and their subsequent involvement in armed conflict, and throughout their demobilization and reintegration into new postwar circumstances. In recounting the experiences of these young women, the primary objective was to generate insights into how conditions might be created in Angolan communities to provide a secure and supportive environment for former girl soldiers, and how practices pertaining to their postwar reintegration could be more responsive to their needs. While the burgeoning literature examining the experiences of female soldiers generally focuses on gender-based violence, this study highlights in particular the nature of gender-based exploitation (including sex labor) not only as a significant factor in facilitating guerilla wars, but also as a foundation of postwar social enormities. As former girl soldiers are frequently disconnected from their erstwhile family ties through death, displacement, or stigmatization, they are acutely vulnerable to continued abuse and exploitation in postwar circumstances. Accordingly, this chapter proposes reforms to disarmament, demobilization, and rehabilitation (DDR) programs[1] in ways that will accommodate the distinctive realities and needs of former female soldiers. The chapter concludes by emphasizing the need for postconflict policies and programs that will counter the tendency to relegate former girl soldiers to the underclass margins of postwar society.

Overview of Child Soldiers in Sub-Saharan Africa

Recent trends in warfare indicate that although children and young persons have always been recruited to take part in conflicts, their involvement has become progressively more widespread and lethal. The magnitude of children's direct engagement in war has significantly increased in the past decades, leading inevitably to increasingly disproportionate victimization of children as perpetrators as well as casualties of violent conflict (Denov, 2010; Honwana, 2006; Wessells, 2006). Within sub-Saharan Africa especially, several factors have come together over the past 30 years that have resulted in a "perfect storm" in the use and abuse of children by fighting forces (Stavrou, 2004). Numerous factors have resulted in the forcible conscription of children as soldiers in civic conflict and in the deliberate targeting of children and women as victims of war atrocities.[2]

In recent decades, substantial areas of the African continent have been overcome by prolonged civil war that has encompassed entire populations and often made it difficult to distinguish between combatants and noncombatants. Attacks against civilians have become a deliberate tactic of war. In such contexts as Rwanda, Darfur, and the Democratic Republic of the Congo (DRC), ethnic cleansing has motivated this struggle, with women and children (generally the most defenseless subsectors of the populace), as deliberate targets of aggression and atrocity. Indeed, sexual and gender-base violence (SGBV) has reached unprecedented proportions in recent years, and in the context of the DRC is now referred to as a "war within a war and a war against women."[3] Historically, while young children have not been the obvious choice for soldiering because of their undeveloped cognitive and physical capacities, the increasingly intractable nature of civil wars, sometimes lasting for decades (e.g., Angola and Sudan), has resulted in the necessity to recruit ever-younger fighters to ensure the continuity of conflict. As adult soldiers are killed, incapacitated, or reluctant to wage war, young children are often seen as prime fodder for fighting units. Since over half of Africa's population is under 18 years of age, and with the proliferation of small arms that can be carried and used effectively by young children, it is not surprising that the demographics of fighting forces in sub-Saharan Africa are reflective of the overall youthful population of the continent, especially among rebel forces and guerrilla groups that lack the administrative means to conscript the adult population. The widely reported reluctance of adults to fight in prolonged violent conflict has meant that child soldiers make up a disproportionate number of war casualties (Crill, 2001; Wessells, 2006).

Moreover, during lengthy civic conflict, as norms regulating social behavior are weakened and traditional institutions and social systems break down, systems of child protection and support tend to be eroded. Not only has this resulted in a growing number of rootless children evincing a willingness to voluntarily enlist in fighting forces, but it has also enabled recruiters to exploit the very underdevelopment of children through verbal and physical abuse, tapping into their malleability and their limited capacity to resist authority. Through a combination of beatings, torture, deprivation, and induced drug and alcohol ingestion, as well as enticements of power, status, and material gain, children are frequently and easily compelled to undertake actions that are often deemed by regular troops to be too dangerous and too barbaric. Despite the array of international protocols concerning warfare (e.g., the Geneva Convention) and human rights (e.g., the UN Convention on the Rights of the Child [CRC]), nonstate entities such as rebel groups, irregular militias, and armed insurgents are not signatories to these formal legal instruments, and are usually either unaware of such protocols or consider themselves not to be officially bound by them (cf. Bennet, 2000). This obliviousness to international law further contributes to the extensive nature of child soldiering.

In sum, the increasing reliance on children to form the backbone of fighting forces in sub-Saharan Africa, and the use of SGBV as a weapon of war, has resulted in a de facto war against children and women. This is a phenomenon that has not only wrought unspeakable devastation and trauma in many regions of the African continent, but has generated enormous challenges for societal reconstruction and the reintegration of agitators and victims alike when conflicts draw to a close (Denov & Maclure, 2006; McKay & Mazurana, 2004). The experience of Angola provides an example of such challenges, particularly for women and girls who have been especially victimized by prolonged armed conflict.

Child Soldiers in Angola's Civil War

Preceded by 500 years of slavery and colonization,[4] Angola's prolonged civil war, lasting from 1975 to 2002, was ruinous for the entire civilian population. An estimated 1 million people died, 4.5 million were internally displaced, and some 400,000 people fled to neighboring countries as refugees (International Crisis Group, 2003; UNHRC, 2002). At its most intense, between 1992 and 1994, fighting centered on the main cities, with both government and rebel forces bombarding civilian populations in a bid to take control of the provincial capitals. During the last phase of the war, most of the violence was directly aimed at civilian populations. Education and basic health care were destroyed, and community social capital was severely undermined. As anarchy and displacement became the norm in much of the country, many children were drawn into the conflict, some willingly, many forcibly, as protagonists in the fighting.

Given the duration of the conflict, a whole generation of young people was affected by the war, either because they were directly and indirectly involved in armed conflict, or because they spent their childhood in camps for internally displaced people (IDP) or for refugees beyond Angola's borders. As the demographics regarding individuals who were actively engaged in the fighting over the years are unavailable, the involvement of children in the conflict has been difficult to document. Often the children who participated in the fighting were located in remote conflict zones away from the public eye and media scrutiny. Vast numbers have been unaccounted for, in all likelihood killed in battle or fatally injured and abandoned.

This lack of accountability has continued in the postwar era, especially in relation to former girl soldiers, most of who were quietly disbanded from fighting units with no effort on the part of either their commanders or DDR officials to engage them in formal processes of demobilization and rehabilitation. Unlike their male counterparts, very few female child soldiers benefitted from DDR-related assistance packages such as vocational training, access to microcredit, and direct material and financial aid, as opposed to many of their male counterparts. As child soldiers, most girls and young women were not visibly prominent, and in the postconflict period they have remained largely marginalized and vulnerable, with their experiences of conflict essentially muted—often intentionally so by former female soldiers themselves for fear of public retribution and stigmatization. Given that they were never formally acknowledged as child soldiers, they were rarely acknowledged in the demobilization processes.[5] This has had significant implications for postwar social policies in Angola. As female soldiers have been a sorely neglected group in terms of research and social programs, there is a fundamental need for a gendered perspective on child soldiers, and an understanding of how it is that the social construction of gender affects male and female child soldiers differently during conflict as well as in postwar circumstances.

In view of the silence and vulnerability of former girl soldiers in Angola, the purpose of this chapter is twofold. First, it highlights the voices of a cohort of former girl soldiers in Angola to recount their experiences before, during, and after the war. In so doing it illuminates the injustices that many of these girls and young women suffered and continue to suffer. Second, the chapter proposes policies for improving their livelihoods in postwar circumstances.

Methodology

Fieldwork for this study consisted of interviews and focus groups undertaken during the period of January to August 2004. Forty in-depth individual interviews were conducted with former girl soldiers, all of whom had been abducted and compelled to join armed rebel groups, and all of whom had ended their affiliation with the rebels within the three years prior to the interviews. The ages of the interviewees ranged from 13 to 34 years old at the time of research fieldwork, and 18 indicated that they were 18 years of age or older. Also, 32 of the 40 girls interviewed were mothers, with an average of 2 children each.[6] In order to facilitate disclosure and put the interviewees at ease with the research process, the research team was managed by and composed of women.

Selection of the 40 girls was based on an iterative process whereby the researchers drew upon information and advice offered from trusted key informants from NGOs, church groups, and community association leaders. Interviews were conducted in two phases. The first consisted of a pilot phase in two regions of the country—periurban Luanda and rural Huambo. A series of meetings and focus groups, along with several hundred individual interviews, enabled the researchers to gain a sense of respondents' understanding of the war and its impact on the lives of communities and women in particular. On the basis of this pilot phase, the research team determined that in-depth interviews would not be effectively conducted in one sitting, but instead required a semi-structured process of one-on-one interaction to be held over the course of a two-day period. In this way, the researchers were able to attain a level of familiarity and mutual confidence with the young women who were interviewed. Participation was voluntary, strict confidentiality was observed, and private interviewing spaces were used in order to avoid increasing the vulnerability of the young women. The participants were remunerated for the costs of their travel to and from the interview sites, and for their time away from their own personal activities. The pace of the interview sessions was matched to the energy levels and needs of the young women, especially for those who were caring for small children. Food and drink was available for the participants and time was set aside for the young women to pause and rest, since interview topics were sometimes difficult to discuss and touched on past traumatic experiences.

Having lived in highly militarized situations where their speech and even thoughts were subject to authoritarian control, some women had difficulty in articulating their experiences and opinions, particularly early on in the interview process. Nonetheless, the interviewers were all experienced community workers, trained in in-depth interviewing and focus group analysis. The practical psychosocial working experience of the researchers enabled them to establish rapport, create trust, detect nuance, and negotiate mutual understanding with the young women whom they interviewed. Each interview was conducted in one of three languages—Umbundu, Tchokwe, or Portuguese—whichever was most comfortable for the interviewees. In addition, in order to gain interviewee confidence, participants were encouraged to go beyond their immediate wartime and postwar experiences, and to suggest policy and program interventions. In this way the study incorporated a participatory, policy-oriented component. In order to alleviate the researchers' own anxieties that interviews concerning the traumatic past of these young women might rekindle their anguish and suffering, monthly structured team debriefings were held for them with a clinical psychologist and two social workers who were familiar with the psychosocial pressures associated with conflict and postconflict situations.

Experiences and Perceptions of Former Girl Soldiers During and After Conflict

Abduction and Immersion in Bush Warfare

Most of the interview testimonies covered war experiences that took place during the period 1998–2002 when the majority of the girls were aged 13–18 years. All of the girls had been abducted from their homes and families, usually at the time of raids on their communities. Upon attacking and entering a settlement, armed groups typically captured or killed the men, left the aged behind, often with the women who had young children, and abducted the children who were 10 years or older.

In areas controlled by UNITA,[7] village leaders were sometimes obliged, at the risk of death, to surrender children and adolescents to the armed forces. All of the 40 young women and girls interviewed were separated from their families when they were abducted, and at the time of the research fieldwork, few had returned to their original family groups.

Following their abduction, girls were routinely separated from family members and others from the same community who had also been captured. Very young girls were generally allocated to houses of high-ranking military commanders where they were forced to work as servants until their early teens. While adolescent boys went on to become active combatants or support soldiers for the frontline troops, girls in their teens tended to work initially as porters and provide domestic help at base camps in support of the frontline troops. This reflected the pattern of deliberately abducting young children not only for the purpose of armed combat, but also for use as pools of conscripted and compliant labor for the military. Over time, however, some were drawn into combat.

The girls quickly learned of the dangerous consequences of attempting an escape from the armed group.

> There in the base where I was, they caught a girl who had left a one year old baby behind when she tried to escape. They went after her and caught her and killed her when they brought her back. Everybody had to assist. They put a red band across her eyes and then they killed her. They did it to make the others afraid so that they would not try to escape.

As recounted by the interviewees, militarized life in the bush was characterized by extreme deprivation and ongoing risks to their health, safety, and security. Fear and fatigue were commonplace. Girls suffered from exhaustion and from lack of sleep, from wounds on the feet during marches, and from head, neck, chest, and back pains from carrying heavy materials day in and day out. Children suffered from many illnesses, including malaria, anemia, malnutrition, tuberculosis, and sexually transmitted diseases. They had no access to any form of education, and health care was practically nonexistent. Many girls stopped menstruating because of the poor diet and constant walking. Sexual assault was rampant and many also died from abortions or during childbirth. The following interview excerpts vividly exemplify the experiences that many of the interviewees recounted:

> We carried the ammunition, the dishes, and pans and [cooked] the food. When they [our soldiers] finished the attack, we carried things to the

> next place we went. We [stole] clothes and food from inside the houses where the people were.
>
> One day they sent me to carry 25kgs of salt and I fell in a hole and sprained something. And I said that I could not get up and they said "we will put you in a hole [kill you] if you do not want to get up."... It was the kwachas (UNITA) that ordered me to carry the salt.... At the time I was only 13.
>
> During the journeys, in the night they take the girls and they sleep with them... in the night every soldier is with one, they just don't sleep with you if you are pregnant or have a baby.
>
> Suffering is lack of clothes, lack of salt, to sleep in the leaves without clothes under the rain, sleep seated near to the fire because of the cold, blemishes on the skin due to the dry skin. I hate my memories mostly of the rain showers and the walking.
>
> Life was just walking from one place to another, by day and by night. At first you were crying, but then you had no more tears left.

Constant movement from place to place frequently led to a loss of the sense of passing time and the sequence of events. Unrelenting surveillance by their captors meant that reminiscent talk about home and family was minimized. Through isolation from former friends and relatives, memories of previous identities, relationships, places, and communities were diminished.

> We used to tell our stories... Oh! When we will find our families... so on. But when you are speaking like that they will call us and say: "You are speaking like that because you are thinking of escape". They didn't let us stay together very often. Everybody stayed in her house because if we are together they thought that we are talking about escaping... they didn't accept that.
>
> They didn't let you speak because they thought "You are thinking too much about your home and speaking about your life with your mother, so you will escape soon". So, they did not let us speak about the past, and we forgot about all of that.

To a certain extent this relegation of females to work in support of males and to be offered in "marriage" at a young age was an extension of conventional community norms. Yet through a combination of factors—harsh living in the bush, exposure to extreme violence, and diminished supplies and sustenance—the traditional allocation of roles and responsibilities broke down. Girls were forced to undertake actions that transgressed the social boundaries and taboos of institutionalized sociocultural norms.

> First you [we girls] were scared, but then you were not afraid anymore. When they finished that attack, they passed each house and checked [them] with guns, shooting under the bed, and opening the closet to see if there was a person inside... [When] they see that [the inhabitants] are dead, you take the things you went for and go away.

To escape the worst forms of brutalization, it was advantageous for a girl to become the "wife" of an influential leader. To be attached to a leader, and to become the mother of his children, was considered to be a means of escaping the misery of long marches, heavy manual labor, and involvement in armed conflict. Yet there was no guarantee that such bonding would alleviate suffering. Pregnancy and motherhood did not necessarily translate into a lightened workload. Moreover, if a father did not acknowledge a child born from this type of union, the mother invariably was obliged to give birth surreptitiously and to face the prospect of raising the child on her own with no support. In such instances, when infants were seen as a burden, especially when military groups had to move quickly and in silence, soldiers perpetrated infanticide in order to reduce the danger of attack. As one participant stated,

> The marches with children were complicated because the children would cry. There was a special group of soldiers for killing children by hitting them against a tree. No one could make any noise at all and they would kill children of any age like that.

The Gender Dimension of Bush Warfare: Girls as "Soldiers" or Peripheral Support for Combatants?

Of the 40 young women interviewed for this study, all of who had been abducted by armed guerrillas and were obliged to become actively involved in their campaigns of violence, only one received recognition as a former soldier by the official postwar DDR Commission and thus was eligible to receive a demobilization grant. The remainder did not participate in the DDR process.[8] In part this was due to the fact that some girls did not want to self-identify as agitators. Yet there was also a tendency to downplay or dismiss the role of girls as genuine soldiers during Angola's protracted civil war, and, therefore, to disallow them from participating in the official DDR process. In some instances recognition of their status as combatants was refused because of a combination of their young age and their gender. While adolescent and young adult males are widely acknowledged as having been involved in most of the fighting, and continue to represent a potential source of postconflict instability in Angola, young girls are not viewed in the same manner. Many young girls did not carry arms during the war and consequently they were seen as dependent minors who were not perpetrators of violence during the war and posed little risk of engaging in postwar violence. In addition, since many had been forcibly attached to one or more male soldiers (as "wives," as sex slaves, or as domestic laborers), they were seen as being akin to "camp followers" or as attached to male soldiers through marriage and, as was often the case, mothers of children born in such circumstances. Accordingly, any benefits accruing from the DDR process were seen as being an indirect outcome from their conjugal attachments brought about by their abduction and subsequent affiliation with fighting groups, rather than through their direct involvement in combat per se.

Yet another singular reason underlying the assumption that most girls could not be considered as bona fide soldiers relates to the tasks that girls generally undertook during the conflict. From the perspective of guerrilla commanders, they were regarded as a low cost, low maintenance source of multiple types of labor. They were efficient and easily controlled, they required only the most basic food, and they could travel quietly over any terrain and leave few tracks and dust clouds to be spotted by the enemy. They worked long hours and, because of the menial tasks required of them, they could be easily replaced. They cooked and prepared camp, they cared for the wounded, cleared paths, served as spies, and for men's entertainment they danced and sang and provided them with sex.

> In the bush it is being a slave... [the girl] must cook, fetch water, and serve the elders. Sometimes she doesn't sleep, [because] she must dance through the night. From one minute to the other [the commanders] decide she must go on a march, then she has to carry the load... if it is too heavy somebody must help to put it on her head. It doesn't matter if it is night, time doesn't exist. It is pure suffering.

What emerges strongly from many of the narratives is how the hard labor of the abducted girl soldiers during the war was an exploitation of their expected gender-based compliance and vulnerability. While much of the literature on recent internecine conflict focuses on gender-based *violence*, in the case of Angola's civil war, gender-based *labor exploitation* (including sex labor) was a key factor in sustaining the agitators for so many years. The critical role of many girls and young women who were abducted by fighting forces was to provide essential logistical support. Accordingly this has been widely regarded as "women's work" rather than as "soldiering," and, therefore, has not qualified as being eligible for demobilization benefits. In short, because so many girls did not carry and use weapons, they were not considered to have truly been child soldiers.

In addition, further exacerbating the marginalization of former girl soldiers has been their perceived lack of *independent* status throughout the conflict. As almost all girls and women caught up in armed conflict are generally seen to have been dependent on male soldiers, they have been labeled with a secondary status as agitators. This is ironic, however, for although far fewer girls than boys were directly engaged in actual combat in Angola, without their involvement the tragedy of Angola's protracted civil war could not have lasted as long as it did. Yet because of the secondary status accorded to them as participants in armed conflict, in postconflict circumstances many of them have been rendered dependent on postwar demobilization allocations accorded to former male soldiers. Consequently, although abducted girl soldiers proved to be invaluable to fighting forces and contributed substantially to the prolongation of a generation of bush conflict, at war's end the vast majority were seen as requiring an official or "goodwill" link to a male soldier's family in order to become secondary beneficiaries of the demobilization process. Invariably, this perception has perpetuated the ongoing marginalization and exploitation of girls and women.

From Conflict to Postconflict: The Continuity of Gender Discrimination

Brutal abduction from home and family, and subsequent immersion in a violent militarized subculture, has left many former female soldiers struggling with the sudden demands of a new social environment, often in circumstances of isolation, poverty, and lingering psychological trauma. The following girl participants explained a few of the many postconflict challenges they faced, particularly in relation to ongoing poverty and a corresponding lack of access to healthcare, psychosocial support, and financial assistance.

> On the days when you have to go to the hospital you do not eat. You need to borrow money to go to the hospital or buy medicines, and you might have to

> work for the person who lent you money so as to pay it off. When a person is ill the only thing that matters is money; without money you do nothing.
>
> Here there is no one to help me. And so I go to sleep without eating. I have no one to go to ask, because people do not give anything. I go to church but just like this [in her one set of clothes]. I go because I want to be buried; I don't want to be buried like a dog.

Unfortunately, the discrimination of girls as a consequence of their roles as former child soldiers has continued unabated in Angola's tenuous postconflict circumstances. Following formal cessation of hostilities, community welcoming and reintegration rituals focused almost entirely on males, the perceived protagonists of war who consequently benefitted from externally financed demobilization and rehabilitation programs. By contrast, because former female soldiers were widely regarded as domestic and manual workers, they continue to be marginalized, valued only for menial work and reproduction. Consequently, as attested to by the participants in this study, many former female soldiers have found themselves in situations that have been anything but "integrative."

The only hope for most of these young women in postwar circumstances has been to reconnect with family members. Indeed, for girl soldiers the reestablishment of normalcy and social integration was connected to the process of recovering, or more commonly reconceptualizing, their identity in new postconflict circumstances. As indicated by the interviewees in this study, reintegration and the (re) formulation of a positive identity were generally bound up with the reconnection with families of origin. Within the cultural context of Bantu society, family support networks are often essential for social security and corresponding access to resources, to remunerative work, and to education (for the former female soldiers themselves, as well as for their children). Yet despite the desirability of reasserting family ties, only 11 of the 40 formerly abducted girls interviewed for this study were living with members of their family of origin. Some had no family or were unable to locate close family members. Some had experienced difficulties reintegrating with family members or had found that their families were already under severe economic pressure and were thus unable to support them. For others, a lack of family reconnection was due to the fear of the stigmatization associated with their involvement in the bush war or—even more difficult—due to their "marriages" to former male combatants and the children they bore as a result.

Yet wartime conjugal attachments have generally dissipated in post-conflict circumstances. Out of the 40 young women interviewed for this study, 17 had experienced enforced "marriages," only to have them severed soon after the end of the conflict. In the words of two interviewees,

> One older man said that it was better to stay with him [rather than providing sexual services to other male soldiers] and this was the father of [my] child. But in the end he was only lying, so last year I left him. He already had three wives in the village.
>
> A woman is always a daughter, she is always subservient to her husband, she always follows her husband, so we came here. But when we got here we found out that actually they had other women from before the war. Now he only wants to take care of his former wives, not us. So I did not meet up with my family because I followed my husband. I did not know where to go to say, 'that's my family'. So now there is a lot of suffering. Girls [like me] do not know who to go to for help, and don't have money to go back to their area of origin.

Unfortunately, despite the disruption of family and community networks that resulted from the Angolan civil war, no substantive alternative networks that are inclusive and mutually reinforcing have emerged for these girls. Prevailing sociocultural norms in postwar Angola continue to be grounded in gender-based discrimination and power differentials. Consequently, the great majority of women—and particularly former female soldiers—who are unattached to husbands and supportive families have been essentially cast off into the margins of society. Without education, and with minimal or no access to credit, these women can support themselves and their children only by relying on their own manual labor, or on poorly remunerated seasonal trading and retail activities. Not surprisingly, as was discerned in this study, low social status combined with limited work opportunities has fostered low self-esteem among many former female soldiers.

Lessons Learned and Recommendations for Postconflict Programming

The current situation for young women and girls in Angola is such that they continue to face challenges to reintegration in postwar circumstances. The great majority of former girl soldiers have not benefited from DDR programming in the same way as have male youth, and so they remain mostly marginalized from many income-generating activities and often from their own home communities and families. While reintegration must be understood as a developmental process with an open-ended time frame, this conception presupposes long-term planning and flexibility, from both governmental and nongovernmental initiatives. Given the uncertainties that arise after civil wars and large-scale population displacement, it is necessary for measures to reach as many returnees and ex-soldiers as possible. Quick impact projects are, therefore, generally placed at the start of reintegration programs, for example, back-to-school programs and public works reconstruction projects.[9] Similarly, accountability on the part of key stakeholders who work in areas of children's rights and protection is critical during the postwar transitional context. Institutional support for returnee populations is particularly important when security concerns are still high and when risks of abuse and exploitation increase during periods of political uncertainty, mass population movements, and rapid social change. Protective mechanisms should include those that are coordinated and are able to quickly identify and flag security and abuse threats against formerly abducted children and women. Likewise monitoring should focus on identifying those individuals and families who are most vulnerable and are excluded from local community environments and access to existing social services.

As programming shifts from emergency to transitional to long-term development, so the focus should be broadened to include other forms of protection. These include improving access to resources and to service-driven interventions such as improved welfare assistance, legal and police protection, and ongoing community-based initiatives. In this respect the capacity building of service providers and the development of livelihood opportunities is particularly significant. The ex-child soldiers in this study were very clear in their recommendations that the types of assistance they required should be related to improving the lives of their own children through opportunities for income generation. Finally, in order to achieve lasting reconciliation and successful overall reintegration of the wider conflict-affected population, supports also need to include programs for internally displaced persons (IDP) in order to allow them to return and resettle.

While the majority of programming should be broad-based and inclusive, a number of specific vulnerabilities need to be targeted to meet particular assistance needs of children and youth. These special needs groups include the following:

- children and youth who have personal or family problems related to drug or alcohol abuse;

- those who have serious health or disability problems;
- those who have experienced sexual assault or sexual abuse;
- those who have witnessed or were forced to participate in atrocities;
- those whose family cannot be found or who have no remaining family members;
- those who are injured, disabled, or terminally ill;
- infants and young children born to girls associated with armed forces, and
- those whose families have rejected them or who face hostility from their family and community.

Programs for these particularly vulnerable groups should thus be tailored to their specific needs and should consist of culturally sensitive community-based rehabilitation and long-term care. Most importantly, youth need to be increasingly involved in socioeconomic reconstruction and rebuilding of their own communities, and processes of reconciliation. Youth involvement in such activities can potentially enhance their long-term efficacy.

Returnees often take a staggered route of return—first to their families and communities of origin, and sometimes, depending on a variety of factors, settling temporarily or for longer periods within other communities with or without extended family members. While settlement solutions need to be available to the returnees, the decision of when, where, and under what circumstances settlement is to take place is so complex that it cannot be the responsibility of resettlement organizations alone. In making resettlement decisions, individuals and families are often influenced by social and economic factors, and many are drawn to urban rather than rural areas, given the greater economic opportunities available to them in cities.

Both national and international organizations also have a responsibility toward former girl soldiers in facilitating their reintegration. In particular, governments and organizations such as the World Bank that support and implement DDR initiatives, must have plans in place for monitoring the progress of child and gender-specific objectives of national and international policies in postconflict programming. The monitoring of these initiatives should involve ongoing research examining the extent to which the unique gender-specific needs of children and young girls are being addressed, particularly in relation to customs such as welcoming ceremonies, purification rituals and other traditional conventions.

Table 5.1 Demographic profile of 40 formerly abducted girl soldiers

No.	Description	Data
1.	Date of Interview	4-month period—April, May, June, July 2004
2.	Location of interview	- 20 in periurban Luanda (Viana; Estelagem, Campo de Descolados, Bairro Miru, Zonas A & B, KM 9) - 20 in rural areas surrounding Huambo city, Huambo province (Campo de Deslocados de Cantao Pahula in Caala; Cachiungo; Tchicala TcholohanFQA; Huambo bairros and city)
3.	Age of interviewee	- Average age at present: 21 (Luanda 22; Huambo 20) - 45% (N=18) formerly abducted girls soldiers were 18 yrs and younger at the time of the interview (7 Luanda; 11 Huambo) - Age range of sample at time of interview: 13–34 (Luanda 13–34; Huambo 16–32)
4.	Province of origin	- **Luanda interviews:** Huambo: 10, Lunda Norte: 3, Uige: 2, Benguela: 2, Malange: 1, Kwanza Norte: 1, Kwanz, Sul: 1 - **Huambo interviews:** Huambo: 10, Bie: 5, Benguela: 2, Kuando Kubango: 2, Kwanza Norte: 1
5.	Age when abducted/ captured	- Average age at capture/abduction: 12 yrs. (45% [18] did not remember their age at time of abduction) - **Luanda:** average age 11.5 (12 did not remember, one was 6 months old when mother was captured, one was born in UNITA area during the war) - **Huambo:** average age 12.7 (6 did not remember, one born in UNITA area during the war)
6.	Abducted/captured by which armed force	- 22.5.% (9) captured by FAA - 72.5% (31) abducted by UNITA - 12.5% (5) experienced multiple abductions both by FAA and by UNITA
7.	No. of years spent with armed forces	- 2–18 yrs (45% [18] did not know how long they spent with the armed forces)
8.	No. of children	- 80% (32) had children (Luanda 16, Huambo 16) - 17.5% (7) pregnant on return (Luanda 4, Huambo 3)
9.	Age of children	- Average age of children – 3.9 yr (some of the formerly abducted girls soldiers did not know their children's ages) - Luanda: 4.5 yrs, Huambo: 3.4 yrs - Average number of surviving children: 2 - Luanda: 2.6, N=42. Huambo: 2, N=33 Huambo) - 3 of the Huambo formerly abducted girls soldiers had children that died during the time spent with the armed forces (2 had 2 children that died, and 1 had 1) - On average girls were 16 yrs old when they had their first child (subtracting age of oldest child from formerly abducted girl soldier's age)

Continued

Table 5.1 Continued

No.	Description	Data
10.	Level of literacy/level of education	60% (24) had no formal and informal schooling whatsoever. Luanda: 7 studied: average was 5.5 yrs of formal education Huambo: 9 studied, average was 4 yrs of formal education Of the 16 who had studied – all had 3 yrs and less education and were functionally illiterate 12.5% (5) Currently at school (Luanda 4, Huambo 1)
11.	Marital status	Single through abandonment by war husbands: 50% (N=20, 10 Luanda and 10 Huambo) Single/never married: 20% (N=8, Luanda: 4, Huambo: 4). Married: 22.5% (N=9, Luanda: 5, Huambo: 4) Widowed: 7.5% (N=3, Luanda: 1, Huambo:2)
12.	Who do they currently live with	Living alone, with or without children: 32.5% (N=13, Luanda: 6, Huambo: 7) Living with husband: 20% (N=8, Luanda: 4, Huambo: 4) Living with family members other than own children: 27.5% (N=11, Luanda: 7, Huambo: 4) Living with other formerly abducted girls soldiers: 20% (N=8, Luanda: 3, Huambo: 5). 53% (N=21) are living in female-headed households (national average is 27%).
12.	Living conditions	80% (N=32) of the sample were living in conditions of extreme poverty 20 % (N=6/20) of the Luanda sample, and 10% (N=2/20) of the Huambo sample reported being able to meet their own and their children's basic needs with respect to shelter, nutrition, clothing; are currently able to work and/or accessing formal education, and being able to follow-through with future plans regarding work, education, and training
13.	Livelihood (work and means of income in areas of return).	87.5% (35) working, and 12.5 % (5) not working (Luanda: 4, Huambo 1). Occasional odd jobs (Luanda 8, Huambo 13), most do more than one job: buying and selling goods/food on the streets, including making and selling traditional drink, cutting wood and making charcoal. Agricultural labourers on other people's lands (Luanda 3, Huambo 8) Other means of financial support, by rank order: 1. Family members (family of origin). 2. Husband. (Amount and type of support received not defined).
14.	Income – daily or weekly	Difficult to calculate, sometimes paid in kind, e.g., 3–4 kgs of maize meal per working day, old clothes, in exchange for rent. When paid in cash, average 100 Kwanzas per day for odd jobs, do an average of 3 days of paid work per week. Weekly income for working formerly abducted girl soldiers: 300 Kwanzas/$ 3.50 per week/$15.00 per month/50 cents per day.

Conclusion

This research has demonstrated that assigned and/or assumed social identities (e.g., daughter, sister, wife, widow, single mother, ex-bush girl, abducted girl soldier, working girl, etc.) strongly influence access to resources and prescribes social status. In view of the history of conflict in Angola and the extensive poverty that has settled upon the country in the postconflict era, the identities of young Angolan women greatly dictates their social position and access to resources in postwar Angola. Gender is thus central to understanding the experiences of former girl soldiers and should play a vital role in any current and future programming initiatives designed for their benefit. As is the case with all other social processes, conflict, peace building, and social reconstruction must be understood as *gendered* activities.

Collectively, the young women's narratives collated for this study painted a picture of extreme deprivation and vulnerability. Beginning with their abduction, and throughout the war period and its aftermath, these girls and young women experienced a profound violation of their rights. This research has shown that in a postwar period, most formerly abducted girl soldiers are not children in a conventional sense. In the aftermath of conflict, in which many have self-demobilized, they do not remain as dependants of male ex-soldiers, but nor do many return to their homes and families of origin. Largely abandoned by their families, by the armies that used them, and by society in general, many of these young women are mired in poverty with few income-generating skills and no social safety net. Sadly the vulnerability of their position is often viewed as the norm, and communities continue to exploit them since there are rarely any legal or traditionally defined social responsibilities for these women. The implications for the DDR process are to recognize former girl soldiers early and to ensure that they do not drift into a postwar underclass status. Recognizing and implementing the rights of girls and young women must be central to postwar reconstruction efforts.

Our understanding of girls' and women's roles during war and in postwar societies must go beyond the common account of "women's experiences of war." Each situation of conflict must be understood on its own terms. The acknowledgment of the specificity and diversity of the experiences of former girl soldiers can enhance our understanding and facilitate comparative assessments of war and postwar reconstruction from both a child and gendered perspective.

Notes

* The research for this chapter took place in Angola from November 2003 to July 2004 by Vivi Stavrou (CCF Angola National Manager), Josefa Dombolo (Field Manager), Natalia Pinto, Ana Samuel, Penina Chiltula, and Christina (interviewers and field workers). Acknowledgments to the Children's' Rights Unit of the Canadian International Development Agency's Human Rights and Participation Policy Branch, for the generous grant and support to CCF Angola that made this research possible.

1. DDR programs are a common feature in postconflict reconstruction, are often led by the United Nations and are aimed at disarming and disbanding warring parties, while also reintegrating them to civilian life. Such programs have occurred from Afghanistan to Haiti, however, the majority can be found in Africa (Hanson, 2007).
2. The use of young children under 15 years of age and of girls as soldiers whilst pervasive, is not a long-standing African tradition and appears to be clearly related to financial and "manpower" shortages, especially in the context of long-standing civil wars (Child Soldiers Global Report, 2004).
3. From Book 5 of the "Inclusive Security, Sustainable Peace: A Toolkit for Advocacy and Action." International Alert and Women Waging Peace, 2004.
4. From the sixteenth to the nineteenth century, Portuguese colonial forces along the Angolan coast profited from a large slave exporting system, to the extent that Angola became the largest source of slaves for many Western hemisphere countries, including Brazil and the United States of America. Within Angola mass forced labor replaced formal slavery by the end of the ninteenth century and continued until it was prohibited in 1961 (United States Department of State, 2003).
5. For example, the 1994 Lusaka Protocol Demobilization Commission, which oversaw the demobilization of 9,133 boy soldiers under the age of 18 systematically excluded girls from such programming. In spite of the fact that girls had participated in both active combat and support roles throughout the war, they were never identified as combatants for demobilization programs, and assistance packages (containing money and offering vocational training and access to microcredit) were made available only to male ex-combatants.
6. See table 5.1 for a more detailed demographic profile of the interviewees.
7. UNITA stands for the National Union for the Total Independence of Angola (Uniao Nacional para a Independencia Total de Angola) and is the second-largest political party in Angola. While it was founded in 1966, UNITA has since fought against the Popular Movement for the Liberation of Angola (MPLA) in the Angolan War for Independence (1961–1975) and also in the civil war from 1975 to 2002.
8. The remainder of the girls received assistance through World Food Programme (WFP) food. The WFP is part of the United Nations system,

voluntarily funded, and provides food and clothing to those in emergency situations around the world.

9. In order to facilitate reintegration for all, target group participation should follow the 40:60 ratio. Thus, any reintegration support activity should aim at having no more than 40 percent of the participants as formerly abducted child and ex-soldiers. This is done in order to benefit other war-affected children and their families who are not ex-combatants, to facilitate the ex-child soldiers' sustainable reintegration, to prevent stigmatization, and to avoid the impression that past participation in armed forces is being rewarded.

References

Bennett, T. (2000). Criminalising the Recruitment of Child Soldiers. In E. Bennett, V. Gamba, & D. van der Merwe (Eds.), *ACT Against Child Soldiers in Africa: A Reader*. Pertoria: Institute for Security Studies.

Child Soldiers Global Report. (2008). *Coalition to Stop the Use of Child Soldier.* Retrieved from www.child-soldiers.org.

Crill, M. (2001). The Demobilisation and Reintegration of Former Child Soldiers in the Democratic Republic of Congo: A Consultancy Report for SAVE UK. In I. McConnan & S. Uppard (Eds.), *Children—Not Soldiers. Guidelines for Working with Child Soldiers and Children Associated with Fighting Forces.* London: Save the Children UK.

Denov, M. (2010). *Child Soldiers: Sierra Leone's Revolutionary United Front.* Cambridge : Cambridge University Press.

Denov, M., & Maclure, R. (2006). Engaging the Voices of Girls in the Aftermath of Sierra Leone's Conflict: Experiences and Perspectives in a Culture of Violence. *Anthropologica*, *48*(1), 73–85.

Hanson, S. (2007). Disarmament, Demobilization and Reintegration (DDR) in Africa: Publication # 12650. Council on Foreign Relations. Retrieved from http://www.cfr.org/publication/12650/

Honwana, A. (2006). *Child Soldiers in Africa*. Philadelphia: University of Pennsylvania Press.

International Crisis Group. (2003). *Angola's Choice: Reform or Regress.* Africa Report No. 61. Luanda and Brussels.

McKay, S., & Mazurana, D. (2004). *Where Are the Girls? Girls in Fighting Forces in Northern Uganda, Sierra Leone, and Mozambique: Their Lives During and After War.* Montreal: International Centre for Human Rights and Democratic Development.

Stavrou, V. (2004). *Literature Review and Analysis of Gender-Based Violence and Children Associated with Armed Forces and Groups.* Report for UNICEF, East and Southern African Regional Office.

United Nations High Commissioner for Refugees (UNHCR). (2002). *Statistical Yearbook 2001.* Geneva

United States Department of State. (2003). *Background Note: Angola*. From the Women's Commission for Refugee Women and Children. Angola Country Report. New York.

Wessels, M. (2006). *Child Soldiers: From Violence to Protection*. Cambridge, MA: Harvard University Press.

CHAPTER 6

Addressing Youth Violence and Aggression in Colombia: Examining a Community-Wide Prevention Initiative*

Luis F. Duque, Michael Ungar, and Beatriz Caicedo

Introduction

Set in the Aburra Valley of the Colombian Andes, the Metropolitan Area of Medellín comprises 10 municipalities and 4.6 million inhabitants. As elsewhere in Colombia, violence has been a significant public health problem for the past two decades (Duque, 2000b; Franco, 2003). In order to promote nonviolence among children and adolescents, the Medellín Early Prevention of Aggression Program (MEPAP) was initiated in 2001. MEPAP was part of a larger program, the Medellín Civic Coexistence Program, funded by the Medellín municipality and the Inter-American Development Bank (IDB). This larger program had five objectives: (1) to prevent aggressive behavior among children and youth; (2) to strengthen justice mechanisms; (3) to develop the mass media as promoters of citizenship and civil coexistence; (4) to observe and monitor occurrences of violence; and (5) to ensure community ownership of the program. Its design was directed by one of this chapter's authors, L. F. Duque, following consultations with 80 public, private, and community institutions and more than 500 individual local leaders. These consultations had identified violence as one of the four main obstacles hindering the economic development of Medellín (Duque, 2000a). Participants involved in the consultations recommended violence prevention initiatives at the local and national levels of government.

MEPAP was designed and conceived to address the first objective of Medellín's Civic Coexistence Program—to prevent aggressive behavior among children and youth. The problem is particularly acute in the areas of the city with the lowest socioeconomic income levels. According to Agudelo et al. (2002), among children ages 5–11 sampled from Medellín's preschools and elementary schools, 13 percent are reported by their teachers to have exhibited serious aggressive behavior (14 percent boys, 11 percent girls) in the past 12 months. Direct aggression, such as assault, was displayed by 9 percent (13 percent boys, 5 percent girls) of the children. Indirect aggression, such as intimidation and bullying, was found among 8 percent of the child population (7 percent boys, 10 percent girls).

In response, MEPAP was designed as a primary prevention effort to develop pro-social behaviors such as solidarity, cooperation, and volunteerism among school age children. It made efforts to prevent violence, aggression, and the use of psychoactive substances such as alcohol, marijuana, and cocaine. Concurrent with these goals, the program sought to enhance children's coping and address low academic performance, particularly among children enrolled in elementary school. To achieve these ends, MEPAP was designed to influence the childrearing practices of parents and the educational and disciplinary practices of teachers. An essential component of the program was to enhance communication between governments, pre-schools, and elementary schools to better integrate their respective aggression prevention projects. Collaboration was also encouraged between families and educators. MEPAP pursued these goals through teacher and parent training and support aimed at assisting children's caregivers to develop among the children in their care necessary pro-social skills, nonviolent behavior and strategies for peaceful conflict resolution. These strategies were targeted particularly at children demonstrating conduct disordered behavior.

By simultaneously addressing children's behavior at home and school, MEPAP reflected the principles of the United Nations Convention on the Rights of the Child (CRC). Specifically, parents and schools are partners in the provision of childcare. Emphasis needs to be on both developing the capacity of parents and creating the social infrastructure (schools and counselling services) that support parents and educators in their roles as children's caregivers. In this sense, MEPAP fulfills Article

19.1 of the CRC, providing "effective procedures for the establishment of social programs to provide necessary support for the child and for those who have the care of the child." Moreover, given that MEPAP is oriented toward influencing parents' childrearing practices, this also addresses children's rights through Article 18.2 of the CRC by rendering "... assistance to parents and legal guardians in the performance of their childrearing responsibilities...." The nature of the program's collaborative intervention was hypothesized to be particularly well-suited to the vulnerability of Medellín's children and the complexity of the violence they experience within their social ecologies (home, school, and community).

In this chapter, we examine the impact of violence on children in Colombia and report on the initial results from an evaluation of MEPAP. We begin by providing an overview of the scope of the problem of violence in Colombia, as well as examining the implications of this violence with respect to children's development and demonstrate how witnessing violence in childhood can have repercussions for later adult relationships. The chapter then outlines the development of an early intervention violence prevention strategy that borrowed from a number of other successful initiatives. The mixed method evaluation of MEPAP that follows examines the results of a survey with school principals, teachers, and parents, a before-after impact assessment of children's aggression and pro-social behavior and the results of focus groups with children, parents, teachers, and school principles. The overall results indicate that MEPAP as an intervention appears to function best as a supportive factor, building on the latent capacity of families. The chapter concludes with suggestions for future research that will continue this examination of other means of preventing and intervening in cases of violence among children and youth.

Violence in Colombia: The Scope of the Problem

In 2004, Colombia's intentional homicide[1] rate was estimated to be between 45.5 and 61.1 per 100,000 population, the highest in South America, followed by Venezuela with an estimated 32.5–37.0 homicides per 100,000, and Brazil, with 26.2–30.08 per 100,000. By comparison, South America's lowest homicide rates are found in Argentina, Bolivia, and Chile, with an estimated 5.3–5.5, 3.7–5.3, and 2.9–5.5 homicides per 100,000 respectively (United Nations Office on Drugs and Crime, 2009). Although the violence generated by armed groups in Colombia has received widespread attention, it is not the primary cause of violent death in the country. Only an estimated 5–20 percent of homicides can be attributed directly to the armed insurgence. Interpersonal violence and organized crime are responsible for the vast majority of violent deaths (Colombia Departamento Nacional de Planeacion, 1998; Comisión de Estudios sobre la Violencia, 1987).

When MEPAP was designed in 2000, Medellín, Colombia's second largest city was ranked among the most violent cities in the world (Colombia Instituto de Medicina Legal y Ciencias Forenses, 2000) (see figure 6.1). Although the number of homicides has dropped dramatically in Medellín over the past 10 years, violence persists as the second leading cause of death after cardiovascular disease (Colombia National Department of Statistics, 2006; Medellín Municipality, 2006). Consequently, violence continues to be a serious health problem and one of the greatest obstacles to the city's social and financial development.

The scope of the problem justified the implementation of MEPAP. A survey of a representative sample of 12- to 60-year-olds in and around

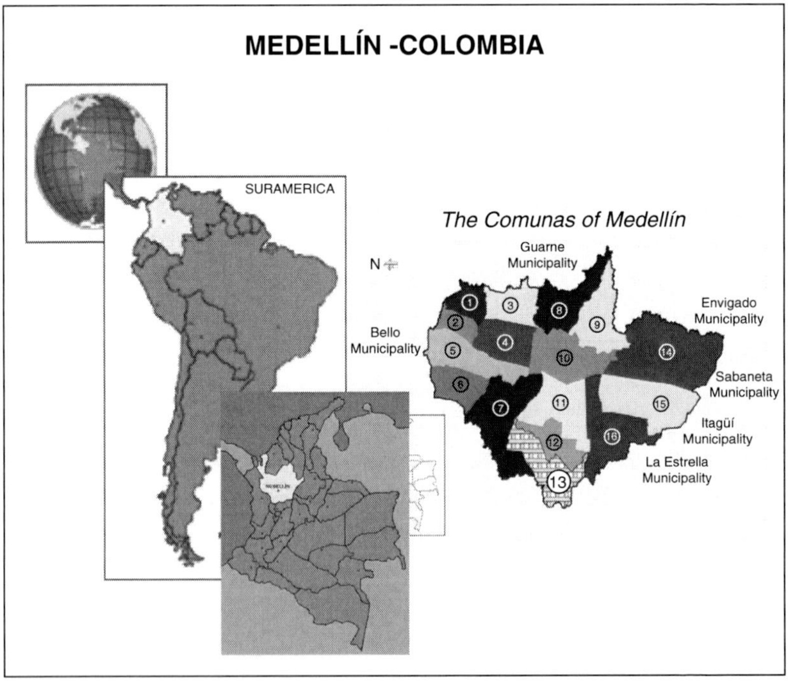

Figure 6.1 MEPAP Program location. Comuna 1, Medellín. Colombia. Phase One-2001.

Medellín showed that problems of violence are more serious in that city when compared to the surrounding districts. Medellín has higher prevalence rates of different forms of violence than the nine municipalities that surround it in the Valley of Aburra (Duque, 2005). In Medellín, 41 percent of inhabitants have witnessed a homicide within their lifetime and 75 percent have witnessed aggression with a weapon. Almost 40 percent have been victims of threats with weapons, or experienced other serious threats such as extortion, forced displacement, muggings with a weapon, and theft. Domestic violence is also a serious problem with one in three Medellín couples reporting that at least one individual caused the other physical harm during the past year (Duque & Montoya, 2008).

Results from the same survey conducted by Duque (2005) show that individuals of all ages have a high level of tolerance with regard to breaking the law and accept the use of violence as a way to resolve conflict. Fifty-two percent agree that it is acceptable to make money by illegal means. Seventy-six percent agreed that it is normal behavior to bribe a public servant or public authority. Seventy-five percent justify severe violence for personal or political aims and half of those surveyed justified the use of homicide to protect their community (Duque, 2005). This pattern of beliefs was most likely to occur among residents of Medellín residing in lower income neighborhoods.

The Implications of Violence: Threats to Children's Development

Aggressive patterns of interaction including violence are established early in life. Research conducted in economically developed countries has shown that physical aggression (such as bullying, assaults, and theft that involves physical assault on another child) during childhood is one of the best predictors of aggression and criminality in adulthood, particularly among male children (Brame, Nagin, & Tremblay, 2001; Keenan & Shaw, 1994; Loeber, 1982; Nagin & Tremblay, 1999; Olweus, 1979). Studies have found significant continuities between boys' childhood aggression and adolescent aggression (Brame, Nagin, & Tremblay, 2001) and adult violence and delinquency (Farrington, 1991). Predictors among girls for aggression and delinquency during adolescence and adulthood have not been as well studied (Broidy et al., 2003).

Evidence suggests that when children are raised in environments where aggression and violence are the norm, the maladaptive behaviors they develop are caused less by individual psychopathology and more by the stress posed by the child's social environment. Violence in the family environment in particular is an important proximal factor that determines future violent behavior (Hawkins et al., 2003). Violence witnessed at home models for children how violence is both normative and instrumental. Although children who experience violence and abuse do not necessarily go on to become aggressors themselves—indeed, the majority do not—abuse during childhood remains an important risk factor for future violent behavior (Widom, 1989).

Childrearing practices have also been found to have an impact on childhood aggression. Parents of aggressive children tend to use coercive strategies such as physical correction, threats, and corporal punishment rather than discipline that is corrective and non-physical (Rothbaum & Weisz, 1994; Olweus, 1979). Furthermore, an aggressive child's parents are less likely to monitor their child's social interactions when the child is with his or her peers and are more likely to ignore their child's pro-social behaviors when they do occur (Patterson, Capaldi, & Bank, 1991). In sum, witnessing family violence and experiencing child abuse, as well as coercive childrearing strategies are factors associated with childhood aggression both in Colombia and internationally (Klevens & Duque, 2002).

The consequences of childhood aggression are varied. Children displaying behavioral problems at the same time experience characteristically high levels of conflict and stress (Loeber & Stouthamer-Loeber, 1986). It has been reported by Tremblay et al. (1996) that in communities where most families score low on measures of sociability such as social capital and have more accepting attitudes toward violence, differences in individual family functioning (i.e., maintaining supportive relationships within the family, attachment between family members, parental monitoring of children, and the expression by parents of clear expectations for children) account for 53 percent of the variation in aggressive behavior among children. Whereas in communities where families show high levels of sociability, individual family functioning is far less important, accounting for a mere 3 percent of the variation between families whose children have positive or negative behavioral outcomes (Tremblay et. al., 1996). Dahlberg and Potter (2001) point out that

> A mutually reinforcing relationship appears to exist between weak family environment, involvement in delinquent peer groups, and school failure. Youths who have little interaction with or attachment to their parents, for example, have higher rates of delinquency, and earlier involvement in delinquency tends to further reduce levels of attachment to parents and to school. (p. 9)

In more dangerous social ecologies or communities that support violence and lack social capital, supportive family interactions would seem to be protective for children most at risk of future aggression.

Aggression in children tends to generate a "snowball" effect: their behavior perpetuates rejection by their parents, who in turn resort to increasingly severe disciplinary measures. A child's negative and violent behavior also tends to elicit rejection by teachers, which, coupled with a child's potential impulsiveness and hyperactivity, hampers learning and further elevates the risk of failure and school dropout (Patterson, Capaldi, & Bank, 1991; Patterson, DeBaryshe, & Ramsey, 1989; Pepler & Slaby, 1996). Likewise, aggression may lead to rejection among schoolmates (Coie & Kupersmidt, 1983). Once isolated, the child who is unattached tends to seek out peers with similar problems (Cairns & Cairns, 1994). During adolescence, these same children have a higher risk of early use of alcohol and drugs, alcohol-related problems, premature and promiscuous sexuality, affective and occupational instability, and violence against women (Caspi, Elder, & Bem, 1987; Nagin & Tremblay, 1999).

Given evidence of the relationship between a child's early environment and future aggressive behavior, the Municipality of Medellín sought to prevent future adult violence through an early intervention program that aims to influence the home and school experiences of children most at risk. By targeting educational and parenting practices, initiatives like MEPAP focus on children to address the overall climate of violence and limit its transgenerational transmission (Widom, 1989).

Early Intervention Violence Prevention Strategies: Drawing from Existing Programs

In economically developed countries, a number of effective interventions exist to prevent or modify the course of early aggression. In a systematic review of the literature on successful early prevention conducted for MEPAP (Klevens & Acevedo, 2000), 21 programs were found that were later drawn upon for the current study. Research that influenced the methodology for this study had assessed a sample of 50 or more children under 12 years of age; used a control group for comparison; and employed standardized instruments, such as questionnaires and tests, that measured the effects of intervention on aggression or antisocial behavior at least one year following the intervention. The programs surveyed came from many different countries, including Canada (Tremblay et al., 2003), the United Kingdom and the United

States (Conduct Problems Prevention Research Group, 1999; Hawkins et al., 2003; Tolan & MacKay, 1996). No studies that met the selection criteria could be found from developing countries.

Seven categories of successful prevention activities were identified through this review (Klevens & Acevedo, 2000). These can be summarized as follows:

1. Interventions that promote *cognitive skills* generate a high impact when carried out with preschool age children and when combined with the development of other types of skills in the child, such as pro-social behaviors. Parental involvement in educational activities constitutes an important component of these early interventions.
2. Interventions for children that consolidate *psychosocial skills*, such as understanding another's emotional states, peaceful conflict resolution, self-control skills development, giving and receiving praise, cultivating friendship, problem solving, and anticipating the consequences of one's behavior. These skills are effective buffers against future aggression for children with behavior problems as well as for children with high a probability of developing behavior problems due to the presence of multiple risk factors. These interventions were most effective for children seven years of age or older.
3. *Parenting workshops* can result in 60–75 percent reductions in aggressive and antisocial behavior among children aged three–eight for a short period of time following intervention (Miller, 1994; Webster-Stratton, 1991). The impact is less among children whose families have lower household incomes or are without social support, and in those families in which there is violence or conflict. These workshops alone will not produce results that generalize to other contexts such as school, and hence, intervention in more than one aspect of a child's social ecology is recommended.
4. *Educator training* decreases problems in the classroom, but does not decrease the incidence of delinquency in other domains such as at home and in the community.
5. *Home visits by health care professionals* during the early years of a child's life are effective, particularly when they succeed in helping mothers adapt their parenting styles to become less punitive and less aggressive.[2] They are also effective when they facilitate parents' development of wider networks of support (Armstrong, Birnie-Lefcovich, & Ungar, 2005).

6. The *administration of medication for aggressive children* contributes to behavioral improvements in children who show symptoms of hyperactivity and attention deficit disorders. Pharmacological treatment is likely to be more effective when employed concurrently with school activities or any other type of family or community intervention.
7. *Establishing mentoring relationships* with high-risk children experiencing behavioral problems at school and home seems to have a positive impact, but existing evidence for this is weak given the limited number of evaluations conducted.

The first five of these seven components of successful aggression prevention were included in MEPAP, while the last two were excluded. The idea of administering pharmacological intervention for aggressive children was not used because when municipal authorities responsible for MEPAP's design consulted parents, they conveyed a reluctance to medicate their children. Mentorship was also not used as it was felt the municipality could neither adequately standardize the intervention (there would be problems with selection of mentors and supervision of their activities) nor ensure fidelity to the program's goals.

Objectives, Structure, and Implementation of MEPAP

MEPAP was conducted in four phases, with each phase expanding the intervention to another group of participants. The first phase began in 2001 and is the subject of this chapter. During phase one, MEPAP provided training and support to educators and parents over a 12-month period. Within that period, educators received 4 months of training, which included 10 workshops, as well as a manual detailing planned classroom interventions with highlights from successful similar programs in other countries outside Latin America (McGinnis & Goldstein, 1990; Patterson, 1976; Shure, 1994; Slaby, Wilson-Brewer & Dash, 1994; Sobel, 1983). The 10 workshops covered the following topics: (1) The role of the teacher in violence management; (2) listening and communication skills; (3) teaching children to respect the views of others; (4) the healthy expression of feelings, assertiveness, and self-esteem; (5) promoting cooperation among students; (6) teacher ethics and values; (7) making the classroom a kind and supportive environment; (8) establishing, maintaining, and negotiating authority in the classroom; (9) strategies for conflict management; and (10) coping with violence outside the school. Following the completion of the workshops, educators attended mentoring sessions every 15 days for a period of 8 months.

Parents and caregivers received group training in alternative non-punitive parenting practices (see Duque, Klevens, Ungar, & Lee, 2005 and Klevens & Montoya, 2003 for details). Mothers and fathers of children showing the most severe symptoms of aggression were invited to receive support, as well as any parents of children having no aggressive symptoms but who expressed an interest in participating. This additional support took the form of workshops for parents and, when possible, in-home visits to help parents develop non-punitive child management strategies. Consistent with the school intervention, group facilitators worked with the parents who received extra support to develop a critical analysis of the ways they interact with their children and their disciplinary and supervisory techniques. Activities were adapted to the sociocultural conditions of Medellín (Duque, Klevens, Ungar, & Lee, 2005; Patterson, 1976). Paralleling the workshops for educators, parents were provided training in the following subject areas: (1) listening and communication as ways to build children's social competency; (2) showing respect for differences by giving children an understanding of other people; (3) enhancing assertiveness, self-esteem, and how to express affection effectively; (4) promoting cooperation at home; (5) parents as children's role models; (6) authority in the family and how to negotiate rules; (6) strategies for conflict management; (7) how to deal with violence that occurs outside the family. In addition to six group workshops, family support also included two visits to each family at their place of residence, and two sessions of family advising offered at the children's school. These activities were carried out by psychology or social work lecturers from a local university (Bolivariana Catholic University) (Duque, Klevens, Ungar, & Lee, 2005).

This first phase of the program was implemented in the poorest zone of the city, Comuna 1, characterized by high degrees of socioeconomic marginalization and violence (Duque, 2000a). All public schools in this zone were invited to participate and all of them accepted, though individual teacher participation was voluntary. Overall, the first phase of the program involved 7,605 children in 33 different primary educational institutions and 24 government childcare homes; 271 teachers participated and 2,442 families received some form of intervention. Based on the success of the first phase of implementation, the program was delivered to a second cohort of 19,209 children in 2003. An explanation of how that success was evaluated, and outcomes from the intervention, are reported later in this chapter. An additional 1,394 teachers were trained and 18,545 families were involved in the program. In total, 160 schools and childcare homes in the City of Medellín participated in the program in 2003. In the following year, the program expanded again adding another 993 educators, 15,129 families, and 129 schools. To our knowledge, this has been the largest Latin American initiative to date to address violence and aggression among children, having reached nearly 90,000 young people and 400 educational institutions in Medellín.

MEPAP Fidelity Monitoring

To ensure fidelity to the model when implemented, staff followed participants for one and a half years after phase one intervention using participant observation, semi-structured interviews, and analysis of field diaries. Two social science professionals who were familiar with the program and research methods conducted monitoring. Together they completed 57 participant observations of teacher and family workshops and family visits, 30 semi-structured interviews with principals, teachers, and families, and a content analysis of 16 field diaries composed by teachers and family advisors. Participants were purposefully chosen to maximize the variability of the sample in order to explore similarities and exceptions to their experience of the intervention. Participants varied by their levels of engagement in the intervention (low and high fidelity) as well as by the degree of engagement demonstrated by their school. Individuals were randomly invited from both low and high fidelity cohorts to participate in the qualitative data collection. The final purposeful, stratified sample, however, represented only those participants willing to be part of the more intensive survey, and, therefore, limits the validity of the findings.

It was particularly important to those implementing the program to assess family and teacher adherence to the program during the first phase of implementation as it was expected that greater participation in the program would lead to better results for the children. Families were classified by the number of sessions they attended, ranging from high (one or both parents attended 9 or 10 training sessions, that is, workshops, home visits, or advising sessions) (22 percent, n = 531), acceptable (one or both parents attended 6, 7, or 8 of the 10 training sessions) (21 percent, n = 513), and low (one or both parents attended 5 or fewer sessions) (57 percent, n = 1398). The classifications reflected findings from previous research that indicated the levels of participation expected to cause a program effect. Teacher adherence during the first phase of the program was classified similarly as high, acceptable, or low. Data from these checks on fidelity helped to inform the evaluation and was integrated into later analyses in order to assess the relationship between program participation and individual child outcomes.

Evaluating MEPAP

Over a period of five years following the intervention (2001–2006), investigators conducted a sequence of mixed method evaluations of the program outcomes that included (1) a survey of school principals, teachers, and parents to document the degree of achieved institutionalization of the program within a school's regular activities; (2) a before-after assessment of children's direct, indirect, and total aggression, pro-social behavior, and school performance; (3) a quasi-experimental follow-up study over three years that compared a group of children who received the program with a control group who did not; and (4) focus groups with children, mothers, school teachers, and principals to investigate their perspectives on the program and its outcomes. In this chapter we report on the before and after impact assessments and the focus groups; the results of the quasi-experimental follow-up study and the survey are still pending.

Before-After Impact Assessment

A component of the evaluation was a 36-month before-after impact analysis conducted using quantitative data gathered from a sample of 339 public school children who had participated in the program in 2001. Baseline "before" assessments identified these children as ranking in the uppermost decile on a test of children's antisocial attitudes and behavior (the COPRAG), ensuring the sample included only the children exhibiting the most severe behavior problems among the entire school population tested. Information was gathered again in 2004. The COPRAG is a 50-item screening instrument assessing aggressive and pro-social behaviors.[3] The COPRAG was validated in Medellín for use with children aged 12 and under (Agudelo et al., 2002). The child's teacher completed it in those cases where the teacher had known the student for at least six months. The measure estimates direct aggression, indirect aggression, prosociality, and academic performance. Test items covered a range of topics as detailed in table 6.1. Cronbach alpha indices were acceptable for all complex variables constructed through a confirmatory factorial analysis.

Table 6.1 Features of the COPRAG test amongst the children participating at Medellín's Early Violence Prevention Program (MEPAP). Medellín, Colombia. 2001 and 2004

*Variable**	*Cronbach Alpha*
SYMPTOMS OF DIRECT AGGRESSION Physically attacks people. Kicks, bites, hits other children. Destroys (voluntarily breaks, knocks down or steps on) objects that belong to his or her family or other children. Gets into a lot of fights. Is cruel, abusive, or mean with other people or animals. Spoils games or activities of others. When another child accidentally hits him or her, child assumes that this was done on purpose, reacting with rage and fighting. Is impulsive, acts without thinking. Takes objects from other children without their permission. Destroys his or her own things. Threatens others with gestures or words. Has difficulty to wait for his or her turn in games or groups. Tells lies, cheats. Imitates the crying of other children.	0,93
SYMPTOMS OF INDIRECT AGGRESSION When upset with someone, tells others not to share with that person. When angry with someone, makes friends with others as revenge. When upset with someone, tells others that person's secrets. When upset with someone, says things behind the person's back. When angry with someone, tries to make others angry at the person too. Tells lies, cheats.	0,90
SYMPTOMS OF HYPERACTIVITY DISORDERS WITH ATTENTION DEFICIT Is impulsive, acts without thinking. Has difficulty to wait for his or her turn in games or groups. Gets distracted, has difficulty to carry out the same activity. Is restless or impatient when seated. Has difficulty paying attention for a long period of time. Stays in any one activity for only a few minutes. Is inattentive, loses concentration easily.	0,90
SYMPTOMS OF PROSOCIAL BEHAVIOR Comforts boys and girls who are crying or sad. At will helps to pick up objects that other children have dropped; for example, a pencil, a notebook, etc. Invites people who are watching to participate in games. Helps other children who are feeling down. Praises the work of less able children. Tries to calm children when they are aggressive. Shares his or her belongings with other children.	0,90

* Based on a scale of: (1) Never; (2) Sometimes; (3) Nearly Always.

Focus Groups

After receiving supplementary evaluation funding, five focus groups were conducted in 2006. Groups were held as follows: two with parents or caregivers (only women chose to attend), two with children who were in the intervention cohort, and one with teachers and principals. Participants were selected at random among families that showed improvement in their childrearing practices based on children's COPRAG scores, and from among those showing no change. Similarly, children were chosen at random from those who improved their behavior and those who did not. Teachers and principals were also chosen at random from those who participated in the program. Each focus group had between 6 and 12 participants. Their objective was to gather feedback on MEPAP as implemented in 2001 and to document what changes, if any, were noticed in children's aggressive behavior or the parental and educational practices of adults over a three-year period.

Program Outcomes

Before-After Study

Based on COPRAG scores, children who participated in MEPAP in 2001 showed a 19 percent decrease in direct aggression, a 39 percent decrease in indirect aggression, and an increase of 47 percent in prosocial behaviors over a three-year period. When compared with children of the same age, children who participated in MEPAP recorded an unexpected 66 percent drop in superior academic performance, though there was no change among youth with average or low levels of school achievement[4] (Duque, Caicedo, Sandoval, Orduz, & Klevens, 2007). All these results were statistically significant. It was based on these relatively positive findings that the intervention was expanded to include additional communities.

In order to estimate if these changes were associated with sex, age, and aggression level of the children or the degree of support provided to families, a logistic regression analysis was performed taking these variables into account (see table 6.2).

This model equation is: $$Ln\left[\frac{Y_i}{1 - Y_i}\right] = \sum_{j=1}^{6} \beta_j X_j$$

Where Ln () is the natural logarithm. Y_i: is a group variable, this is Y_i = 1 when measures were in 2004 and Y_i = 0 in other case. X_1, X_2, X_4 are respectively symptoms of direct aggression, indirect aggression,

Table 6.2 Odds Ratio (OR) of aggression and academic performance, before-after (2001–2004) measurements, according to family adherence to program, and age, sex, and initial aggression level of children

VARIABLES	*General*	*Family adherence to the Program*		*Sex*		*Age (years)*		*Initial level of aggression (COPRAG test)*	
		Highest	*Lowest*	*Boys*	*Girls*	*<=10 years*	*> 10 years*	*Low*	*High*
Direct aggression	0,8*	0,9	0,8	0,9	0,8	0,9	0,8	1,0	0,6***
Indirect aggression	0,7***	0,6***	0,8	0,8	0,5***	0,9	0,7***	0,8*	0,5***
Prosocial behavior	1,5***	1,9***	1,2	1,4**	1,8***	1,3*	1,5***	1,4***	1,4
Academic performance (similar to same age students)	0,8	1,2	0,6	0,7	0,9	1.0	0,7	1.0	1,0
Academic performance (superior to same age students)	0,9	0,8	0,9	0,9	1,0	0,8	1.0	0,9	1,5
Level of significance Model power	0,05 0,99	0,05 0,99	0,05 0,80	0,05 0.80	0,05 <0.80	0,05 <0.80	0,05 <0.80	0,05 <0.80	0,05 <0.54

OR: Odds ratio = 2004 / 2001. * = p-value 0.05 or less ** = p-value 0.01 or less *** = p-value 0.001 or less.

prosocial behavior, and two dummy variables: similar academic performance of the child in comparison to worse children of the same age and superior academic performance of the child in comparison to worse children of the same age.

A positive association was observed between degree of family adherence to the program and symptoms of prosociability. Positive behaviors increased with greater participation by parents in the program. There was also a negative association between family adherence and symptoms of indirect aggression.

Direct aggression significantly decreased among individuals who showed a higher degree of aggression at the outset of the intervention. A statistically significant reduction in indirect aggression among girls (but not boys) was found along with a reduction in indirect aggression among children over 10 years of age. Results reflect the cumulative scale score for each dimension of the study.

The intervention appears to have had a greater effect upon those who showed a higher degree of indirect aggression in 2001, though changes were observed among children at all levels of aggression. Increases in prosociability were observed for both sexes and all ages among the intervention group, particularly for those who showed fewer pro-social traits initially. No statistically significant differences in direct aggression were observed between boys and girls. However, a significant reduction in direct aggression did occur among the group as a whole. The reduction in indirect aggression was observed in children aged 12 and older, but not in children under 12.

Children with higher levels of aggression showed a reduction in both direct and indirect aggression. Among children with lower levels of aggression, the reduction was not statistically significant. However, an increase in pro-social behavior was observed in both groups.

Focus Groups

Focus group participants indicated a persistent cultural belief that physical punishment is the most effective childrearing method. While many parents accepted the need to decrease their use of physical punishment, the practice was not discarded completely and in the majority of cases, participants continued to consider it an effective method of childrearing.

The participants in both of the parent and caregiver focus groups, with and without improvement in care practices and disciplinary strategies, said that their use of physical punishment decreased, as did their children's aggressive behavior. Participants attributed this change to participation in the program. Children who showed the least improvement in behavior after the intervention tended to have parents with low levels of adherence to the program and multiple family problems, including histories of severe physical punishment. Children who showed a decrease in severe aggressive behavior attributed the change to the fact that their mothers had improved their care and supervision and were using non-violent alternative punishments (i.e., removing something the child likes).

Interesting differences were also seen among the mother and caregiver focus groups. Those who reported the most change in their childrearing approach were parents of children attending a school that had participated in the program for the past five years. In contrast, parents of children who did not report a change in their use of physical punishment were more likely to have changed schools. These transfers occurred either because the school had requested that the child leave or because the parents had chosen to move the child in order to try and address his or her aggressive behavior, or to prevent or correct the child's consumption of illegal drugs.

Convergence of Findings

Combined, the quantitative and qualitative findings suggest that the intervention was most successful diminishing children's aggression in families that demonstrated the best childrearing practices before the program began and were more active in the program. Change in scores on the COPRAG and qualitative data from focus groups both suggest that families already characterized by greater degrees of instability and more aggressive childrearing and educational practices were more likely to show poor results. Therefore, MEPAP as an intervention appears to function best as a supportive factor, building on the latent capacity of families. Moreover, in families under greater stress, MEPAP may not be preventive. It is likely these families need more intensive and focused interventions that help families individually while also addressing contextual challenges.

Program Effects on Institutions

Teacher and principal meetings were used to analyze the results of the intervention and discuss the program's progress and sustainability. Even though the Municipality of Medellín did not continue its financial support, 74 percent of the schools that participated in phase one reported continuing to offer the school-based component of the intervention five years later. More than half of the 51 interviewed principals and 131 interviewed teachers agreed that content from MEPAP had been integrated into their schools' educational programming. Also, almost 80 percent of the school principals and teachers reported making an effort to carry out activities, such as training of teachers, and discussion and follow-up meetings that would help institutionalize MEPAP in their schools and daycare centers.

Survey and focus group data provide evidence that a large number of the principals and teachers considered that the overall functioning of their schools and daycare centers had improved. Anecdotal evidence highlights an improvement to the work environment and relationships among teachers, between teachers and their superiors, and between teachers and their students and the students' families. Participation of families in community and school activities, such as attending teacher parent meetings and school support committees, were similarly reported to have increased. Overall, discipline in the school had also improved. Importantly, teachers said the program helped them to improve the way they looked at themselves as educators and were more satisfied with the work they were doing with all children, not just those with aggression problems.

MEPAP's success suggests that it is possible to offer community-wide prevention initiatives through schools and for children at home in economically less developed countries like Colombia that share similarities with programs offered in other economically developed countries. Such programs can import best practices from other contexts that show potential to increase pro-social behavior and reduce aggression among vulnerable children and adolescents.

Findings also suggest, however, that unique outcomes are to be expected from programming that is shared between contexts. In the present evaluation, the children with the most significant behavioral problems who participated in MEPAP come from families with greater socioeconomic and cultural barriers and with care patterns and disciplinary strategies in which severe physical punishment was more likely to be used. Children from these families may not benefit as much from a program like MEPAP as do families that were better functioning before the program. Change was still positive (though not statistically significant) for almost all individual children who received the intervention. Regardless of the level of vulnerability shown at the start of the program, the effect of the intervention was supportive of existing strengths, to varying degrees.

This evaluation of MEPAP demonstrates the importance of researching program effectiveness in developing countries. Adequate funding of pilot programs and their evaluations is crucial. Programs adapted from a developed country context for use in the developing world require the resources to examine their impact longitudinally. Thorough evaluations such as this one permit the expansion of programming that is ultimately sustainable within particular communities. Furthermore, given the challenges encountered by this evaluation, the activities carried out with the families of MEPAP show that it is necessary to ensure a sufficiently large "dose" of an intervention if results are to be judged reliable and valid.

Finally, MEPAP's results suggest that programs addressing childhood aggression in developing countries should not focus exclusively on personal growth, but should also emphasize parent and educator training in strategies and practices that will help them teach children prosocial skills. Interventions that are more ecological in nature, balancing personal and environmental change, and more organic, relying on the efforts of frontline professionals and families for implementation, seem to predict greater efficacy (Ungar, 2005).

Conclusion: Future Research and Next Steps

Effective research programs help support public policy initiatives to prevent early aggression and other risky behaviors among children. In the case of Medellín (and similar contexts), we recommend future research to

- Further investigate the impact of multipurpose early prevention programs addressing aggression, tobacco use, sexual risk behaviors, and drug and alcohol abuse on school performance among vulnerable children and youth.
- Differentiate the impact of such multipurpose interventions for boys and girls.
- Differentiate the impact of such programming among early and severe aggressors and low aggressors or those young people who stop their aggression in their later teens.
- Disseminate findings across Latin America and introduce audiences in developed countries to the unique aspects of research and programming in developing countries.

Studies on the epidemiology of violence in Medellín (Duque, 2005; Duque, Montoya, & Sierra, 2006) show how some social groups, including youth, teachers, and caregivers, are highly tolerant of lawbreaking and social norm transgressions. Many of their behaviors demonstrate acceptance of violence in their communities, legitimating its use as a viable means of solving problems. When children are raised with these values and violence is tolerated and promoted, aggressive and risk-taking behaviors are transmitted across generations. As such, Medellín needs more than just a violence prevention program; what is required is a concerted effort to recognize the rights of children and families to both the protections and health promotion supports identified by the UN Convention on the Rights of the Child (CRC). Both the government and the family share in the "performance of their child-rearing responsibilities" (UNCRC, Article 18.2). Promoting a child's access to pro-social modelling and school and home environments that teach alternatives to antisocial behavior is fundamental to protecting children's rights. Given that many of MEPAP's young participants had histories of victimization both at home and in their communities, the program sought to expand children's limited skillset to cope with violence and provide accessible supports within their schools and homes.

Longitudinal research (and the researchers' relationships with policy makers) has contributed to a thoughtful reflection on the needs of Medellín's children and the actions required to address those needs. Recently, the mayors of Medellín and its nine surrounding municipalities approved an eight-year common public policy to promote civic coexistence and prevent violence. Among its priorities are early aggression prevention in children from *in-utero* to three years of age, early violence prevention and development of civic mindedness in preschool and school children, and domestic violence prevention. Given the success of MEPAP, we anticipate further gains for children and their families from these new initiatives.

Notes

* The authors wish to thank the Canadian International Development Agency and the Pan-American Health Organization for their generous support of this research.

1. The United Nations Office on Drugs and Crime defines intentional homicide as "unlawful death purposefully inflicted on a person by another person" (UNODC, 2009).
2. The focus of these studies is almost exclusively on mothers.
3. It is based on the work of Dr. Richard Tremblay and his colleagues at the Université de Montréal, Laval University, and McGill University. Dr. Tremblay holds the Canadian Research Chair on Child Development.
4. The 66 percent drop was unexpected, and we are currently studying this finding in greater depth in order to understand it further.

References

Agudelo, L. M., Giraldo, C. A., Gaviria, M. B., Sandoval, C. A., Rodríguez, M. Á., . . . Gómez, J. F. (2002). *Características de las familias y escuelas relacionadas con los comportamientos agresivos y prosociales en niños y niñas de 3 a 11 años. Medellín* (Characteristics of Families and Schools Related to Aggressive and Prosocial Behaviours among 3 to 11 Years Children. Medellín). Medellín: Colciencias, CES, Universidad de Antioquia.

Armstrong, M., Birnie-Lefcovich, S., & Ungar, M. (2005). Pathways between Social Support, Quality of Parenting and Child Resilience: A Transactional Model. *Journal of Family and Child Studies, 14*(2), 269–281.

Brame, B., Nagin D. S., & Tremblay, R. E. (2001). Developmental Trajectories of Physical Aggression from School Entry to Late Adolescence. *Journal Child Psychology Psychiatry, 42*, 503–512.

Broidy, L. M., Nagin, D. S., Tremblay, R. E., Bates, J. E., Brame, B.,... Dodge, K. A. (2003). Developmental Trajectories of Childhood Disruptive Behaviors and Adolescent Delinquency: A Six-Site, Cross-National Study. *Developmental Psychology, 39*, 222–245.

Cairns, R. B., & Cairns, B. D. (1994). *Lifelines and Risks: Pathways of Youth in Our Times.* New York: Cambridge University Press.

Caspi, A., Elder, G., & Bem, D. (1987). Moving against the World: Life-Course Patterns of Explosive Children. *Developmental Psychology, 23,* 308–313.

Coie, J., & Kupersmidt, J. (1983). A Behavioural Analysis of Emerging Social Status in Boys' Groups. *Child Development, 54,* 1400–1416.

Colombia Departamento Nacional de Planeacion. (1998). *La paz: El desafío para el desarrollo.* Bogota: Tercer Mundo Edit.

Colombia Instituto Nacional de Medicina Legal y Ciencias Forenses & Centro de Referencia Nacional sobre Violencia. (2000). *Forensis 1999 Datos para la vida.* Instituto Nacional de Medicina Legal y Ciencias Forenses. Santa Fe de Bogotá: Author.

Colombia National Department of Statistics (DANE) (2006). Retrieved May 22, 2006 from http://www. dane.gov.co.

Comisión de Estudios sobre la Violencia. (1987). *Colombia: Violencia y democracia.* Bogotá: Universidad Nacional de Colombia.

Conduct Problems Prevention Research Group. (1999). Initial Impact of the Fast Track Prevention Trial for Conduct Problems: I. The High Risk Sample. *Journal of Consulting and Clinical Psychology, 67*, 631–647.

Dahlberg, L. L., & Potter, L B. (2001). Youth Violence: Developmental Pathways and Prevention Challenges. *American Journal of Preventive Medicine, 20*(1) Suppl. 1: 3–14.

Duque, L. F. (2000a). *El Programa de Convivencia Ciudadana de Medellín.* Medellín: Medellín Cargraphics.

Duque, L. F. (2000b). La Violencia Cotidiana en Colombia y el Papel de la Universidad. *Revista Facultad de Salud Pública, Universidad de Antioquia, 18*(1), 57–70.

Duque, L. F. (2005). *La Violencia en le Valle de Aburra. Su magnitud y programa para reducirla.* Medellín: Universidad de Antioquia y Área Metropolitana del Valle de Aburra.

Duque, L. F., Caicedo, B., Sandoval, J., Orduz, J. F., & Klevens, J. (2007). Lecciones del Programa de Prevención Temprana de la Violencia. Medellín, Colombia. *Pan American Journal of Public Health, 21*, 21–29.

Duque, L. F., Klevens, J., Ungar, M., & Lee, A. W. (2005). Violence Prevention Programming in Colombia: Challenges in Project Design and Fidelity. In M. Ungar (Ed.), *A Handbook for Working with Children and Youth: Pathways to Resilience across Cultures and Contexts* (pp. 455–472). Thousand Oaks, CA: Sage.

Duque, L. F., & Montoya, N. (2008). La violencia doméstica en Medellín y demás municipios del Valle de Aburrá. 2003–2004. *Revista Facultad de Salud Pública, Universidad de Antioquia, 26*(1), 27–39.

Duque, L. F., Montoya, N., & Sierra C. A. (2006). Características de la Familia: Relaciones con los Padres en la Niñez. Universidad de Antioquia. Área Metropolitana del Valle de Aburrá. Serie de documentos de Información para la Acción para los Comités de Convivencia y Seguridad Ciudadana de los municipios del Valle de Aburrá, número 8. Medellín: Acción para los Comités de Convivencia y Seguridad Ciudadana de los municipios del Valle de Aburrá.

Farrington, D. P. (1991). Childhood Aggression and Adult Violence: Early Precursors and Later Life Outcomes. In D. J. Pepper & K. H. Rubin (Eds.), *The Development and Treatment of Childhood Aggression* (pp. 5–30). Hillsdale, NJ: Lawrence Erlbaum.

Franco, S. (2003). A Social Medical Approach to Violence in Colombia. *American Journal Public Health, 93,* 2032–2036.

Hawkins, J. D., Smith, B. H., Hill, K. G., Kosterman, R., Catalano, R. F. & Abbot, R. D. (2003). Understanding and Preventing Crime and Violence: Findings from the Seattle Social Development Project. In T. P. Thornberry & M. D. Krohn (Eds.), *Taking Stock of Delinquency: An Overview of Findings from Contemporary Longitudinal Studies* (pp. 255–300). New York: Klewer Academic/Plenum.

Keenan, K., & Shaw, D. S. (1994). The Development of Aggression in Toddlers: A Study of Low-Income Families. *Journal of Abnormal Psychology, 22,* 53–77.

Klevens, J., & Acevedo, O. (2000). Estrategias para la prevención temprana de la violencia en ninos. Alcaldía de Medellín, Secretaria de Educación y Cultura, Programa de Convivencia Ciudadana, Corporacion Presencia Colombo Suiza. Medellín: Contrato Municipio de Medellín-BID.

Klevens, J., & Duque, L. F. (2002). The Victim Perpetrator Overlap and Routine Activities: Results from a Cross-sectional Study in Bogotá, Colombia. *Journal of Interpersonal Violence, 17*(2), 206–217.

Klevens, J., & Montoya, E. (2003). Un Abordaje de la Violencia desde la Salud Pública: el Proyecto de Prevención Temprana en Medellín. *Rev. Salud Pública, 5*(1), 24–39.

Loeber, R. (1982). Stability of Antisocial Behaviour: A Review. *Child Development, 53,* 1431–1446.

Loeber, R., & Stouthamer-Loeber, M. (1986). Family Factors as Correlates and Predictors of Juvenile Conduct Problems and Delinquency. In N. Tonry & M. Norris (Eds.), *Crime and Justice: An Annual Review of Research*, vol. 7 (pp. 29–150). Chicago: University of Chicago Press.

McGinnis, E., & Goldstein, A. P. (1990). Skill-Streaming in Early Childhood: Teaching Prosocial Skills to the Preschool and Kindergarten Child. Champaign, IL: Research Press.

Medellín Municipality. (2006). *Observatorio de la Violencia. Vigilancia epidemiologica de homicidios.* Medellín: Violence Observatory, Homicide surveillance.

Miller, L. S. (1994). Preventive Interventions for Conduct Disorder: A Review. *Child and Adolescent Psychiatric Clinics of North America, 3,* 405–419.

Nagin, D., & Tremblay, R. E. (1999). Trajectories of Boys' Physical Aggression, Opposition, and Hyperactivity on the Path to Physically Violent and Nonviolent Juvenile Delinquency. *Child Development, 70,* 1181–1196.

Olweus, D. (1979). Stability of Aggressive Reaction Patterns in Males: A Review. *Psychological Bulletin, 86,* 852–875.

Patterson, G. R. (1976). *Living with Children. New Methods for Parents and Teachers.* Champaign, IL: Research Press.

Patterson, G. R., Capaldi, D., & Bank, L. (1991). An Early-Starter Model for Predicting Delinquency. In D. J. Peplar & K. H. Rubin (Eds.), *Development and Treatment of Childhood Aggression*. Hillsdale, NJ: Lawrence Erlbaum.

Patterson, G. R., DeBaryshe, B. D., & Ramsey, E. (1989). A Developmental Perspective of Antisocial Behaviour. *American Psychologist, 41,* 432–444.

Pepler, J., & Slaby, R. (1996). Theoretical and Developmental Perspectives on Youth and Violence. In L. D. Eron, J. H. Gentry & P. Schlegel (Eds.), *Reason to Hope: A Psychological Perspective on Violence and Youth,* (pp. 27–58). Washington, D.C. American Psychological Association.

Rothbaum, F., & Weisz, J. (1994). Parental Cregiving and Child Externalizing Behaviour in Non-clinical Samples: A Meta-analysis. *Psychological Bulletin, 116,* 55–74.

Shure, M. (1994). Raising a Thinking Child: Help Your Young Child Resolve Conflicts and Get Along with Others. New York: Pocket Books.

Slaby, R. G., Wilson-Brewer, R., & Dash, K. (1994). *Aggressors, Victims and Bystanders.* Newton, MA: Education Development Center.

Sobel, J. (1983). *Everybody Wins: 393 Non-competitive Games for Young Children.* New York: Walker.

Tolan, P. H., & MacKay, M. M. (1996). Preventing Serious Antisocial Behaviour in Inner-City Children: An Empirical Based Family Intervention Program. *Family Relations, 45,*148–155.

Tremblay, R., Boulerice, B., Harden, P. W., McDuff, P., Pérusse, D., Pihl, R. O. & Zoccolillo, M. (1996). Do children in Canada Become More Aggressive as They Approach Adolescence? In Human Resources Development Canada & Statistics Canada (Eds.), *Growing Up in Canada: National Longitudinal Survey of Children and Youth.* Ottawa: Statistics Canada.

Tremblay, R., Vitaro F., Nagin, D., Pagani, L., & Séguin, J. R. (2003). The Montreal Longitudinal and Experimental Study: Rediscovering the Power of Description. In T. P. Thornberry & M. D. Krohn (Eds.), *Taking Stock of Delinquency: An Overview of Findings from Contemporary Longitudinal Studies* (pp. 205–254). New York: Klewer Academic/Plenum.

Ungar, M. (2005). Introduction: Resilience across Cultures and Contexts. In M. Ungar (Eds.), *Handbook for Working with Children and Youth: Pathways to Resilience across Cultures and Contexts* (pp. xv–xxxix). Thousand Oaks, CA: Sage.

United Nations Office on Drugs and Crime (UNODC). (2009). International Homicide Statistics (2004). Retrieved January 5, 2001 from http://www.unodc.org/documents/data-and-analysis/IHS-rates-05012009.pdf.

Webster-Stratton, C. (1991). Annotation: Strategies for Helping Families with Conduct Disordered Children. *Journal of Child Psychology and Psychiatry, 32,* 1047–1062.

Widom, C. (1989). The Cycle of Violence. *Science, 244,* 160–166.

PART III

Child Rights, Education, and Participation

CHAPTER 7

The Dynamics of Youth Participation: Insights from Research Fieldwork with Female Youth in Senegal

Richard Maclure

The Evolving Discourse of Child-Centered Development and Youth Participation in West Africa

Children are valued and loved by adults for a host of reasons—family ties, their perceived innocence, their capacity to learn and adapt, and the hope they provide for the future. Yet in most societies they are also widely regarded as the property of their parents or immediate guardians who are responsible for socializing them according to the prevailing norms and values of the adult world. In such circumstances the opinions and desires of children carry little weight. Their role is to listen, obey, and learn from their parents and other adults who are charged with the responsibility of managing their growth and development, and integrating them into the established structures of the adult world.

Concurrently, however, in contrast to long-standing perceptions of children as necessarily subservient to adult direction, an alternative perspective has emerged that portrays children as having both the capacity and the right to participate in the decisions and the actions that directly affect their well-being. This perspective has gained considerable ground since the promulgation of the UN Convention on the Rights of the Child two decades ago. As outlined in Article 12.1 of the CRC, children under the age of 18 years who are capable of forming their own views have "the right to express those views freely in all matters affecting the child" and to have these views "given due weight in accordance with [their] age and maturity." Although phrased as a rights-based imperative, this assertion is founded on a growing acknowledgment of children's agency and their natural proclivities to engage actively with the world around them (Arches & Fleming, 2006; Campbell & Trotter, 2007; Kirk & Shutte, 2004). When provided adequate information and opportunity to participate, young people are often "capable of making well-informed and responsible judgments" (Bessant, 2004, p. 394). Consequently, the participation of young people in decisions and actions that directly affect their own welfare is widely seen as pragmatic and just.

In West Africa this alternative perspective of children's agency and capacity has been increasingly endorsed by NGOs and international aid agencies. References to child-centered approaches that aim to engage young people in public discourse and civic action are now commonplace (Bucholz, 2002; de Boeck & Hanwana, 2005; Leiten, 2003; Ubi, 2007). In part this is due to regional demographics—an estimated 50 percent of the population across West Africa is now under the age of 18 years and, therefore, constitutes a profound influence on economic and cultural developments in the region (Wiwa, 2010). Yet heightened interest in youth has also emanated from an array of structural problems that have undermined conventional processes of youth socialization and protection. Global market forces have diminished the significance of small household farming and community-based social economies, and this in turn has eroded the significance of the family as a unit of collective production and social security. The quality of public schooling has likewise deteriorated, leaving many young people disillusioned with the returns that they had expected from their attendance at school. At a time when the materialist aspirations of youth are being stoked by media-fed consumerism, particularly among those living in urban centers, vast numbers of young people are confronted with prospects of unemployment or seasonal low-paid informal sector work. Equally troubling are the entrenched gender disparities that diminish girls' access to good quality education and eventual economic independence.

These conditions are particularly acute in Senegal, a country in West Africa that is encumbered with a weak economy and stark social inequalities, and where the median age of its population is 18.6 years[1] (République du Sénégal/UNICEF, 2009). The mass marketing of a youth-oriented culture of music, dress, and style contrasts sharply with the emergence of a growing youth proletariat that is susceptible to the effects of widening class divisions and exploitation (Fall & Ndiaye, 2003). With few opportunities beyond piece-meal low-wage labor or prolonged unemployment and dependence on kin relations for their subsistence needs (Biaya, 2000), most youth have neither political clout nor strong institutional support systems. In this somber context, growing numbers of urban youth have become susceptible to social networks that perpetuate risky and frequently illicit activities—for example, begging, petty theft, drug dealing, sexual exploitation and abuse, and violent crime (Delaunay, 1996).

The challenges of the growing youth demographic in Senegal have, therefore, become a central social policy concern. As an early signatory to the CRC, the Senegalese state has promulgated various child protection laws that include parental codes of conduct, sanctions against child pornography, the establishment of juvenile courts, and programs of youth training and job creation.[2] Yet legislated child protection measures are only sporadically enforced, and state-sponsored youth training and employment creation schemes have been hampered by poor coordination, lack of transparency, and disconnectedness from informal, private sector job markets.

Increasingly, therefore, much of the dynamic for youth development and support has emanated from an array of international aid agencies and NGOs that have embraced the discourse of child rights and child-centered development programs. While directing resources toward tangible goals of disease prevention, and more and better education, most child-centered development initiatives have also embraced the language of child rights and the ideal of youth participation as a means, as well as a goal, of development assistance. This acknowledgment of the participatory potential of youth signifies a laudatory shift in perception and policy. Yet there remains substantial ambiguity surrounding the purposes and practices of youth participation. This stems from two inherently contradictory perspectives—the tendency on the one hand to romanticize the notion of participation as a transformative process that alters young people's social and economic status, and on the other to regard youth participation as a set of utilitarian practices that can enhance the efficacy of child-oriented social assistance programs.

Conceptualizations of Child and Adolescent Participation

From a transformative perspective, the participation of children and adolescents presupposes the engagement of young people in mutually beneficial decision making with adults, and is informed by principles of power sharing and democratic governance (Cockburn, 2005; Stasiulis, 2002). For organizations that espouse child-centered approaches to development assistance, a transformative view of children's participation, therefore, implies a set of structures and procedures that are open to the involvement of children in policy deliberations and in program implementation. Within such alternative institutional contexts, youth are regarded not as individuals for whom responsibility lies in the future, but as bona fide citizens whose opinions and recommendations directly affect organizational activities. In practice, however, the transformative ideal of children's participation is difficult to achieve. In challenging structures of adult control and generating uncertainty regarding the extent to which children's participation should or can be an inherent aspect of hitherto adult-dominated decision making, the transformative perspective can be particularly unsettling for organizations with established hierarchical structures and procedures.

Invariably, therefore, the transformative ideal of children's participation tends to be overshadowed by a utilitarian perspective that portrays children and adolescents as constituting a valuable human resource capable of contributing to social programs and services designed to enhance their development (Ginwright & James, 2002). From this perspective, children's participation is a social investment that simultaneously enables them to gain experience and skills on the way to productive citizenship within an existing social and institutional order. As exercised within the framework of discrete projects and activities, it may certainly contribute to enhancing the efficacy of services for children and youth. Yet power remains vested with adults who bestow opportunities to participate upon youth for specified utilitarian ends rather than for purposes of heightening youthful autonomy and responsibility. Participatory processes may involve open-ended dialogue and shared decision making, but their effect is merely to reinforce predetermined institutional goals and existing hierarchies of authority.

Between these two contradictory perspectives, the practice of child and adolescent participation is affected considerably by diverse contexts, objectives, activities, and actors. In an effort to counter the ambiguity surrounding youth participation, a number of scholars have formulated conceptual models that attempt to illustrate its variations and complex dynamics. Hart's (1992) well-known "ladder" depicts eight levels of youth participation, beginning at the bottom with "tokenistic" participation that essentially does little more than legitimize an established set of policies and practices, and reaching an apex representing "child-initiated" decisions that are integral to organizational processes. Shier (2001) has postulated a model consisting of five levels of participation, ranging from children's voices being heard (but not necessarily acted upon) to children's appropriation of power and responsibility for decision making. Within each level, there are three stages of commitment—openings, opportunities, and obligations—that determine the relative depth of youth participation. Somewhat in contrast to Hart and Shier, both of whom have conceptualized youth participation as a hierarchical set of relations and undertakings, Cashmore (2002) has depicted a series of concentric requirements of youth participation. These include (1) opportunity and choice; (2) access to information; (3) mentorship; (4) supportive policies and legislation; (5) forums for youthful critiques and complaints; and (6) services for monitoring and evaluating participation (p. 841).

While such models assist in illuminating the complexities and limitations of youth participation, there has been scant empirical research on the engagement of youth in contexts in which incentives and norms of democratic practice are scarce. Consequently, in an effort to contribute to a burgeoning knowledge base relating to the role of youth in development activities in West Africa, the author and a research assistant, Moussa Diagne,[3] undertook a study that sought, in part, to examine the processes of youth participation among Wolof youth in ruralvillages and town neighborhoods. This project specifically sought to establish how young people organize themselves, how they function as groups (whether autonomously and of their own volition, or whether guided or even coerced by interested adults), and how their collective deliberations and actions relate to their own interests and/or to those of aid organizations and adult community leaders. Adopting a qualitative, somewhat serendipitous approach to research fieldwork, we attained particular insights into the functions of mentorship and constructivist pedagogy as stimuli for youth participation.

The Study

Methodology

Funded jointly by the Social Science and Humanities Research Council of Canada (SSHRC) and Plan Senegal, the study focused on two objectives. The first was to encourage cohorts of rural and urban youth to articulate through various narrative forms their personal preoccupations and their views on issues that they believed were affecting the current and long-term well-being of Senegalese youth. The second was to examine the particular dynamics of participation as the youth engaged in discussions and the development of their own narratives. This chapter focuses specifically on the activities conducted with and by four groups of female adolescents living in different neighborhoods of the town of Thiés, the capital of the similarly named region.[4]

Methodologically the research was conducted as an action-oriented ethnography, relying on youth voices and the different forms of collective narratives we encouraged them to develop and articulate. Field research was carried out in two distinctive phases over a period of approximately eight months.

Phase 1: Working with Designated Representatives of Groupes de Base

During the first phase, through the cooperation of a local NGO, ENDA Jeunesse Action (EJA), we contacted the four groups of girls, most of whom were loosely associated through EJA-sponsored training in skills such as needlework, sewing, and hair dressing. About a third of the girls worked as domestic servants in the homes of relatively well-to-do urban dwellers. These girls had all immigrated to Thiés from their home villages in search of employment: 3 of the female domestics resided in the homes of their employers; the remaining 11 lived either with extended family relations in Thiés or together in rented lodgings. The other girls contacted for this project (approximately 35 in number) were unemployed, generally in search of work or further education, and all living in their own homes or with relatives. The selection of these girls, which was undertaken in conjunction with EJA staff, was entirely determined by their association with EJA, which provided them with opportunities for training and socializing. Although not a random sample, these young women were typical of Senegalese female youth—bright, aware of their obligations to parents and siblings, yet keen to attain a degree of independence through education and remunerative work. In view of the fact that EJA served as the institutional mediator for our research, the girls were quite happy to participate and received no objection from their parents or guardians or employers in the case of domestic workers.

By agreement with EJA, we first began meeting on a periodical basis with 12 representatives (aged 16–21 years) of the four groups. These meetings were held at the EJA training center in Thiés. Discussion initially focused on the aims and open-ended nature of the research, but eventually settled into informal dialogue in the Wolof language. Topics centered primarily on issues of interest to the girls. They spoke about their communities and families, about their own daily activities, about schooling,[5] and about their concerns, anxieties, and aspirations. While these meetings were conducted in order to gain an appreciation of the lives and diverse experiences of these young women, a key purpose for us was also to foster a rapport with them.

Participant attendance at these meetings was excellent, in part because they were scheduled to coincide with the days when the girls attended a series of EJA-sponsored workshops. Yet full attendance was also due to the participants' genuine interest in speaking with us, and in eventually developing their own collective narratives, which we explained was an objective of the research. They always ensured that the meeting room was neatly set up prior to each gathering, and discussions were generally lively and candid. On two occasions, following postponements of scheduled meetings because of our own travel constraints,[6] the girls themselves proposed to reschedule the meetings.

Once the rapport was established between the researchers and the participants, topics for discussion were generally defined by the young women. These usually related to issues that were national and even international in scope, and were often the subject of popular media attention—rising food prices, youth unemployment, growing youth alienation, the sexual harassment of girls, and the migration of youth away from home and family. A common refrain among the participants was the Wolof notion of *daan doole*—the "sweat of one's brow" that must accompany the resolution of problems. Broadly interpreted, this reflected the girls' acceptance of the necessity of hard work and self-reliance if their personal goals were to be attained or the difficulties they confronted were to be overcome. Another common desire was to obtain steady employment in a skilled occupation (unlike the customary manual labor of house maids). Yet most of these young women believed that people cannot succeed on their own. Instead, there was a general consensus that if *daan doole* was to be fruitful, young people—girls in particular—need support from parents, older siblings, or other relations, especially in the form of resources for education and training. This reflected what the young women regarded as a sort of ideal moral social contract, one that entailed efforts by senior or well-placed individuals to provide the resources needed for their dependants to eventually become successfully productive and independent.

Examples of this perspective are indicated in the following two vignettes, one articulated by a girl who saw herself in a role enabling her to provide for dependent siblings, the other expressed by a girl who regarded herself as having to rely on others:[7]

> I am the oldest in my family and I work as a domestic servant because I have no desire to cross my arms and simply watch others work. I have to

> assist my mother and take charge of things. I don't count on my parents to buy me clothes because they do not have the means to do so. Nowadays parents cannot provide many things for their children. So it is up to us to work for things, and make sacrifices. At each Tabaski festival I want my brothers and sisters to wear fine new clothes. So I have told my mother that it is not necessary for her to buy me new clothes; [instead] she can save money in order to buy new clothes for my brothers and sisters. It is so comforting for me to see them dressed in their nice new clothes.
>
> I am the second eldest girl in my family. I am not going to look for work because physically I cannot manage—I'm ill. My parents look after my needs so I don't have to go work as a domestic servant. At the time of Tabaski [festival], my parents buy the clothes that I like, but I will only wear them if they also buy clothes for my cousins. Otherwise I will wear my old clothes so that the others won't feel left out.

In order to facilitate discussions that combined personal recollections with critical reflections on broad social issues, in the third meeting with the group, the researchers proposed an iterative process involving a mix of role-playing and discussion. In effect, each time different points of view on a particular issue emerged, the researchers suggested that opposing groups exemplify their perspectives through role-playing as a basis for further argumentation. For example, on two different occasions, while there was agreement about the seriousness of rising food prices and high levels of unemployment, different perspectives centered on the ways that youth respond to these issues. Some girls felt that in the face of such problems too many youth were idle and lackadaisical. Others, however, felt that most youth in Senegal are energetic and resourceful, even if they are unable to fully overcome what are clearly major structural hurdles. Both these issues were highlighted by the girls through impromptu role-playing. The first issue was considered through a short skit prepared by the girls, with four girls acting out roles and the others singing at the end of the skit. The second issue was examined through role-playing commonly known as *journal futur*—a mock radio phone-in format involving a radio "host," a "guest interviewee," and an audience of radio "listeners" who participate by "phoning in" their queries and commentaries on specific social topics. These forms of role-playing tended to facilitate more vocal participation among the girls, especially among those who were naturally reticent, than simply informal seminar-style exchanges. Discussions after each role-playing scenario were always animated.

In demonstrating these different perspectives through role-playing, followed by discussion, the participants often came to see that generally they were in agreement on the main issues. Often, for example, girls arrived at a consensus concerning the status and comportment of youth—that though behavior is a function of individual choice, the choices one makes are strongly influenced by existing opportunities and constraints, for example, gender, family background, the extent of parental support, levels of education, access to resources, and skills training.

During the first phase of the project, as the weeks went by, our relationship with the girls evolved into one of mutual friendship and trust. In particular they looked on Moussa, a native Wolof speaker and a musician who is attuned to popular Senegalese culture, as a friend and mentor. As time progressed, Moussa periodically confirmed meeting times with several of the group representatives through text-messaging and occasional phone contact (cell phone use is ubiquitous in Senegal, and some of the girls either owned or had easy access to cell phones).

Phase 2: Working Directly with the Neighborhood "Groupes de Base"

After the first four months of the project, with a firm rapport established between ourselves and the 12 group representatives, the project moved into a second phase during which responsibility for group activity shifted to the girls themselves. We began by meeting all four neighborhood groups. The groups ranged in number from approximately 12 to 20 adherents, with the youngest about 11 or 12 years old, and the oldest in their early twenties. Similar to the informal discussions of the earlier meetings with their representatives in the first phase, the girls were invited to identify and talk about specific issues that were of concern or interest to them. Again, our aim was to gain an appreciation of the diversity of life experiences among these girls, some of whom were originally from Thiès, but many of whom had migrated from home villages and were either living with extended family members or together in small groups (which was common among the domestic servants). As with the first phase of the project, once a good rapport had been established, we invited the girls to inject creativity into their discussions through role-playing and any other form of collective expression. As an incentive for their engagement in these self-directed activities, we agreed to audiotape their "performances" (a point of genuine appeal for these girls) and eventually to help organize public presentations of their narratives in their own communities and to a broader audience of governmental and nongovernmental officials having an interest in youth issues.

In contrast to the first phase of the project, during which we had initiated and generally led all the meetings, after the first two encounters with each group, this phase of the project required little direction and almost no input from us. Because of our fieldwork schedule elsewhere with other rural youth, our presence in Thiés diminished and the groups of girls developed their own narratives whenever they met, usually—but not always—according to an informal schedule they themselves had set up for crocheting and knitting together. Emulating the experiences of discussion and role-playing during the first phase, the representatives of each of these groups assumed the role of animators (essentially the role that we had played in the first phase). On occasion, some girls contacted us by telephone, asking when we planned to visit them, or requesting advice or suggestions regarding their emerging narrative presentations. Frequently as well, conscious that they would be presenting publicly, the girls expressed an interest in what other groups were doing, indicative of an element of competition that emerged as members of each group began to consider how their narrative performance would be compared to the others.

During the last two weeks of research fieldwork, particular days were selected for each group of girls to present their narratives publicly in their respective neighborhoods. Overall, a series of short sketches and *journaux futurs* dealt with the following issues:

- family violence;
- official corruption;
- illicit drug trafficking;
- forced marriage;
- sexual harassment of female workers;
- anxiety related to a lack of education and employment opportunities; and
- mistreatment of the poor.

Several of the theatrical presentations included music, song, and dance. As agreed upon with the girls, we filmed these dramatizations. The organization of public neighborhood presentations, which required availability of refreshments, chairs, and sound systems for music, necessitated genuine collaboration between the girls and ourselves.

Following the recording of the girls' narratives, Moussa and I hosted a day-long seminar in Thiés for the staff of various NGOs and for representatives from other government units and aid agencies working on youth issues. Selected photos and film footage of the youth narratives (those of the girls in Thiés as well as those of other rural youth) served as a basis for animated discussion centering on the conditions of young people in Senegal and their ostensible rights as citizens and participants in development policies and programs.[8]

The Pedagogy of Youth Participation: An Evolving Relation between Youth Insiders and Adult Outsiders

Through this modest set of discussions and activities, and the research fieldwork that accompanied the process over several months, we gained insights into the lives and the preoccupations of a group of girls coming to terms with the challenges and constraints of approaching adulthood in a town to which many of them had migrated. Despite limited formal education, collectively they were mature, articulate, inventive, and capable of organizing themselves and responding to opportunities. Toward the end of research fieldwork, in view of the enthusiasm they demonstrated in presenting their dramatized narratives, a genuine feeling of camaraderie had developed between ourselves and these young women. Simultaneously, on our part at least, was a sense of regret, that because of our position as outsiders and researchers (not government or NGO staff charged with the responsibility of working with young people), there was no possibility of carrying this relationship further into program activity or even a policy context. As is almost always the case, the relationship that developed during the research process faded rapidly following the termination of research fieldwork.

Yet it was through this relationship, between outside (adult) researchers and young people, that we discerned some fundamental insights into youth participation in a context in which the rhetoric of youth participation and the broader notion of child-centered development do not easily correspond with established institutional practices. It is not my purpose here to launch into a critique of such practices, but rather to highlight what we learned from our fieldwork about the nexus of youth participation, mentorship, and constructivist pedagogy, and its implications for programs that aim to assist children and adolescents.

In this study of female youth in Thiés, necessitating as it did an evolving collaborative relationship between researchers and young women, and the development of narratives animated from the girls' own interests and concerns, the nexus between the processes of education and participation became evident. Central to this nexus was an adult-youth relationship that was not bound by an immutable power framework. Instead, as the project progressed, the relationship between ourselves (the adult researchers) and the youth participants underwent a subtle, yet profound, shift, with the youth assuming greater control over their own involvement in the project, and we the researchers willingly ceding the pace and direction of fieldwork to the youth participants. To elaborate more fully, it is useful to consider two aspects of the process of youth engagement, and one key aspect of the shifting adult role.

Youth Engagement

Youth Participation as Learning-by-Doing

At the outset of each of the project phases, our first meetings with the girls were characterized quite naturally by a strong element of reticence on their part. Anticipating direction from us as adult outsiders, they exhibited an aura of passive responsiveness. This lasted, albeit to a diminishing degree, over the course of one or two subsequent meetings in each of the two project phases. This is not to say, however, that the young women were mute or even shy. On the contrary, early on they demonstrated a willingness to talk about themselves and their experiences. Yet initial discussions generally followed from our own questions and prodding. Gradually, however, as friendliness and a sense of mutual informality developed, most of the girls gained confidence to speak independently without trepidation of deviating from what they may at first have assumed was an agenda that we had not fully disclosed.

Midway through each of the two phases of the project, when the groups of girls were asked to decide for themselves the specific issues that they would like to relate in their own narrative fashion, the dynamic for continuing project fieldwork shifted toward the girls themselves. Once this occurred, our questioning and prodding almost completely ceased, and the girls manifestly assumed control over the issues to be discussed and the ways they would articulate their perspectives. Relying on their own knowledge and experiences, the girls demonstrated a collective ability to present a broad range of social problems in interesting and creative ways. Through a *learning-by-doing* process they became empowered, albeit within the limited parameters of a modest ethnographic research project. Having initially been stimulated by adult outsiders, they assumed control and encouraged one another through interaction and a collective desire to accomplish something together. This was the epitome of education as experiential (socially creative) learning.

Youth Leadership

At the outset of the project the adult researchers were clearly in a leadership position, recruiting youth participants, initiating meetings, and facilitating discussions. Gradually, however, as a trusting and friendly rapport developed, and as we ceded the initiative to the girls for deciding the issues to be highlighted and the manner in which they were to be presented publicly, specific individuals emerged as natural leaders within each group. Where we had defined the parameters of discussion in the early meetings of each of the two phases, stipulating that discussion should stem from what was important to the girls themselves, group leaders began to manifest a strong influence in identifying thematic issues for presentation, and in organizing and coaching their peers as the groups developed their own narrative presentations. Generally, too, these were the individuals who maintained contact with us through cell phone use.

This element of leadership helped underscore the truism that members of social groups, no matter how superficially alike, are rarely homogeneous in terms of their relationships and their capabilities. This was evident among the groups of girls whom we came to know. Group participation was a reflection of the leadership qualities that emerged within each group. Leadership was a characteristic that not only facilitated the participatory process, but also manifested itself because of the stimulus afforded by the opportunity to exercise agency as a collective activity. As we came to recognize firsthand, youth cannot be considered as an amorphous sector or group, nor can youth participation succeed in practice unless scope for individual expression and agency emerge *from within* the collective. Effective leadership among youth, in other words, is often a manifestation of internal group dynamics rather than an allocation of power from outside the group.

Mentorship and Flexibility: The Shifting Nature of Outsiders' Intervention

The relationship between ourselves—most notably Moussa—and the girls was essentially a form of mentorship. In talking with the girls in familiar naturalistic settings, and in fostering an atmosphere of inclusiveness and collegiality with them, we strove to engage them in a process of informal dialogue that would allow each side—researchers and young women—to learn from and about each other. Honesty, openness, and a sense of growth and development characterized all the meetings. Mutual learning derived not only from the issues and social problems that groups identified as topics of discussion, but it also stemmed from the process of collective engagement, particularly when this led to the increased responsibility that the girls assumed in the latter stages of each of the two phases of research fieldwork. It was a relationship predicated on a shift toward *shared* project ownership, which implied a diminishment of our initial monopolistic direction of the project. As the study progressed, our roles became interchangeable, with the young women assuming a more dynamic collaborative role in the fieldwork process, and our own position as outside researchers being transformed from that of protagonists in the early focus groups to a more supportive status as monitors and observers.

In effect, this was a process of mentorship. It was by no means an easy or a straightforward task; it required patience and self-effacement. It was time-consuming, with schedules for meetings often having to accommodate other diverse youth interests and obligations. Over the course of eight months of research fieldwork, we traveled long distances and frequently withstood lengthy delays before the girls arrived for designated meetings. Yet despite occasional frustrations and setbacks, we developed and maintained friendly relations with all four groups of young women in Thiés. For our part, we were naturally motivated by the commitment to gain insights into their concerns and aspirations, and to facilitate and monitor manifestations of their participation as we shifted the onus of constructing and presenting narrative forms of expression to them. For their part, the girls came to trust us and developed an interest in availing themselves of the opportunity to develop and articulate their collective narratives that were subsequently recorded. The ingrained dimension of mentorship that characterized the evolving researcher-youth relationships had helped substantially to stimulate youth agency and to foster a participatory process that was amenable to observation and analysis.

Conclusion: The Interconnectedness of Education and Youth Participation

In the broad realm of development studies, education and participation are generally accepted as instrumental for the growth and long-term welfare of children and adolescents. Curiously, however, youth education and participation have rarely been considered as interconnected aspects of development intervention.

To a large extent this dichotomy would appear to stem from official as well as popular perceptions regarding education and participation in developing countries. On the one side, for decades, education has mainly been considered as a service to be delivered (a "deliverable"). As such, it is deemed to consist of the buildings, classrooms, and desks that comprise school infrastructure, the books, and materials that are used for teaching and learning, the teachers who work in school classrooms, and the certificates to be attained at the end of schooling (Maclure, Sabbah, & Lavan, 2009). Similarly, nonformal ("nonschool") education tends to be regarded as a vast array of workshops and information sessions designed to enhance the vocational and life skills of learners. While not completely erroneous, such views of education as a service that is delivered and intended to result in specific outcomes, usually measured in years of enrolment and test results, almost never fully encompass the notion of education as a process of human interaction between teachers and learners, and among learners themselves.

On the other side, as discussed earlier, despite almost universal endorsement of the UN Convention on the Rights of the Child and the considerable import now given to the notion of child and adolescent participation as one of the key precepts of the CRC, there is considerable ambiguity concerning the ways that young people are engaged as participants, particularly in processes that have hitherto been initiated and managed by adults. This is largely due to the surprising dearth of in-depth knowledge concerning the mobilization of children's agency for development purposes, and the conditions that facilitate young people's involvement in community and organizational decision making and action. In particular, although it is generally understood that adult support and organizational adjustments are necessary if the participation of young people is to be realized in any meaningful way, so far little demonstrable connection has been made between the ideal of youth participation and the pedagogical processes that underlie the aptitudes and skills necessary to participate in development activities.

As Moussa Diagne and I came to discern in our research fieldwork, education and participation are two sides of the same coin. Youth participation is invariably an educational process. Conversely, good quality education is invariably a learner-centered activity, with learners functioning as active *participant* discoverers and practitioners of knowledge rather than as passive repositories of information delivered to them. Unfortunately, however, although perennial appeals are made for improvements in educational quality, rarely is much attention devoted to the reciprocal possibilities of teaching and learning, or to the potentiality of learning as a participatory learner-directed process. At the same time, while there is a growing body of literature on the dynamics of participation as we have indicated, most of the focus has been to ascertain the levels or typology of participation, and the extent to which voices and actions are representative of particular subgroups. Yet in view of the need to facilitate children's acquisition of knowledge and of the skills to engage in open discussion and debate, and to make decisions collectively, the pedagogical dynamic of youth participation requires far more consideration than it has received to date. And here is where the role of the (adult) mentor is significant.

Though the role of adults in supporting children's participation is widely acknowledged, what is generally far less understood is the nature of adult support. If it is to be truly effective, it should not be static or indefinite, but rather be clearly focused on facilitating young people's acquisition of knowledge and skills through a learning-by-doing process (Smith, 2002). This is essentially a pedagogical approach that aims to develop children's competence through encouragement and the creation of opportunities to deliberate and make decisions collectively. The task of the mentor in this situation is to demonstrate flexibility, to hear and understand children's own modes of expression, and to communicate in ways that are familiar to children (Mahoney, Eccles, & Larson, 2004; Smith, 2002). The mentor must likewise continue to adjust to children's expanding abilities, and be committed to fostering the autonomy of young people through a gradual transfer of power—from youth dependency to a relationship of interdependency and bona fide partnership.

This view of education and participation, as symbiotic processes essential for youth development and welfare, has significant implications for systems of education and for externally supported development assistance programs alike. Ministries of education, teachers, parents, and young people must overcome adherence to antiquated rote forms of teaching and learning, and strive to embrace the more dynamic perspective of learning as a manifestation of individual and collective agency engrossed in knowledge discovery and dissemination. Simultaneously, national and international organizations, and community groups, must increasingly recognize youth participation as an *educational* process that necessitates an alteration of conventionally static top-down relationships between aid agency benefactors and (youthful) beneficiaries.

Such an appeal for sweeping changes in institutional and policy approaches with regard to youth would seem to be presumptuous on the basis of modest insights attained from a small action-research project. The informal nature of the relationships and activities that characterized our research fieldwork, involving a limited number of young people over a relatively short period of time, is certainly a far cry from proposed shifts in institutionalized procedures, administrative arrangements, and power dynamics that are inherent to development organizations, be they government departments, international aid agencies, or even local grassroots associations. Yet almost all governmental and nongovernmental development organizations do espouse the discourse of good quality education and youth participation. And at the core of all development practice, indeed the fundamental raison d'être of most such organizations, is the human interaction between outsiders (organizational staff, educators, and animators) and their intended beneficiaries (the poor, the vulnerable, and increasingly youth). Organizational change, therefore, should be driven by consideration of the primacy of such interaction. Without such change, it is difficult to ponder how the nexus between education and youth participation can be fully realized.

Notes

1. Senegal had an estimated population of 13,711,597 in July 2009 and a growth rate estimated at 2.35 percent. Despite its relatively open democratic political system, an affluent 10 percent of the populace commands an estimated 44 percent of national income, while a majority of households live in poverty and have little access to good quality social services (Polgreen, 2008).
2. The Plan d'Action pour l'Emploi (PAE), which emphasizes the promotion of youth employment on a national scale; le Fonds National de Promotion de la Jeunesse (FNPJ); le Fonds National d'Aide à l'Emploi (FNAE) ; and l'Agence Nationale pour l'Emploi des Jeunes (ANEJ).
3. Initially a female research assistant worked with us, but for family reasons she was obliged to leave the project early into the fieldwork.
4. The study also focused on groups of male and female youth in four rural communities, but for reasons of length this aspect of the research is not covered in this chapter.
5. Most of them had attained some level of primary schooling, but none was attending school at the time of the study.
6. We were based in the capital city of Dakar, roughly a two-hour drive from Thiés.
7. Translation from Wolof to French to English.
8. Currently a DVD compiling the youth narratives is being produced.

References

Arches, J., & J. Fleming. (2006). Young People and Social Action: Youth Participation in the United Kingdom and United States. *New Directions for Youth Development (111),* 81–90.

Bessant, J. (2004). Mixed Messages: Youth Participation and Democratic Practice. *Australian Journal of Political Science, 39(*2), 387–404.

Biaya, T., (2000). Jeunes et culture de la rue en Afrique urbaine (Addis-Abeba, Dakar et Kinshasa), *Politique africaine*, n° 80 – décembre 2000, 12–31.

Bucholz, M. (2002). Youth and Cultural Practice. *Annual Review of Anthropology, 31*, 525–555.

Campbell, C., & J. Trotter. (2007). "Invisible" Young People: The Paradox of Participation in Research. *Vulnerable Children and Youth Studies, 2*(1), 32–39.

Cashmore, J. (2002). Promoting the Participation of Children and Young People in Care. *Child Abuse and Neglect*, *26,* 837–847.

Cockburn, T. (2005). Children's Participation in Social Policy: Inclusion, Chimera, or Authenticity?. *Social Policy & Society, 4*(2), 109–119.

De Boeck, F., & Honwana, A. (2005). Introduction: Children and Youth in Africa. In De Boeck, & Honwana (Eds.), *Dans Makers & Breakers : Children & Youth in Postcolonial Africa* (Trenton, NJ: Africa World Press, 2005).

Delaunay, V. (1996). Le travail des fillettes en Afrique sub-saharienne. Conditions de vie et de travail des jeunes migrantes Sérére à Dakar. In Schlemmer Bernard (Eds.), *L'enfant exploité, oppression, mise au travail, prolétarisation*. Paris: Karthala, ORSTOM

Emslie, M. (2009). "Practice What You Teach": Researching Youth Work Education: Teaching Participatory Casework Practice. *Journal of Youth Studies, 12*(3), 323–336.

Ginwright, S., & T. James. (2002). From Assets to Agents of Change: Social Justice, Organizing, and Youth Development. *New Directions for Youth Development, 96*, 27–46.

Hart, R. A. (1992). *Children's Participation: From Tokenism to Citizenship*. Florence: Innocenti Research Centre, UNICEF.

Kirk, P., & Shutte, A. M. (2004). Community Leadership Development. *Community Development Journal, 39*(3), 234–251.

Leiten, G. K. (2003). *Children as Agents in Development: Field Realities across the World*. Plan Netherlands.

Maclure, R., Sabbah, R., & Lavan, D. (2009). Education and Development: The Perennial Contradictions of policy discourse, in P. Beaudet, P. A. Haslam, & J. Schafer (Eds.), *Introduction to International Development: Approaches, Actors, and Issues* (pp. 367–383). Toronto, ON: Oxford University Press.

Mahoney, J. L., Eccles, J. S., & Larson, R. W. (2004). Processes of Adjustment in Organized Out-of-School Activities: Opportunities and Risks. *New Directions for Youth Development (101),* 115–144.

Polgreen, L. (2008). Once a Bright Point, Senegal Teeters toward a Arisis. *International Herald Tribune*.

République du Sénégal & United Nations Children's Fund (UNICEF). (2009). Étude mondiale sur la pauvreté et les disparités chez les enfants au Sénégal. Ministère de l'Economie et des Finances (MEF) et UNICEF.

Shier, H. (2001). Pathways to Participation: Openings, Opportunities and Obligations: A New Model for Enhancing Children's Participation in

Decision-Making, in Line with Article 12.1 of the UN Convention on the Rights of the Child. *Children and Society, 15*, 107–117.

Smith, A. B. (2002). Interpreting and Supporting Participation Rights: Contributions from Sociocultural Theory. *The International Journal of Children's Rights, 10,* 73–88.

Stasiulis, D. (2002). The Active Child Citizen: Lessons from Canadian Policy and the Children's Movement. *Citizenship Studies, 6*(4), 507–538.

Ubi, E. N. (2007). *African Youth Charter: Prospects for the Development of the African Youth.* Sahel & West Africa Club/OECD/Economic Community of West African States (ECOWAS).

United Nations. (1989). *UN Convention on the Rights of the Child.* New York.

Wiwa, K. (2010, May 7). Africa's Youth: An Energy to Liberate or Detonate. *Globe & Mail.*

CHAPTER 8

From Education to Equality? Bolivian Adolescent Males' Understanding of Gender Equality in the Wake of Sensitivity Workshops*

Christine Gervais

Introduction

In the late twentieth and early twenty-first centuries, the involvement of boys and men in increasing awareness and education about discriminatory treatment of women and girls has been emphasized internationally as essential to the achievement of overall gender equality. Many scholars and activists have insisted on the centrality of males to feminist movements, and on the necessity and viability of solidarity between females and males (Chittister, 1998, p. 4; Hooks, 2000, pp. 69, 71). In addition, the growing prominence of profeminist male scholars and "meninist"[1] activism has helped to expand gender-oriented education for males as well as females, and to encourage the engagement of boys and men in support of women's rights and in the struggle to end violence and discrimination against women (DeKeseredy, Schwartz, & Alvi, 2000; Flood, 2010).

On the world stage, several international meetings have drawn attention to the inclusion of males in proequality pursuits. The Fourth World Conference on Women[2] (1995), the World Summit on Social Development (1995, 2000), the Dakar Framework for Education for All (2000), and the 48th session of the United Nations Commission on the

Status of Women (2004) all focused on the significance of engaging males as partners in efforts toward gender equality (Connell, 2003, pp. 4–5; UNESCO, 2004, p. 1). As hooks (2000), Chittister (1998), and Connell (2003), among others, have maintained, it is imperative to move beyond the antimale sentiment of earlier decades and to include both women and men in feminist pursuits toward equality. As proequality scholars and activists have contended, while patriarchal conditions and their corresponding stereotypes are particularly damaging to girls and women, they also have adverse effects on males (Connell, 2003, p. 12; UNESCO, 2004). In this light, both women and men, as well as society as a whole, would benefit from a shared responsibility in striving to overcome patriarchy and its emotional, social, political, and economic constraints.

This broad citizen-oriented approach parallels the growing academic and grassroots emphases on human rights education, empowerment, and engagement of youth. It resonates, for example, with Mihr's (2009) insistence that for the purpose of respecting human rights and protecting people's dignity, "[e]ducating people in their human rights should empower them to know and use their human rights to protect themselves and others from human rights violations" (p. 177). This corresponds to arguments advocating the education and involvement of young people in the struggle for their own rights and those of other vulnerable social groups (Kaiser, 2005; Silva & Salles Souto, 2009). Such youth advocacy stems from the conception of youth citizenship as a social position, rather than as simply a legal one, from which youth can create alliances to promote social change (Quijada, 2008).

Nevertheless, although studies have shown that attitudes improve when young men are educated on and engaged toward gender equality, progress remains uneven in view of the complexities of entrenched patriarchal systems (Flood, 2010, p. 2). Consequently, while the inclusion of boys and men in all attempts to achieve gender equality is considered to be imperative, there is a need for corresponding research that monitors those processes and their long-term optimal outcomes (Connell, 2003; Flood, 2010; UNESCO, 2004).

In Latin America, efforts to increase youth awareness of human rights and issues pertaining to gender equity have coincided with burgeoning postconflict and postdictatorial transitions (Mihr, 2009; Quijada, 2008; Silva & Salles Souto, 2009). Several conferences on gender equality and masculinities have been led by the Latin American Federation of Social Sciences (FLACSO), and proequality education projects for boys and men have become increasingly common in a number of Latin American countries[3] (Valdés & Olavarría, 1998). It is within these international and regional contexts that Bolivia's recent state and nongovernmental support of gender equality has emerged.

Within the past 10 years, in a concerted effort to move beyond repressive military rule and lay the foundations of long-term democratic governance, Bolivia has introduced significant constitutional[4] reforms that have sought to promote and protect the political, social, and economic rights of Bolivians. In particular, constitutional provisions have been introduced that specify the rights of indigenous peoples and women, two groups that have suffered centuries of repression under successive colonial and patriarchal regimes.[5] The promotion of gender equality is exemplified in clauses upholding women's right to land ownership, to health and reproductive services, to protection from discrimination and violence, and to workplace and pay equity (Lanza, 2009).

From a human rights perspective, the past decade has, therefore, been one of relative optimism in Bolivia. It was in this context of progressive legislative change that in 2006 a women's NGO in Cochabamba launched a grassroots-level education program that consisted of a series of community-based workshops focusing on gender equality and human rights for a group of Bolivian adolescent girls and boys of Quechua descent.[6] This chapter explores the ensuing effects of this educational program on the evolving perceptions of human rights and gender equity among the adolescent male participants. This was part of a broader research project that explored the connection between informal education and heightened awareness of human rights among women and men in Bolivia, Honduras, and Nicaragua.[7] By featuring their voices through a series of vignettes drawn from questionnaires and focus groups transcripts, the chapter illustrates the capacity of young indigenous Bolivian males to experience attitudinal changes concerning key aspects of social justice and the causes of gender equity. In so doing, the chapter aims to highlight the connection between educational activities designed to enhance critical awareness of gender and human rights issues, and boys' subsequent perceptions and experiences related to fundamental rights and the struggle for gender equality.

The Human Rights Education Workshops in Cochabamba, Bolivia

The participants in this study took part in a set of forty five three-hour-long human rights workshops that were held at a women's NGO in Cochabamba, Bolivia.[8] The workshops were intended to create awareness about human rights, gender equality, and citizenship. Besides highlighting national and international human rights frameworks such as the UN Convention on the Rights of the Child (CRC), the Universal Declaration of Human Rights and the Constitution of Bolivia,[9] the content of the workshops also included themes related to citizenship, health, peace-building, social responsibility, and environmental sustainability. Workshop activities were varied, and included guest speakers and lectures on current affairs, video documentaries, photo essays, art, popular theatre, team-building, leadership games, and reflective dialogue. Emphasis was on continual social interaction among workshop leaders and participants as a basis for ensuring effective learning, problem solving, and teamwork (Silva & Salles Souto, 2009).

Data Collection and Analysis

This examination of adolescent boys' engagement with human rights and gender equality draws upon data collected[10] between April 2006 and October 2008. In total, 69 male adolescents,[11] representing a second generation of displaced[12] Quechua families living in Cochabamba, participated in a series of questionnaires and focus group sessions cofacilitated in Spanish by the author, her research assistant, and three youth participant-leaders. These individuals helped in creating the research instruments by providing advice on relevant content and the inclusion of language that could be easily understood by adolescent respondents. Their experiences in the workshops led to the clarification and editing of questions on themes related to citizenship, civic duty, personal conduct, and perceptions regarding gender. Sensitivity was accorded to the dignity of the young participants. Their involvement in the design of research instruments also greatly facilitated the researchers' access to the young male respondents and the consistency of their responses in questionnaires and focus groups.

The Canadian–Bolivian research team frequently adopted a social approach to data collection by engaging youth participants in singing, story-telling, and doing exercises. This is what Chevalier and Buckles (2008, pp. 11, 66) refer to as "creative expression" in research, an approach that involves youth through narrative forms that are familiar to them.[13] The questionnaire responses and recorded discussions of focus groups were subsequently translated[14] into English by the author and her research assistant. In order to ensure faithfulness to the sentiments and experiential accounts of the youth respondents, the youth narratives were inductively analyzed in adherence to grounded theory (Denov & Gervais, 2007; Glaser & Strauss, 1967). By grounding analysis of the boys' articulation of their perceptions and experiences in relation to their involvement in the human rights/gender equity workshops, the study yielded insights into the boys' evolving knowledge of human rights and their growing acknowledgment of gender differentiation.

Postworkshop Perceptions of Human Rights

The following sections of this chapter are intended to provide a broad sense of the postworkshop perceptions of adolescent males concerning human rights and gender equity. A judiciously selected set of short verbatim statements that reflect the overall authenticity of the scope and range of the respondents' perceptions of their recent educational experience and the issues covered in the workshops form the basis of the commentary. Consequently, the narrative adheres to this edited collection's spirit of "essays from the field."

Realizations and Personal Benefits

Overall the male participants in this study developed a greater understanding of citizenship and a related sense of responsibility through their training experience. Although not without their moments of tension and contradiction, the workshops generally fostered a positive social network derived from the collective learning experience. This social dimension of the workshops, and the spirit of solidarity that emerged, seems to have surprised many of the participants. Indeed, at the outset, many of the boys admitted to being initially skeptical of the value of the workshops. Yet as time progressed, most (90 percent) also concurred that the learning they derived from the grassroots-level workshops, largely through dialogue and social interaction, was novel and compelling:

> Before the workshops, I thought that they would be a waste of time and only be a help to girls, but after I realized that they were for everyone and they helped us all to better ourselves and be aware of our reality.
>
> I thought the workshops were going to be boring but afterwards I realized that they were very interesting and fun.
>
> I learned to understand things that we do not cover in school. . . . I consider things in a different way.

The workshops provided these adolescent males with the space to learn about human rights and how to articulate their own evolving perspectives on rights issues. Consequently, there was a general consensus that the workshops enabled them to become conscious of rights discourse not only as it applied to them personally, but also to others in their community, and to other social groups.

> I have many more rights than I thought.
>
> They helped us value ourselves as people regardless of gender and I believe that the objectives were achieved because I feel capable and ready to face the world.

Such statements revealed how the workshops affected the boys cognitively and emotionally, and as such fostered among many of them a sense of personal growth and heightened self-confidence. With knowledge and self-confidence came an increasingly reassuring sense of safety for many of these boys.

> Now I consider that I am somebody in life and that I have the same rights as everyone else.
>
> The teaching was excellent and because of that I am more sure of myself and it helped me a lot to claim my rights as a person.
>
> Before I did not have the courage to argue but now I can raise my voice and defend my opinion and defend myself verbally . . . I go out with my head held high and with very high ideals.
>
> I feel more secure because now I have my rights respected and if someone violates them I can denounce them.

Numerous (83 percent) respondents indicated that their personal conduct had changed and that they had started to behave differently in relation to others. While there were clearly differences of opinion, and tensions sometimes emerged during the workshop discussions, such divisions were eventually overshadowed by the solidarity and spirit of camaraderie that developed through the social and supportive dynamic of the workshops. This unity of purposes was rooted in the boys' enhanced understanding of their own rights and of the broader impetus to respect the rights of other vulnerable groups.

> Each person thought differently but in the end we all arrived at an agreement.
>
> Over the course of time people [the workshop participants] became more affectionate and united.

> My personal life has been affected in a good way because thanks to the workshops I have been able to get rid of the ignorance that I had.
>
> We united to search for solutions to make problems disappear.

Citizenship Duties and Respecting the Rights of Others

An underlying lesson of the workshops that most boys came to understand was that the counterpoint to rights was responsibility. Through repeated articulation of the notions of duty and obligation, it was evident most of them had inculcated the idea that citizenship did not signify the prioritization of their own rights alone, but instead entailed a balance between advocacy of their own rights and support for the rights of others.

> I learned that as citizens we need to know our rights to demand respect for ourselves and our obligations to respect others.
>
> I grew internally as much with understanding of obligations and duties as with rights.
>
> I have many rights and just as many duties as a citizen.

When questioned about the meaning and responsibilities of citizenship, the youth reiterated what they had learned in the workshops, that citizenship duties included being engaged so as to help others, to improve their communities, and to set a good example through civic actions.

> To be a better citizen in daily life, I need to participate, to work in my community with my neighbors... [to be] an example so that the rest will follow.

In relation to the idea of citizenship as the fulfillment of collectively oriented duties, some boys indicated how their growing attentiveness to the plight of others had resulted in changes within themselves. They spoke about being more considerate, listening to others, respecting others, and being tolerant. As one boy said,

> Before I was always right and... only my opinion mattered. Now I know that I have to respect the rights of other people.

Through interviews and focus groups, it was clear that for most (87 percent) boys, the growing sense of citizenship-based responsibility toward others' rights and their frequently repeated articulation of the imperative of respecting others served as the impetus underlying heightened consciousness of rights and reflection on related social actions.

Postworkshop Perceptions of Gender Equity

In addition to enabling the boys to become fully aware of their own human rights, the workshops encouraged them to become attentive to the plight of others, and particularly to that of females. The following sections summarize the boys' changing perceptions regarding gender differences, and their attitudes toward girls and women.

Heightened Gender Consciousness

Almost all (96 percent) the respondents indicated that the workshops had fostered a shift in their views about women. For many this was tantamount to discovering that "women are equal to us and cannot be used as objects" and that "we must respect women's decisions." Two statements in particular sum up what many of the boys felt.

> It surprised me to know many things about women that I had no idea about before, but I feel much better knowing them.
>
> I thought [before the workshops] that women did not have the same rights as men, but now I know that it is not that way and that we all have the same rights.

Claims of improvements in their relations with young women were also indicative of the Bolivian adolescent boys' growing belief in gender equality. Gender-related barriers appeared to diminish through the workshop experiences, and increased comfort with females in communication seemed to foster greater mutual understanding and respect among boys and girls. For some participants, their acknowledgment of the merits of gender equality, a direct result of their involvement in the workshops, seemed to have yielded social benefits, and several openly stated that their relations with young women had improved.

> I am not as reserved in my communication with female friends. I have become much more open.
>
> [My] relations have improved a lot because I have more female friends. . . . [and] I now understand some of their worries.

Such sentiments reflect attitudinal changes that are the building blocks for improvements in gender relations. One boy spoke of the need "to be more honest" as a basis of enhanced respect and responsibility toward females. Another claimed that his relations with girls improved because of his deliberate attempts to create awareness about respect and equality. At the very least, these aforementioned examples are testaments to the boys' awareness of the need to actually translate their newfound knowledge into practice.

Actions Taken in Support of Human Rights and Gender Equality

All the boys who participated in this study acknowledged that social activism through advocacy and involvement in rights-based activity was necessary to create awareness, respect, and solidarity, particularly among the most vulnerable who do not know their rights. Undoubtedly, reflecting the enthusiasm engendered by the workshops, the majority of participants conveyed confidence regarding the prospect of personal engagement in rights-oriented social action.

> [It's important] to change...family violence and most importantly machismo, [and to] denounce people who violate rights and protect the victims.
>
> I take my younger sisters into consideration knowing that we have the same rights and responsibilities.
>
> I would like to get more of these human rights started because I do not want to listen anymore about abuses against children.
>
> [The workshops taught me] to protect others and encourage them to go forward.

While the boys frequently referred to "sexism" and "patriarchy" (terms they had learned in the workshops) as being the underpinnings of many of the injustices suffered by women, they nonetheless often expressed their concerns with real conviction about specific problems such as violence against women, the powerlessness of women in the face of discrimination and abuse, and the lack of education and mass level sensitization concerning the rights of women.

> Sexism...I never realized how selfish it was.
>
> I am worried that many women do not know their rights and are abused, raped, and they do not denounce [their violators] for fear of retaliation.

> I am worried that people are not interested in women's rights... that these workshops are not in all of Bolivia.

When asked if their conduct in relation to girls and women had actually changed, four boys indicated quite specifically that in their efforts to be good citizens they were refraining from being "sexist," and two openly claimed that they had started "to be feminist."[15] Such assertions certainly echo the admonishments that the boys heard in the workshops and perhaps in part reflect a response bias. Yet there was also a tendency to regard "nonsexism" as largely equivalent to protecting girls and women from nefarious acts without any broader conceptualization of full female rights. This would suggest minimal departure from dominant paternalistic perceptions of women as wholly vulnerable and thus incapable of supporting themselves without a male presence. On the other hand, most of the young male respondents did reveal an overt inclination to support the principle of gender equity, and a willingness to understand and strive to redress the discriminatory practices directed toward the opposite sex.

Similarly, most (93 percent) boys expressed a desire to disseminate their own burgeoning consciousness of human rights and gender equity. To some extent, of course, this was a natural sentiment of pride and enthusiasm that stemmed from enhanced knowledge and self-confidence. Some (90 percent) of them asserted that they had already shared information from the workshops with friends and family members, even to the point of encouraging them to participate in similar workshop sessions in the near future.

> I have spoken with my parents and siblings in simple chats.
>
> I shared it with my mother because she always asks me how the workshop went.
>
> I talk about everything I learned about human rights because they are important in our daily life and people need to know their rights.
>
> I told my aunt about my experience in the workshops, telling her everything that was explained to us.... that a man is not more than a woman because a woman has the same rights as a man and that a woman must hold her place to have her rights respected.

Still others spoke about their participation in other human rights discussion groups, and three boys mentioned their involvement in community gatherings in support of women's rights and an end to violence against women. While only a few (4 percent) of the respondents claimed to have engaged in any form of social activism (e.g., public protests) following their involvement in the workshops, their apparent acceptance of the need for citizens to participate actively in the struggle for social justice is an indication of the salutary effect of human rights education among youth. This lends further credence to the oft-cited argument that young people (male and female) are the vanguard of human rights activism, capable of exercising their agency in opposition to discriminatory attitudes and practices, and in support of the discourse that propounds a more equitable future (Quijada, 2008).

Skepticism, Resistance, and Uncertainty

Despite the respondents' overall rhetorical endorsement of human rights and the cause of gender equity, which understandably were still in the forefront of their minds even after the end of the workshop, some boys nonetheless did express some reservations about the implications of rights discourse and its effects on them. In both the focus group sessions and questionnaire responses, a small number (4 percent) of boys flatly stated that the influence of the workshops on their attitudes and behaviors had been minimal. This contrariness was largely due to skepticism and outright resistance.

> I don't know if I have really changed.... I don't have a clear opinion about this [workshop] material.... I need more information.
>
> I am not convinced that everything that they told us is all true.
>
> No, I didn't change because I am who I am.

For others (28 percent), it appeared that the content of the workshops, particularly references to the abuse of rights, triggered a nerve. Although subject to the methodological pitfalls of self-reporting, these individuals indicated that they had experienced, or continued to experience, varying forms of psychological, physical, and sexual abuse, generally within family contexts. In particular, considerations of child abuse as a workshop topic appears to have stirred up residual memories of abuse among some boys. For at least one boy, the way to ward off lingering trauma was to keep silent about his own history of neglect and abuse.

> The experience I had was something traumatic because when I saw the abuse of children by the parents in the [workshop] videos, it agitated me because I saw myself in those children who were being beaten...

> The truth is that I do not want to talk about the abuse that I have had and still have because it makes me very sad in every way.

The boys' reservations about the lessons of rights-oriented education, however, related to the perceived personal costs or risks that they might face if they stood up openly for the rights of others. Underlying this caution were personal difficulties in simply trying to relate the *ideas* of human rights and gender equity to the day-to-day lives of their mothers, sisters, and other female friends. This was also closely related to lack of confidence in the ability to openly articulate reasons to compel others to abandon entrenched attitudes and behaviors. Some of the boys acknowledged what they felt to be their limited capacity to express views sympathetic to the notion of gender equity, or even to act in ways that were deemed contrary to customary male behavior. As one boy indicated, the pressures and constraints of the sociocultural context were the greatest hurdles to overcome if he was to articulate support for gender equity "in public without fear."

This lack of confidence, candidly expressed, was not unexpected in light of the fact that male adolescence is often a period of uncertainty, when boys are struggling to define their own identities and interests. In response to the query "Do you participate in community activities to improve women's and others' human rights?" a few responses revealed obstacles impeding change within the boys.

> I am really not prepared yet because I need a little more training, but I will make sure I learn more.
>
> They [workshops] did not help me a lot. . . . I do not yet have the courage to criticize my parents or my teachers [for abuse].
>
> No, one cannot change that rapidly, a person needs time.
>
> My greatest difficulty is that . . . . I prefer to keep quiet rather than cause problems.
>
> It is hard to change my bad thoughts for the good ones which I should have because I have been accustomed to the old ways.

For a few boys as well, deep-rooted norms of paternal chauvinism, interconnected with the domineering presence of unsympathetic fathers, underscored their lack of confidence. To depart from the norms of strict gender division and to dare to speak out not only on behalf of one's own rights, but of the rights of others, particularly of the opposite sex, was to invite ridicule and fear of sanctions.

> My father is very macho and that is why he bothers me a lot when I help my mother in the kitchen.
>
> He almost never helps me.... he discourages and demoralizes me.
>
> I could be a better person, but without him, it is very hard to achieve things.... there are times when I feel alone without anyone.
>
> My father was always macho ... when I cried he would tell me that men do not cry.
>
> My father has tried to raise me as a man like him.

In contrast, two other boys indicated that the workshops had had little influence on their perceptions, simply because they had already been familiar with most of the issues covered in the workshops, and had always been in agreement with the principles of human rights and gender equity.

Conclusion

> Moving towards a gender-equal society is therefore a complex task, involving profound institutional change as well as the small details of everyday life. (Connell, 2003, p. 4)

This sample of verbatim statements elicited in questionnaires and focus groups at the end of the NGO workshops accurately depicts the variability and tenor of the responses from the male adolescents who participated in this study. With very few exceptions, the boys articulated their new-found interest in, and quite often agreement with, the ideals of human rights and gender equity. Despite their relative youth and impressionability, they were clearly capable of reflecting on these issues and acknowledging the widespread presence of social injustice. This in turn appeared to foster among many of them an inclination to stand up for their own rights and to respect the rights of others. The sentiments they expressed were nascent, of course, and in many instances it is quite possible to surmise that the connection between responses to survey questions and subsequent long-term attitudes and actions would be tenuous. At the same time, however, precisely because of their youth and impressionability, their general endorsement of the principles of human rights and gender equity confirmed the rationale of providing rights-oriented education for children and adolescents. In addition, as was clear in the perspectives that most boys in this study articulated, the engagement of young males in educational programs designed to enhance their critical consciousness of gender issues can be most effective when boys are viewed not as youthful protagonists of a patriarchal culture defined by gender inequity and obliviousness to the advancement of human rights, but rather as young citizens having the potential to participate actively in redressing prevailing structures and norms of divisiveness and injustice. From this perspective, rights-oriented education should be grounded in the ideal of reconceptualized citizenship that extends beyond a person's legal status and portrays individuals as social beings whose citizenship is animated through the discourse of civic participation (Quijada, 2008).

While underscoring the significance of awareness workshops, this case study also points to areas of further, more in-depth research. As indicated at the outset of this chapter, the study was reliant solely on questionnaires and focus groups with young male respondents following their involvement as workshop participants. As such, conceptually and methodologically the study was clearly limited. At best, the study has shown how education programs, if well executed, can foster heightened consciousness of rights and gender issues among young people. Yet it is not possible to pronounce confidently on the boys' subsequent actions, nor whether the generally positive perceptions they articulated concerning human rights and gender equity remained with them long after the workshops were over. To ascertain this progression would naturally entail research capable of illustrating more comprehensively[16] and accurately the complex changes and challenges related to human rights education. Such research would have to move beyond limited self-report data elicited through postworkshop questionnaires and focus groups. Instead, what is required are longitudinal ethnographic studies that monitor in greater depth both the ways in which, and the extent to which, young males apply newly acquired knowledge and sensitivity to gender equality in their social environments of family, school, workplace, and community. Such research must likewise examine the broader contexts and influences that affect the subsequent posteducational struggles, challenges, and accomplishments of young males. The extent to which the young men engage in organized proequality movements in civil society and strive to foster public awareness of social injustices and promote policy changes aimed at greater social and economic equity should also be monitored over the long term to demonstrate the transformative potential of preactivist educational efforts.

By extension, too, young males who participate in research related to human rights and gender equity should also be included in the dissemination of the research results. In this way, research can serve to facilitate their ongoing reflections on the issues that they confront and the actions that they undertake. Indeed, this underscores a key point highlighted in this chapter: that gender equality initiatives can best succeed in promoting their goals of respect for girls' and women's rights when they are undertaken collaboratively with men, young and old alike, both individually and collectively.

Notes

* I would like to thank Claire Turenne-Sjolander, Shoshana Magnet, Myriam Denov, and especially Richard Maclure for their insightful comments on earlier drafts of this chapter. I also acknowledge the collaboration of the Interdisciplinary Research Laboratory on the Rights of the Child, the financial support of the Faculty of Social Sciences and the Research Development Fund at the University of Ottawa, as well as the invaluable research assistance of Betsy Estevez and the exemplary support of Ruth Mery Arancibia in Bolivia. This chapter was first presented at the International Conference on the Rights of the Child held at the University of Ottawa on November 18, 2009. Parts of this chapter appear in an article in *Children & Society* entitled "When Boys Meet Girls' Rights: Bolivian Adolescent Males' Claims of Commitment to Gender Equality" by Christine Gervais. Permission to reproduce excerpts has been granted by John Wiley & Sons Ltd. This chapter is dedicated to the gender equality pursuits of the Bolivian boys who participated in this project and to a resilient "baby girl."

1. See, for example, http://www.whiteribbon.ca/, http://www.feminist.com/resources/links/men.htm, http://www.michaelkaufman.com/man-talk/ and http://www.stephenlewisfoundation.org/ and http://www.xyonline.net/links, among others.
2. The resulting Beijing Declaration called on governments to encourage males' full participation in equality-oriented initiatives.
3. See, for example, www.promundo.org.br in Brazil.
4. The reforms began in 2006 and ended in February 2009; they were led by Evo Morales, the country's first indigenous president since the Spanish Conquest.
5. There is a separate chapter and 33 Articles in the constitution that address women's rights.
6. This chapter concentrates on the boys' experiences. For analyses on the girls' experiences see Gervais (2011).
7. Since 2005, this study has explored the workshop-based experiences of over 547 participants. The 69 Bolivian boys featured in this chapter constitute the only male participants in the entire study. For developments in other countries such as Honduras, see Gervais (2010).
8. The name of the women's center is withheld to protect the identity of the participants.

9. During the course of the workshops between 2006 and 2008, the Constitution of Bolivia underwent considerable reform. Throughout the reform process, the workshop participants were made aware of the pro–human rights emphases being developed in the new constitution that included the promotion and protection of indigenous and women's political, social, and economic rights, among others. While the new constitution only came into force in February 2009, the emerging reforms instilled optimism for change among the participants.
10. This research was undertaken after the workshops had already begun. Since data were not collected prior to the workshops, before and after comparisons on the boys' progress were not established in this study. The girl participants' observations of the boys' evolving attitudes and actions toward gender equality were also not explored.
11. In this study, the participants were between the ages of 13 and 17 and while they are adolescents, they are considered children as defined under the United Nations Convention on the Rights of the Child. According to Article 1 of the convention, a child is defined as "every human being below the age of eighteen years" (UNHCR 1989).
12. The boys' families previously lived as indigenous peasant farmers in remote mountainous regions and moved to Cochabamba to overcome abject poverty and to gain access to basic resources such as water, education, and health care.
13. The "doing it socially" approach is part of Chevalier and Buckles' (2008) Social Analysis Systems² methodology that guides collaborative inquiry and multistakeholder dialogue that cogenerates practical and authentic "living knowledge" through "social" interaction in order to advance "social" change.
14. Considerable care was taken through ongoing communication between the Canadian and Bolivian research teams to ensure that meanings were translated accurately.
15. Since this response was given on a written questionnaire, it was not possible to obtain further clarification on what being "a feminist" implied for the boys. It is likely that some of the terminology employed by these youth reflected their immediate learning and perhaps a limited understanding of these complex terms.
16. I acknowledge that the relatively few examples illustrated in this chapter do not capture the totality of the boys' complex experiences related to learning about, and acting upon human rights and gender equality.

References

Chevalier, J. M., & Buckles, D. J. (2008). *SAS² A Guide to Collaborative Inquiry and Social Engagement.* Sage India: IDRC.

Chittister, J. (1998). *Heart of Flesh: A Feminist Spirituality for Women and Men*. Ottawa: Novalis.

Connell, R. (2003). The Role of Men and Boys in Achieving Gender Equality. United Nations Division for the Advancement of Women. Retrieved from http://www.un.org/womenwatch/daw/egm/men-boys2003/Connell-bp.pdf.

DeKeseredy, W., Schwartz, M., & Alvi, S. (2000). The Role of Pro-Feminist Men in Dealing with Woman Abuse on the Canadian College Campus. *Violence Against Women, 6*, 918–935.

Denov, M. & Gervais, C. (2007). Negotiating (In)Security: Agency and Resistance among Girls Formerly Associated with Sierra Leone's Revolutionary United Front. *Signs: Journal of Women in Culture and Society, 32*(4), 885–910.

Flood, M. (2010). Working with Men and Boys: Engaging Men in Building Gender Equality. *Working Together for Equality*. Retrieved from http://www.xyonline.net/sites/default/files/Flood,%20Working%20with%20Men%20and%20Boys%20-%20Jera%20Int'l%20Beijing+15.pdf

Gervais, C. (2010). From Discovery to Dissidence: Honduran Women's Conceptions and Claims of Human Rights. *Journal of International Women's Studies, 11*(4), 19–36.

Gervais, C. (2011). On Their Own and in Their Own Words: Bolivian Adolescent Girls' Empowerment through Non-governmental Human Rights Education. *Journal of Youth Studies, 14*(2), 197–217.

Glaser, B., & Strauss, A. (1967). *The Discovery of Grounded Theory,* Chicago: Aldine.

hooks, b. (2000). *Feminist Theory From Margin to Center* (2nd ed.). London: Pluto Press.

Kaiser, S. (2005). To Punish or to Forgive? Young Citizens' Attitudes on Impunity and Accountability in Contemporary Argentina. *Journal of Human Rights, 4*(2), 171–196.

Lanza, T. (2009). Bolivia: New Constitution means New Reality for Women and Girls. *Association for Women's Rights in Development*. Retrieved from http://www.awid.org/Issues-and-Analysis/Library/Bolivia-New-Constitution-Means-New-Reality-for-Women-and-Girls, accessed May 25, 2010.

Mihr, A. (2009). Global Human Rights Awareness, Education and Democratization. *Journal of Human Rights, 8*(2), 177–189.

Quijada, D. A. (2008). Reconciling Research, Rallies, and Citizenship: Reflections on Youth-led Diversity Workshops and Intercultural Alliances. *Social Justice, 35*(1), 76–90.

Silva, I., & Salles Souto, A. L. (2009). *Democracy, Citizenship and Youth: Towards Social and Political Participation in Brazil,* IDRC Publication. Retrieved from http://www.idrc.ca/en/ev-138691-201-1-DO_TOPIC.html

Valdés, T., & Olavarría, J. (1998). Masculinidades y equidad de género en América Latina. *United Nations Fund for Population Activities*. Santiago: FLASCO-Chile.

United Nations Educational, Scientific and Cultural Organization [UNESCO]. (2004). *Role of Men and Boys in Promoting Gender Equality*. Bangkok: UNESCO Bangkok. Retrieved from http://www2.unescobkk.org/elib/publications/Role_of_Men_and_Boys/Role_of_Men_and_Boys.pdf

United Nations Office of the High Commissioner for Human Rights [UNHCR]. 1989. Convention on the Rights of the Child. http://www.unhchr.ch/html/menu3/b/k2crc.htm

PART IV

Community-Based Approaches to Child Rights and Protection

CHAPTER 9

The Wayo Program in Northern Uganda: Building on Traditional Assets in Supporting Acholi Young Women and Girls in the Context of War and HIV

Sheetal Patel, Patricia Spittal, Herbert Muyinda, Geoffrey Oyat, and Nelson K. Sewankambo

Introduction

In contexts of violent armed conflict, civilian populations are often forced to contend with a myriad of challenges, including a lack of basic resources, widespread diseases, displacement, extreme poverty, and rampant physical and sexual abuse. These hardships have proven particularly striking in Northern Uganda or Acholiland,[1] where the two-decade-long war has resulted in countless deaths, widespread human rights violations, the destruction of the social and economic fabric of society, and the displacement of more than half the population of Acholiland (Save the Children, 2001). The burden of war has been shouldered by the civilian population, and has been especially brutal for the over 30,000 children who have been conscripted into the main rebel group, the Lord's Resistance Army (LRA), as combatants and sex slaves, forced to commit unthinkable atrocities, including rape, maiming, slaughtering, and looting. They have perpetrated these acts against each other, against their families, and against their communities.

Further intensifying the conflict, in March 2002, the Ugandan government launched "Operation Iron Fist," a military offensive directed against the LRA. In response, the LRA strengthened its attacks on civilian communities and increased the abduction and forced recruitment of children. The number of abducted young people under 18 years of age soared from approximately 12,000 in June 2002, to nearly double that by June 2003, and to at least 30,000 by May 2004 (Nannyonjo, 2004). Given these realities, unprecedented numbers of young people and their families in the area fled their homes and settled in internally displaced camps, with limited access to international humanitarian support. While in August 2001 there were 480,000 internally displaced persons (IDPs) living in camps, by 2004, there were 1.6 million IDPs, accounting for over 90 percent of the population in the affected region (Mazurana & McKay, 2004). Nearly 70 percent of the displaced population was under 25 years of age (Women's Commission, 2004). As of 2009, 235,000 IDPs remained in the camps and an additional 200,000 were residing in transit sites (Internal Displacement Monitoring Centre &Norwegian Refugee Council, 2010). In these temporary settlements, access to education, health care, and other basic necessities is, at best, minimal and inconsistent. Insecurity is widespread, especially for girls who are vulnerable to abuse, rape, sexual exploitation, enslavement, and gender-based violence that are so often characteristic of armed conflicts (Mazurana & McKay, 2004). Such prevalence of sexual assault inevitably has increased women's and girls' likelihood of contracting HIV/AIDS and other sexually transmitted infections (STIs) in disproportionate numbers to their male counterparts. The disparity between boys' and girls' rates of HIV in Uganda is striking; in 2002, six girls were reportedly infected with HIV for every boy (UNICEF, 2002). Moreover, of the estimated 530,000 Ugandans living with HIV in 2003, over half were women and girls (UNAIDS, 2004).

In an effort to fight HIV/STIs among displaced populations in Northern Uganda, a number of interventions have been implemented. These include peer education, rapid testing initiatives, condom distribution, and STI treatment and care. Nevertheless, despite southern Uganda's international recognition for progress in HIV research and prevention, the Gulu district of Northern Uganda, a region ravaged by decades of armed conflict, is severely lacking in HIV/AIDS research and prevention, and is now considered to be one of the worst-affected districts in the country (Ugandan Ministry of Health, 2001). Given the persistent insecurity in the region, technical support for program delivery has proven difficult to sustain. When program personnel withdraw from the camps during periods of escalating violence, for example, large gaps in HIV programming remain. In an attempt to address these challenges, the Paramount Chief of Acholi recommended that programs be administered by local leaders and draw upon cultural and traditional familial mechanisms for support and education. An example of this is the Acholi *ssenga* model (to be discussed below) as a way to increase sexual knowledge and implement child protection against the risk of HIV/AIDS (Liu Centre, 2002).

This chapter explores the experiences of girls in Northern Uganda in relation to their understanding of gender-based violence, levels of sexual knowledge, HIV vulnerability, and traditional systems of child protection. Employing both quantitative and qualitative research methods for the years between 2002 and 2006, the research team focused on girls living in three displacement camps (Palenga, Awer, and Pabbo) in Gulu district. The research also examined the potential coupling of traditional and contemporary mechanisms for creating awareness ofsexual practices, for example, STI prevention, condom use, and reproductive health among Acholi women and girls of Northern Uganda. In particular, the research focused on the application of the traditional *ssenga* model, and the role of the paternal aunt, the *wayo*, in transmitting sexual health information and protection for young girls (Muyinda, Kengeya, Pool, & Whitworth, 2001). The research and its subsequent application have demonstrated that the inclusion of both traditional teachings and contemporary health and sex education can provide a "middle road" between tradition and modernity. Moreover, despite upheavals brought on by war and displacement, traditional systems and concepts that promote children's rights and protections can be effectively used.

Traditional Cultural Mechanisms for Transferring Knowledge: The *Ssenga* Model

Prior to the civil war in Uganda, the Acholi people resided in their ancestral homes. Their households were often surrounded by the huts of paternal relatives, situated on allocated tracts of land that were largely agricultural. An Acholi man usually cultivated his fields in close proximity to his father's compound, on land shared by extended family members, but also quite distant from the nearest neighbors.[2] Traditionally, Acholi households were polygynous, with each wife responsible for supervising her own family's hut. Each woman was given her own land to cultivate, as well as various crops and her own granaries. Men were responsible for the general security of the homestead, the construction and maintenance of huts, the supervision of animals, and plant cultivation. They were also responsible for the financial support of their children's schooling, while the mother provided more informal education to her children. For mothers a key responsibility was to raise their female children so that they eventually would be able to cook, clean, and harvest. Paternal female relatives also participated in the socialization of girls.

Excerpts from old ethnographic texts on Acholi culture written in the 1950s provide invaluable information on the nature and scope of children's socialization in Acholi culture and on traditional Acholi mechanisms of child protection and education. For example, a text entitled *The Luo Girl: From Infancy to Marriage* contains the following critical passage:

> Traditionally, among the Acholi people of Northern Uganda, grandmothers and the huts in which they reside, were pivotal in the transmission of sexual health knowledge and mentoring of young girls...Girls in the old traditional society had a more deliberate or conscious sex education than they receive in modern times. An old woman of the village, whose hut served as a communal sleeping place for girls, formerly gave instruction on the nature of sexual relationships. This old woman was one who must have stopped giving birth to children. She was either a grandmother or an elder wife in a polygamous homestead. (Ominde, 1952, p. 39)

Upon finding this excerpt, our Acholi researcher partners consulted with their grandmothers and aunts who confirmed that an intricate child protection and mentoring system had existed prior to the social upheaval wrought by armed conflict. This system centered on the idea of "the grandmother's hut," and involved mentoring from three women: the *maa* (biological mother), the *wayo* (paternal auntie), and the *adaa* (grandmother). Known as the *ssenga* system, this socialization process was a preparatory system for many girls who had been living in Northern Uganda prior to the war, and had offered them an informal system of support, education, and safety as they developed into young women.

Traditionally, children would stay with their mother until they were old enough to understand that upon their father's visits, they had to make room for the privacy of their parents. Girls were shifted, at approximately four years old, out of the mother's home and into the paternal grandmother's hut where they resided until their own marriage. The boys were sent to a separate structure called the *otogo*.[3] Though girls were officially raised by their mothers and fathers, grandmothers (*adaa*) played a significant role in the upbringing and mentoring of their granddaughters, largely through story-telling in the privacy of the *adaa's* hut. Accordingly, the grandmothers were pivotal in the transmission of sexual health knowledge and in the socialization of young girls. They generally taught the girls about men, social expectations, the importance of waiting until menstruation prior to engaging in sex, marriage, the clan system, and incest taboos.

Traditionally, the *wayo*, the father's sister, assumed a "sister"-like role in a girl's life and was responsible for socializing her into culturally approved womanhood . While there were no highly structured "puberty rites" per se for Acholi girls, the onset of puberty and menstruation signaled a transition to maturity. The *wayo* helped guide the young girl through this transition and thus became a trusted secret-keeper, a mentor, and a confidant.

The *ssenga* model of socialization was widely implemented because it carried tremendous moral authority in family and community life (Muyinda, Nakuya, Whitworth, & Pool, 2003). Unfortunately, however, the conflict in Northern Uganda and the ensuing horrific conditions experienced by the majority of internally displaced people have contributed to an erosion of traditional familial structures and value systems that centered around child protection. The current realities of armed conflict and displacement, along with socioeconomic changes in the extended family system, have all but nullified the *ssenga* system of socialization and other traditional social practices (Muyinda, 2001). Consequently, as a study conducted by the Women's Commission for Refugee Women and Children (2001) concluded, for children living in IDP camps the idea of a "safe passage" or transition from childhood through adolescence to adulthood is no longer evident.

Nevertheless, despite the decline of the *ssenga* socialization process, leaders in Acholiland have become increasingly interested in the reintroduction and valorization of traditional Acholi cultural practices that facilitate adolescent socialization and protection. This interest has been reinforced by increased international attention on human rights instruments that aim to codify standards for children's rights and child protection in Uganda.

Children's Rights and Research Objectives

The international community has recognized the need to promote and safeguard the rights of the child within culturally gender-sensitive frameworks (UN Convention, 1989). The UN Convention on the

Rights of the Child (CRC) enshrined the rights of those under 18 years old on an international level. Spanning a host of rights, including the right to dignity, to education, and to health and safety, the CRC stipulates the following key principles:

> the best interest of the child should be a primary consideration [Article 3]...[to] ensure to the maximum extent possible the survival and development of the child [Article 6]... to protect the child from all forms of physical or mental violence, injury or abuse, neglect or negligent treatment, maltreatment or exploitation, including sexual abuse [Article 19]... to recognize the right of every child to a standard of living adequate for the child's physical, mental, spiritual, moral and social development [Article 27]... [to] protect the child from all forms of sexual exploitation and sexual abuse [Article 34]... [and from recruitment of] any person who has not attained the age of fifteen years into their armed forces [Article 38]. (UN Convention, 1989)

In view of growing attention to children's rights and a resurgence of interest in traditional forms of child socialization and protection, the authors conducted a study that sought to highlight vulnerabilities of young girls living in Northern Uganda's displacement camp settings and to examine traditional intergenerational methods of transmitting sexual knowledge to young girls and dealing with sexual matters in a family context. In so doing, the study aimed at exploring the use of traditional mechanisms for developing culturally sensitive HIV/AIDS programming for former female war abductees and young girls living in IDP situations in Northern Uganda.

The following section highlights the ways in which these research objectives were addressed.

Methodology

The Informed Consent Process

Given the highly sensitive nature of this study, ethical considerations were integral to every stage of the research process. In order to participate in the study, every adolescent under the age of 18 was required to obtain the consent of a parent/guardian. A number of adolescent girls qualified as mature minors (girls under the age of 18 who lived independently of parents or guardians) and, therefore, were permitted to give their own consent. The consent forms were discussed in the local language of Luo to ensure consistency and clarity in the consent process. It was made clear to all involved that they could refuse to answer any question and that their withdrawal from the research at any point would warrant no negative consequences. These consent forms increased the participants' understanding of the project, and facilitated the support that influential camp elders and officially instated zonal leaders provided for this initiative. Given the influence of camp leaders, their endorsement was important for it enhanced respondents' willingness to participate in the study.

Sampling Strategy

Participants were recruited using convenience sampling, on the basis of proximity, age, and consent. An approach that is often used in circumstances where the target populations are difficult to reach (Kalton, 1983), this sampling strategy enabled the researchers to select informants who were easily accessible, either by nature of their geographic proximity or their connection to other research participants (Green & Browne, 2005).

Quantitative Data Collection

This study was initially designed to be qualitative in focus, aiming to explore the HIV-related vulnerabilities of girls and women living in IDP camps, some of whom were former war-abductees. Yet early into the study it became very clear to the researchers that quantitative background data on the respondents' prior and current circumstances were required before embarking on qualitative fieldwork. As such, three bilingual (Luo and English) female Acholi interviewers were hired to administer a 20-page questionnaire with 515 girls[4] between the ages of 13 and 19 living in Palenga, Awer, and Pabbo, all IDP camps heavily devastated by overcrowding and disease. The questionnaire was designed to address and explore HIV- and STI-related knowledge and sex-related vulnerabilities of girls and women.

In this chapter the variables of interest are organized into three broad categories: (1) sociodemographic characteristics; (2) sexual activity and vulnerabilities; (3) HIV/AIDS prevention and condom use. Data analysis was conducted using SPSS software, and this in turn helped to inform the subsequent qualitative data collection.

Qualitative Data Collection

One of the main objectives of this study was to explore, in the context of ongoing conflict, girls' experiences in the IDP camps and how the *ssenga* model of child protection might be used to inform culturally sensitive HIV/AIDS programming for internally displaced girls and former war abductees who were likely to have suffered repeated sexual abuse. As such, we interviewed a broad sample of girls and women whose lives were characterized by entrenched hunger, poverty, and spatial congestion in IDP camps.

Over a period of 10 months, 130 in-depth interviews and 16 focus group discussions were held in the three camps with girls and adult women.[5] Disaggregated, these consisted of 50 in-depth interviews and 6 focus group discussions with adult women over the age of 30 years; 60 in-depth interviews and 6 focus group discussions with adolescent girls over 14 years; and 20 in-depth interviews and 4 focus group discussions with girls who were formerly abducted and were also over the age of 14 years. The in-depth interviews and group discussions explored issues such as: IDPcamp living; knowledge, perceptions, and experiences with HIV and other STIs; availability of, and barriers, to prevention services; and traditional ways of communicating and learning about sex and sexuality. With participants' permission, all interviews and group discussions were audiotaped and subsequently transcribed by the Acholi research team in Uganda. The qualitative data were then analyzed using the Atlas software program to compare and contrast themes and categories generated in the focus groups and subsequent interviews.

Research Findings

Quantitative Results

Sociodemographic Characteristics

As previously mentioned, the quantitative study focused on girls ranging from 13 to 19 years of age. The vast majority (64.5 percent, n=332) of the girls sampled had been living in the IDP camps for over 5 years, and 13 percent (n=65) reported having been abducted into war. In terms of their formal education, 42 percent (n=220) of the girls were in school, 40 percent (n=204) had previously been in school but had subsequently dropped out, and 18 percent (n=91) of the girls had never attended school. The main reasons given for school abandonment included marriage/pregnancy (43 percent), a lack of financial options to support tuition and other educational costs (38 percent), and enrolment ineligibility due to their older age.[6]

Sexual Activity and Vulnerabilities

A number of survey questions were used to explore the sexual vulnerability of adolescent girls in IDP circumstances. These included incidences of forced sex, early sex, and marriage and pregnancy. Of the 515 girls sampled, 53 percent (n=273) were nonvirgins, with a mean age of 15 years when the girls first engaged in sexual activities. Of the sexually active girls, 26 percent (n=71) had been younger than 15 years at the time of their initiation into sexual activity, and 22 percent (n=59) reported having their first experience as nonconsensual sex. The mean age of those coerced into their first sexual experience was younger than those who had not experienced this form of sexual initiation (13 years versus 15 years). Although 45 percent (n=231) of the sexually active girls admitted to being aware of techniques to avoid pregnancy, 75 percent (n=206) had become pregnant. First pregnancy occurred anywhere between 12 and 19 years of age. In addition, 80 percent (n=218) of the sexually active girls in the sample had been with 1–5 sexual partners in their lifetime. 46 percent (n=236) of the girls had been married at one point in their lives, with first marriage having occurred between the ages of 10–19 years .

Knowledge of HIV/AIDS/STI Prevention and Condom Use

When asked about their HIV/AIDS/STIs-related knowledge, all of the girls revealed a high degree of HIV/AIDS awareness and a generally strong understanding of infection prevention. For example, 93 percent (n=472) of the girls knew that HIV could be transmitted through unprotected sex with an infected person and 95 percent (n=502) of the girls knew that HIV could also be transmitted through blood contact with an infected person. Furthermore, the majority of girls in this study knew that using condoms and limiting one's number of sexual partners would help to prevent HIV infection. The girls also displayed an awareness of the common misconceptions about HIV. For example, 92 percent (n=472) knew that exchanging clothes, dish sharing, or handshaking could not transmit HIV. Importantly, the majority of girls in the sample, 57 percent (n=235), indicated that the media (i.e., radio and newspapers) were their primary sources of information on sex and HIV/STIs. Only 25 percent (n=127) of the girls had discussed sexual relationships with anyone, and only 24 percent (n=126) had been shown how to use a condom.

Nonetheless, many of the respondents were quite optimistic about their abilities to protect themselves from HIV/AIDS/STI. Data concerning HIV/AIDS/STI prevention intentions and condom use revealed that 59 percent (n=305) of the girls thought they could protect themselves from HIV/STIs, and 69 percent (n=355) thought they could refuse sexual advances. However, disparities were uncovered between the girls' knowledge of infection prevention, their beliefs about their ability to self-protect, and their subsequent sexual practices. Exemplifying the power dynamics in sexual relationships, half the girls (n=256) thought that discussing HIV/STIs or condom use with their partner could destabilize their relationships, and 67 percent (n=346) of them admitted to feeling uneasy about suggesting condom use to a partner. Significantly, only 13 percent (n=35) of the sexually active girls had ever used a condom.

Discussion of Quantitative Findings

Displaced people, particularly females, are at a much higher risk of exposure to communicable diseases, including HIV/AIDS, than populations that are more sedentary (Cohen, 1998). In times of war especially, a combination of economic, social, biological, and behavioral factors increase girls' sexual vulnerability and render them highly susceptible to HIV/AIDs. Drawing from our quantitative analysis, we discuss several context-specific factors that explain girls' sexual vulnerability.

Sex, Marriage, and Youth Pregnancy

As the Uganda AIDS Commission and our own data have shown, Ugandan youth generally begin sexual activity in their teens, a time when most have sparse information on sexuality and safe-sex practices (Human Rights Watch, 2005). As previously mentioned, 53 percent of the girls sampled in this study said they had previously engaged in sex, with their age of sexual initiation ranging from 9 to 19 years. Much of this early sexual initiation, which is indicative of relationships between older men and younger girls, tends to stem from two underlying factors. First, and particularly in times of societal unrest, girls may depend on sex for economic support, either in a marriage setting or in a more informal relationship. A recent report released by an NGO working in Northern Uganda reinforced this finding by establishing that families with girls between the ages of 15 and 18 years often urge them to marry for economic gain (i.e., "bride price") (Francis & McKibben, 2008). Similarly, in our own study the respondents frequently noted that because of the lack of alternative avenues of financial support, their families often urged them to marry for financial reasons. Unfortunately, however, the payment of bride price often fosters the perception that a husband "owns" his wife and can demand sex from her without her consent. These relationships may inhibit the girls' ability to control the terms of their sex lives (including negotiating condom use), thereby potentially increasing their exposure to HIV (Human Rights Watch, 2003).

A second important factor perpetuating these relationships rests on the fallacy held by older men that younger girls are less likely to be infected with HIV/AIDS (Uganda AIDS, 2001). As a result, older men often target young girls for sexual relationships in hopes of minimizing their exposure to HIV. These age disparities and economic dependence increase the likelihood of sexual coercion and limit girls' willingness to demand fidelity and condom use. The young age at which girls are thus sexually initiated underscores the economic challenges and lack of physical security many of them face, a pattern that is further exacerbated in times of conflict. The marginalized positions of these female youth in this context of armed conflict may exacerbate sexual exploitation and the spread of HIV/AIDS and STIs.

Moreover, experiences with sexual activity among female teens likewise increased the risk of early pregnancy. In our sample, 75 percent (n=205) of girls who were sexually active had been pregnant, with the youngest being 12 years old at the time of her first pregnancy. As other studies have shown, motherhood at an early age often results in reduced opportunities for formal education or for the development of these girls, further fueling their risk of poverty and sexual exploitation (Women's Commission, n.d.). Combined, these high levels of early sexual initiation and early marriage and pregnancy are important contributors to the sexual vulnerability of adolescent girls living in internal displacement camps.

Challenges to Education, Self-Subsistence, and Child Protection

UNICEF (2004) has found that second only to their families, schools are children's most important protective environmental perimeter. One aspect of the protective nature of schooling is that the longer girls are kept in school, the lower their vulnerability to HIV infection(De Walque, 2004). In our study, however, many girls in the IDP camps reported having dropped out of school either because of an inability to pay fees[7] or due to early pregnancy and marriage. Inevitably, lacking education, the girls had fewer subsequent options for self-subsistence. This was aggravated by the fact that in the camps the Acholi people, who were traditionally agriculturalists and livestock breeders, have been reduced to near-total dependence on donated food and other humanitarian aid.

When families become food-aid dependent, the daughters become the most vulnerable members. 33 percent (n=171) of the girls sampled in our study indicated that relief supplies were their main means of livelihood, and only 8.5 percent (n=44) had to support themselves and their children by engagingin petty trade and casual labor[8]. In this context of entrenched poverty and absence of adequately paid-labor opportunities in the camps, many adolescent girls had come to depend on sexual relationships to procure money and goods (see also Francis & McKibben, 2008). This naturally had increased their sexual vulnerability.

Sexual Exploitation and HIV/AIDS/STIs Risk-Minimization Knowledge and Practice

In conflict situations the main perpetrators of sexual abuse and exploitation are often soliders or other armed combatants (Maçhel, 1996). In our study, however, findings indicated that a girl's first sex partner, whether the sex was consensual or forced, was less likely a member of an armed force and more likely a subsistence farmer or a student. This suggests that in times of conflict, the sexual exploitation of adolescents does not result solely from interactions with soldiers or belligerents involved in abduction but may also be the result of living in the harsh physical conditions of IDP camps.

Indeed, as previous research has shown, overcrowding, insufficient night-time lighting, close proximity of male and female latrines and bathhouses, and poor or unequal access to resources can contribute to the likelihood of sexual violence against women and girls living in displacement camps (UNICEF, IRC, Christian's Children Fund, & Legal Aid Project, 2004). 22 percent of the sexually active girls in this study reported that their first sexual experience involved nonconsensual sex. It appears as though the camps' physical set-up and overcrowding contributed to an environment where young girls were vulnerable to exploitation by camp residents, market traders, farmers, and businessmen, in addition to armed individuals (see also Francis & McKibben, 2008).

Although the young respondents indicated a high degree of knowledge regarding HIV/AIDS/STI-related transmission, most either shunned or were ignorant about harm-reduction techniques. As noted above, while 93 percent (n=472) of the girls knew that HIV could be transmitted through unprotected sex with an infected person, only 13 percent of the sexually active girls had ever used a condom. Unfortunately, because of security concerns, the number of humanitarian agencies, NGOs, and organizations capable of providing preventive education in displacement camps had diminished (WHO, 2007). This, in turn, had resulted in resource shortages and subsequent constraints to delivering sexual health programming.

As the results from the quantitative analysis have shown, there had been numerous risk factors facing the Acholi adolescent girls living in displacement camps in Northern Uganda. These findings confirmed existing research on the vulnerabilities of girls in times of armed conflict, and also contributed to a preliminary context-specific data base that further informed the subsequent qualitative component of the study.

Qualitative Results and Discussion

As we manually coded the data from the interviews and the focus group discussions with the girls and adult women, three themes emerged that depicted the experiences of girls living in camps: (1) jeopardized security, most notably fear of abduction and HIV vulnerability; (2) sexual health information; and (3) Acholi traditional child protection systems. Below we summarize the qualitative trends as found in the Palenga, Pader, and Awer IDP camps.

Jeopardized Security: Fear of Abduction and HIV Vulnerability

"Vulnerability in the Light of Day"

The qualitative interviews with the adult women revealed that, prior to the war, an Acholi girl who did not attend school would generally assist her mother in earning an income, usually through small market gardening. With the advent of the war, however, many parents have adapted to the threat of abduction by armed groups by opting to leave their daughters within the relative protection of the IDP camps. As one woman explained:

> Ever since the government ordered everybody into the camp, due to the escalation of rebel activity, I haven't allowed my children to move far away from the camp. It's I who volunteers and exposes myself to carry firewood, cassava, and anything with which to feed them, so they could remain in the camp. They shouldn't go anywhere; they should remain in the camps to avoid abduction. (Adult woman, Pabbo Camp, 2005)

At the same time, however, participants commonly reported that, in the absence of either adult supervision and/or consistent schooling, girls were aimlessly wandering around the camps during the day. Essentially, the girls were exposing themselves to various potential risks, including unprotected sexual relationships. One woman shared her experiences with her own daughter:

> Supposing you leave for the garden, she will also leave for an unknown destination. You return from the garden only to hear rumours about her bad conduct all over the camp. In our absence she will have gone to have sex with a boy in the day time. (Adult woman, Palenga Camp, 2005)

As previously mentioned, extreme poverty may cause girls to barter sexual relations with older males in exchange for goods. Complementing the quantitative data, our interviews revealed that some of the girls may have engaged in sexual relations at the behest of their parents and/or siblings, particularly when these relationships were seen as enabling the girls to procure basic necessities that they might not otherwise have been able to obtain. As one girl explained:

> Conditions within the camp are like war, [especially] if you do not have parents and you are alone to care for your younger brothers and sister. For your older brother …you are still young but in his mind you look mature to him or if you had your menstrual period once and he noticed it, he will say you are now mature enough to go to a man. And because he said so, you would go to a man who has AIDS or you end up getting pregnant and that leads to early marriage. (Adolescent girl, Pabbo, 2005)

"Vulnerability at Night": A Night Commuting Phenomenon?

Despite the ever-looming threat of war, particularly outside the camps' borders, a large number of girls whom we interviewed chose to engage in what is known as "night commuting." At the peak of the war, in the spring of 2004, there were 40,000 children commuting to the town of Gulu every night, and returning home the next morning to be with their families, and then again traveling to Gulu at nightfall (Medecins Sans Frontières, 2006). Consistent with this trend, many of the young interviewees in this study noted that they and their friends flocked nightly from their family compounds and villages to the nearest town of Gulu to sleep in churches and on verandas in order to avoid abduction by armed groups and other forms of violence. In particular, children whose families lived on the periphery of the camps, where huts tended to be isolated, were at increased risk for abduction. At night, therefore, they would move from the outskirts of the camps to seek shelter in more central locations, some in Gulu and some well within the camps' perimeters. According to both the women and the girls, the vulnerability of young girls to predation by men offering goods for sex was common in these night commuting circumstances. Indeed, many girls whom we interviewed reported that their first sexual experiences occurred in these encounters.

This phenomenon had spurned a sense of hopelessness among the girls. Many noted that their night commuting offered relative protection from the direct armed hostilities, but left them vulnerable to other forms of influence and subtle coercion. One girl respondent explained:

> Their lives are spoilt. At night they roam about the camps, going out to visit their boy friends. They spend the night [with their boyfriends] and come back in the morning. This is because they don't sleep in the same house with their parents. So the parents don't know what the girls do at night. (Adolescent girl, Pabbo Camp, 2004)

Unfortunately, child rights advocates have too often failed to appreciate the numerous threats facing commuting children and have not been able to propose effective strategies for protecting girls from sexual exploitation.

Sexual Health Information

Although numerous studies and technical reports claim to be cognitive of the needs of girls living in IDP camps (Barton & Mutiiti, 1998; Nannyyonjo, 2005; UNAIDS, 2004; UNICEF, 2004), in our study we found that there is often substantial dissonance between research and program delivery. A common finding arising from both the interviews and focus groups was the urgent need for sexual health information and services that are adaptive to the current realities and needs of girls living in the IDP camps. Although many participants reported the availability of HIV/AIDS information, they had limited access to other sexual health information related to puberty, safe sex, pregnancy, and abortion. Some participants attributed this lack of information to a lack of awareness by NGOs and IDP camp leaders of the difficulties and risks facing young girls.As one adolescent girl explained, although sensitization workshops on condom use had been offered in the camps, such services rarely targeted the most vulnerable populations:

> When they [family planning services] are teaching about condoms, they usually restrict it to people of 18 years and over. They are the ones who are advised to use it. The use of family planning is for married women

> (those with husbands) not for girls…young girls in the ages of 12–14 years don't have any knowledge about condoms. (Adolescent girl, Awer Camp, 2005)

Similarly, while FM radio stations were reported to be the main sources of sex/HIV/AIDS information, some adolescents noted that the impact of radio was mitigated by redundancy, repetition, and an evident incongruence between the broadcasters' assumptions and the young people's realities. For instance, radio presenters took for granted that condoms and medical services were readily available in the IDP camps, yet this was rarely the case. As our respondents reported, condom availability in the camps was largely nonexistent.

Moreover, many of our female adult interviewees articulated the imperative for additional sexual health information in the IDP camp settings. Exemplifying this need, some of the young respondents spoke of their "condom fears." One girl respondent indicated that "most girls fear that if the condom slips off in you, the boy will not help you to remove it… so they [condoms] would [get] stuck and you would die…condoms cause you to die" (Adolescent girl, Awer camp, 2005). Unfortunately, many of the respondents noted that none of these "condom myths" have been successfully challenged by the current grassroots interventions. The girls and women who were aware of the fallacy of these myths claimed that they further perpetuated the youth fears and fostered ignorant about girls' condom use.

Acholi Traditional Child Protection Systems

In the qualitative component of this study we aimed to explore aspects of the traditional Acholi socialization systems which may be relevant to addressing the vulnerabilities highlighted in the quantitative component. In the interviews and focus group discussions, many of the adult participants drew on their own experiences with Acholi child and youth socialization. The women reiterated the importance of their grandmothers' (*adaas*) socializing efforts and their paternal aunts' (*waya*) provision of sexual education. One woman eloquently explained the *wayo*'s teaching of Acholi rites of passage:

> [The] *wayo*'s role was to teach her niece everything, . . . even how to have sex with her husband, because the niece may have grown up in ignorance. She would teach the young girl that when [you] are having sex you are supposed to do this and that, otherwise you may not be good enough for your husband. She [would] teach girls about respect and about welcoming

> any visitors into the home, so that when you are married, you can respect your mother-in-law, father-in-law, and brothers-in-law, and that you will take care of all children without discrimination. She would emphasize discipline in a relationship. (Adult woman, Palenga Camp, 2005)

As articulated in this way, traditional Acholi socialization mechanisms can provide girls with sexual health information as well as delineated social boundaries for "appropriate" sexual relations. As explained by our participants, the age of sexual initiation according to Acholi cultural norms was anywhere between 14 and 18 years and it was permitted only after the female child had had a number of regular menstrual cycles. In Acholi culture, "premenstrual sex" was forbidden as it was thought to yield stillbirth and infertility, thereby bringing much consternation and stigma for both families involved. In fact, if a child was discovered to be having sex prior to menstruation, the incident became a kin and community issue and was dealt with in the same manner as a sexual assault, wherein the reconciliation involved compensation from the male's family. The respectability of a marriage, therefore, depended on the presence and participation of the *wayo* who was honored with gifts in recognition of her services in socializing the girl and assisting in the marriage process, the *wayo* at the marriage ceremony.

Our respondents provided additional details on the protective features of the Acholi system. They explained that once a young woman began receiving suitors, the young men would first arrive at the family compound, where the mothers, grandmothers, and aunts would determine the feasibility of a relationship. Following the women's acquiescence, the suitor would seek permission from the girl's father in order to propose. The next step would require the girl's expressed *consent* to the relationship and to the sexual relations.

According to the adult women, the traditional Acholi system likewise emphasized familial input in mate-selection, as well as the girl's own consent to both marriage and sexual relations. In fact, as we interviewed more women throughout the three IDP camps, it became clear that traditionally, and in the not too distant past, Acholi girls experienced significantly high levels of personal and sexual security. Taken together, the Acholi compounds of the grandmother's hut, the highly structured roles played by female relatives, the belief systems that forbade premenstrual sex and the sexual violation of girls, all represented a child protection system that placed a high value on the Acholi girl child's personal and familial dignity. There also appeared to be particular emphasis on the culturally imbued concept of personal and community consent. As emphasized by our women interviewees, any deviation from these cultural *morés* would be cause for familial discord.

The interviews and focus group discussions allowed both the women and the girls to contrast their current living conditions with the traditional ideals imposed by the Acholi system. One woman differentiated between the traditional Acholi *ssenga* system and the current state of affairs in the camp:

> If a boy began to court you he had to first present himself at your home and your mother would have to see him so that she could advise you when it's necessary...When you consented to a boy's proposal it was done by giving him such articles like beads, handkerchiefs, bangles...But the girls of today, they consent with their bodies...By the time you get to know your son's fiancée he will have had relationships with many girls...In the past a boy couldn't just come and use a girl. (Adult woman, Pabbo Camp, 2005)

Adding to this shift in behavioral norms was the powerlessness that girls and women in our study described as being associated with the congestion of IDP camp living. Within the camps their sexual decision-making exhibited a shift from *control and consent* to passivity and acquiescence. The personal security that families had once provided young girls, and the associated socialization processes of the *ssenga* system, had largely dissipated because of their war-induced displacement. In IDP camp settings, the mentoring systems were limited by the close proximity between families,[9] thus restricting the traditional comfort that had been associated with the grandmother's hut.

Many of the adult respondents indicated intense frustration following the breakdown of the traditional systems, and expressed grave concern about the vulnerability of their daughters who were living in squalor, impoverishment, and hunger. These conditions and the lack of child protection mechanisms stood in stark contrast to the systems of protection that had existed prior to IDP camp relocation.

Implications and Strategies for Change: "Culture as Intervention" in the Context of War

Our findings on the girls' vulnerabilities, coupled with inquiries into the traditional Acholi *ssenga* system, have contributed to the initiation of a modified form of child rights and protection spearheaded by community members. In this section we describe the scope and process of this system, which combines both traditional and contemporary elements of child rights and protection systems.

As part of our data analysis we organized several community-wide feedback sessions with over 600 members of the Pabbo, Awer, and Palenga IDP camps in order to discuss our preliminary research findings. These meetings centered on the current status of the communities' girls, the relevance of the traditional Acholi systems within this context, and the viability of implementing a sexual education program derived from traditional roles and responsibilities. Representatives from each IDP camp agreed that a *ssenga*-inspired model of sexual education, to draw upon traditional Acholi practices related to girls' personal and sexual security, would provide a sense of hope in battling the HIV/AIDS epidemic. As such, guided by the research outlined in this chapter, community members, study participants, and cultural leaders decided to implement a program that would combine traditional aspects of the *ssenga* model with modern techniques and processes that could be adaptive to the girls' current realities. Below is a brief description of the ways in which this program was thereupon carried out.

Identification and Training of a Nuanced Wayo

Community members were first asked to help select Acholi women who could combine both traditional and contemporary sex-related socialization for the IDP girls. Accordingly, adults and youth alike nominated women with social standing whom they could trust as potential *wayo* candidates.[10] These individuals were then invited to participate in a *wayo* training program.[11]

In total, 40 women were identified to be trained as sex counselors using a modern adaptation of the *wayo*.[12] The selected women were brought together in two separate groups of 20 and enrolled in a Training of Trainers (TOT) course for 7 days. The TOT trainers represented several organizations, including the AIDS Support Organization (TASO), Save the Children, Family Planning Association of Uganda, and the Directorate of Health Services in Gulu. Conducted in the local language of Luo, the curriculum for the training program was developed on the basis of the findings from this study concerning child protection issues and the sexual health information needs of girls in IDP situations. The training materials included visual aids, simple medical training models, role-plays, videos on STIs, and information on traditional Acholi *ssenga* systems and marriage protocols. Upon completion of the training, meetings were held in each community to introduce this modern adaptation of the *wayo* program to the young people and to their families and communities. In order to highlight awareness of the new program, each camp's *waya* drew upon social communication tools, including songs and theater, to present the role and function of the program. Once the information was presented successfully, the *waya* assumed their roles of sex counselors and mentors in their communities.

Successes, Concerns, and Challenges of Program Implementation

Although we did not formally evaluate the initiative's impact, we encouraged the *waya* to keep track of various program aspects, including the number of individual and group contacts made with girls, the common problems and key issues that the girls were confronting, and the *waya's* challenges throughout the process.

In the three-month period lasting from February to May 2006, the *waya* conducted a total of 522 individual meetings and 163 group meetings with girls in all 3 IDP camps.[13] The common issues addressed in the individual meetings included referrals and access to STI care, sexual violence, suicide prevention, abortion counseling, prevention of early marriage, birth control and family planning, condom information, access to rapid HIV testing, abductee support, and advocacy for school enrolment and retention. Concurrently, the common issues addressed in group visits included Acholi traditions related to the role of the grandmother and aunts, traditional songs and courtship processes, child marriage, incest taboos and menstruation, condom and HIV/AIDS education, rape avoidance strategies, and birth control and family planning.

The preliminary feedback about the follow-up sessions from the *waya* suggested that they were largely accepted as the main source of reproductive health information and were considered as the primary authorities on children's rights issues, including justice system advocacy. The *waya* noted that girls and young women often expressed a sense of safety when accessing their services. At the girls' request, the *waya* dealt with barriers to sexual and reproductive health services by facilitating referrals to care, and escorting girls to the treatment facilities.[14] The *waya* were further accessed by various community groups, including schools and churches, as the first point of contact for sexual health and child protection issues such as sexual violence and child rape. They were likewise actively involved in caring for young women who were victims of rape, facilitating access to care and ensuring that the police heeded the voices of these young women.

Finally, our initial assessments, the *waya* have facilitated an integrated approach to traditional and contemporary sex education, and have emphasized the important linkages between sexuality, family planning, and the transmission of HIV/STIs through one-on-one and group mentoring. Involvement of the community in the development of *waya* socialization, integrating the traditional role of the *wayo* with current concerns related to sexual health and protection, certainly contributed to its initial success, as it enabled us to address issues of community concern without violating cultural sensibilities. These initiatives have also indirectly addressed children's rights regarding freedom from sexual exploitation (CRC, Article 34 and Article 19), enjoyment of an elevated level of good health (CRC, Article 24), adequate protection and care from the state (CRC, Article 3 and Article 25), and a reaffirmation of the "inherent right to life" (CRC, Article 6).

The *waya* nonetheless have faced some significant challenges. For example, although incest and intra-family sexual abuse have been disclosed to the *waya*, which is indicative of trust girls have placed on the *waya*, the latter have felt ill-equipped to deal with these issues, and instead have tried to raise awareness about abuses within family households through the traditional justice system and in communication with clan elders. The *waya* likewise face difficulties in their health care referral activities, particularly as the NGOs mandated to provide condoms and related information and HIV/STI care have often been unavailable. These initial indicators thus offer significant feedback for the potential success of the nuanced *wayo* program, particularly in these IDP settings.

Conclusion

This study explored the experiences and realities of girls in IDP settings in Northern Uganda. Our findings indicated that although young girls may have had a great deal of information on HIV/AIDS and its transmission, they have often lacked the tangible support necessary to protect themselves against HIV/AIDS. Our evidence also revealed a large gap in the cultural process of sexual and reproductive health mentorship traditionally provided to adolescent girls by women in the Acholi homestead. This traditional socialization had been significantly disrupted by the war and by the subsequent nature of IDP camp living. With this knowledge, and in partnership with Acholi representatives, we assisted in the development of a nuanced *wayo* program. Spearheaded by the representatives of the three displacement camps, Pabbo, Awer, and Palenga, the *wayo* program included a contemporary, yet culturally sensitive, sexual health system that emphasized child rights and protection. This was a critical departure point for mitigating the impact of HIV/AIDS. Preliminary observations indicated that the community largely supported the *wayo* activities, and that the girls were readily accessing this traditional support system.

Our findings support the notion that despite ongoing conflict, the inclusion of both traditional teachings and contemporary health and sex education can provide a "middle road" between tradition and modernity (Muyinda, Nakuya, Pool, & Whitworth, 2003). The existing roles and obligations in Acholi family systems can be seen as resilient mechanisms for furthering children's rights and protections, particularly in relation to the provision of information and as a means to address barriers to information, testing, and STI treatment in the context of war. Given that the values and principles mirrored by familial and clan obligations can be revived despite the turmoil of war, kinship-related interventions may provide the most appropriate opportunity for consistent programming for young girls, particularly in their post-conflict resettlement.

Notes

1. This region is made up of three districts: Gulu, Kitgum, and Pader, which compromise an area of 28,000 square kilometers, approximately the size of Rwanda. Over a million people reside in these three districts, representing 25 percent of the national population of Uganda. Prior to the current conflict, 90 percent of these people lived in rural areas, which allowed for farming as their primary means of self-subsistence. This area of Northern Uganda is also referred to as Acholiland and is inhabited predominantly by people of "Acholi" ethnicity—from the Acholi tribe.
2. Often, the clans' homesteads were as far as 3 kilometres from one another, allowing each family both privacy in their child-rearing, as well as agricultural autonomy.
3. The traditional sexual education of boys was less of a focus in this research and thus provides a fruitful avenue for further research.
4. A total of 515 questionnaires were collected from three camps in Gulu district: Palenga (64 cases, 0.006 percent of the population, noted as 10,591 residents), Awer (92 cases, 0.005 percent of the population, noted as 18,543 residents), and Pabbo (359 cases 0.007 percent of the population, noted as 54,000 residents).
5. The adult women's participation in the study was rather imperative, as these respondents helped frame the current vulnerabilities of girls and provided complementary perspectives to the information gleaned from the

girls. They also provided a significant amount of information on the traditional Acholi *ssenga* model, a fundamental component of the research.

6. For girls who had been abducted into war, and thus had missed several foundational years of schooling, any subsequent attempt to return to school often led them to feel further removed from education. Forced to rejoin school at an older age than the average student, many girls felt out of place, and subsequently abandoned their education.
7. While the Universal Primary Education (UPE) policy decrees that primary education in Uganda be tuition free, fees for school books, uniforms, and meals remain the responsibility of the student and his or her family.
8. The amount of money girls make in Northern Uganda through casual labor or petty trade only supplements their household income. This sum provides the girls with merely enough to survive but does not allow for disposable income that can be used for education and other necessities.
9. Whereas in the past, distance between family compounds was approximately 10,000 feet, currently, neighboring compounds are separated by a few feet only.
10. Although both boys and girls put forth recommendations for the modern *waya* (the plural form of *wayo*), the girls' selections were particularly emphasized in the process, particularly as the *waya* would specifically mentor the girls.
11. For example, if a woman had a reputation for drinking and/or spreading gossip, it was highly unlikely that she would be placed on the list of potential candidates by the youth.
12. In each of the two smaller camps, Awer and Palenga, 10 *waya* were identified, and in Pabbo (which was almost double in size compared to the two other camps), 20 *waya* were identified.
13. The *waya* in the Awer camp conducted 130 individual and 34 group meetings with young girls, while the *waya* of Palenga carried out 134 individual and 32 group sessions. In the largest camp, Pabbo, the *waya* arranged 258 individual and 97 group meetings in the same period of time.
14. This kind of support had not existed in the camps prior to the introduction of the nuanced *wayo* model.

References

Barton, T., & Mutiiti, A. (1998). *Northern Uganda Psycho-social Needs Assessment Report.* New York: UNICEF.

Cohen, R. (1998). *Protecting Internally Displaced Women and Children: Rights Have No Borders.* Global IDP Survey of the Norwegian Refugee Council: Stylus, LLC.

De Walque, D. (2004). *How Does Educational Attainment Affect the Risk of Being Infected by HIV/AIDS? Evidence from a General Population Cohort in*

Rural Uganda. (World Bank Development Research Group Working Paper). Washington, DC: World Bank.

Francis, O., & McKibben G. (2008). *Abused: Child Sexual Abuse in Northern Uganda*. Gulu, Northern Uganda: Gulu Support the Children Organisation's Research Team.

Green, J., & Browne, J. (2005). *Principles of Social Research*. Maidenhead, UK: Open University Press.

Hackenberg, M. L. (2000). Can the Optional Protocol for the Convention on the Rights of the Child Protect the Ugandan Child Soldier? *Indiana International and Comparative Law Review, 10*(2), 417–455.

Human Rights Watch. (2005). *The Less They Know the Better: Abstinence-Only HIV/AIDS Programs in Uganda*. *17*(4)(A). New York: Human Rights Watch.

Human Rights Watch. (2003). *Just Die Quietly: Domestic Violence and Women's Vulnerability to HIV in Uganda*. *15*(15)(A). New York: Human Rights Watch

Internal Displacement Monitoring Centre & Norwegian Refugee Council. (2010). Uganda. In *Internal Displacement Global Overview of Trends and Developments in 2009 (Uganda)*. Retrieved from http://www.internal-displacement.org/8025708F004BE3B1/(httpInfoFiles)/8980F134C9CF4373C1257725006167DA/$file/Global_Overview_2009.pdf Irish Aid. (n.d.) *Revealing the Female Face of the Epidemic*. Retrieved April 29, 2006 from http://www.dci.gov.ie/article.asp?article=478.

Kalton, G. (1983). *Introduction to Survey Sampling*. Beverly Hills, CA: Sage.

Liu Centre for the Study of Global Issues. (2002). *Assessment Mission to Northern Uganda*. Uganda-Liu Centre for Human Security Initiative.

Maçhel, G. (1996). *The Impact of Armed Conflict on Children*. Retrieved November 28, 2005 from http://www.unicef.org/graca/a51-306_en.pdf

Mazurana, D., & McKay, S. (2004). *Girls in Fighting Forces: Policy and Program Recommendations*. Ottawa, CA: Supported by CIDA's Child Protection Research Fund.

Medecins Sans Frontieres. (2006). *Beyond Night Commuting: The Daily Lives of Children Who Commute*. Retrieved July 20, 2008 from www.msf.ch

Muyinda, H., Kengeya, J., Pool, R., & Whitworth, J., (2001). Traditional Sex Counselling and STI/HIV Prevention among Young Women in Rural Uganda. *Culture, Health and Sexuality, 3*(3), 69–79.

Muyinda, H. Nakuya, J., Pool, R., & Whitworth, J. (2003). Harnessing the Ssenga Institution of Adolescent Sex Education for the Control of HIV and STDs in Rural Uganda. *AIDS Care, 15(*2), 159–167.

Muyinda, H., Nakuya, J., Whitworth, J., Pool, R., (2004). Community Sex Education among Adolescents in Rural Uganda: Utilizing Indigenous Institutions, *AIDS Care, 16*(1), *69–79.*

Nannyonjo, J. (2004). *Conflicts, Poverty and Human Development in Northern Uganda*. Uganda: Bank of Uganda, Research Department.

Ominde, S. H. (1952). *The Luo Girl: From Infancy to Marriage*. St. Martin's Street, London, UK: Macmillan.

Save the Children. (2001). *The Long Road Home.* Report from a cross-border mission to Sudan and Uganda.

Uganda Aids Commission. (2001). *National Young People HIV/AIDS Communication Program for Young People: Concept Paper.* Kampala, Uganda.

Uganda Bureau of Statistics (UBOS) & ORC Macro. (2001). *Uganda Demographic and Health Survey 2000–2001.* Calverton, MD: UBOS and ORC Macro. Ugandan Ministry of Health. (2001). *HIV/AIDS Surveillance Report.*

UNAIDS/WHO. (2004). *Epidemiological Fact Sheets*: Uganda. p.2.

UNAIDS. (2004). *HIV and Young People: The Threat for Today's Youth. Report on the Global Aids Epidemic.* Retrieved June 28, 2008 from http://www.unaids.org/bangkok2004/GAR2004_pdf/Focus_youth_en.pdf

UNAIDS Inter-Agency Task Team on Gender and HIV/AIDS. (n.d.). *HIV/AIDS, Gender and Conflict Situations.* Retrieved July 4, 2008 from http://www.unfpa.org/hiv/docs/hivpercent20factsheets/factsheet_conflict.pdf.

UN Convention on the Rights of the Child. (1989). *UN: Office of the High Commission for Human Rights.* Retrieved April 27, 2009 from http://www.unhchr.ch/html/menu3/b/k2crc.htm.

UNICEF. (2002). *Education and HIV Prevention.* New York: UNICEF.

UNICEF. (2004). *State of the World's Children: The Multiplier Effect of Educating Girls,* pp. 44–57. New York: UNICEF.

UNICEF, IRC, Christian Children's Fund, & Legal Aid Project. (2004). *Protected Yet Insecure.* Unpublished document.

Women's Commission for Refugee Women and Children. (2001). *Against All Odds: Surviving the War on Adolescents.* New York: WCRWC.

Women's Commission for Refugee Women and Children. (2004). *No Safe Place to Call Home: Children and Adolescent Night Commuters in Northern Uganda.* New York: WCRWC.

Women's Commission for Refugee Women and Children. (n.d.). *Adolescent Girls Affected by Violent Conflict: Why Should We Care?* Retrieved July 25, 2008 from http://www.womenscommission.org/pdf/AdolGirls.pdf.

World Health Organization. (2007). *Health Action in Crises: Uganda.* Retrieved from http://www.who.int/hac/crises/uga/sitreps/uganda_bi_monthly_1_18may2007.pdf

CHAPTER 10

Rethinking the Orphan Crisis: Community-Based Responses to Orphan Care in Malawi

Liam Riley and Esther Lupafya

Introduction

Within the past two decades, sub-Saharan Africa (SSA) has experienced an unprecedented rise in the orphan population. An estimated 14 million orphans alone have lost parents to AIDS (UNICEF, 2009). With 81 percent of the world's AIDS orphans living in SSA, the phenomenon of African AIDS orphanhood has attracted considerable global attention in recent years. Paradoxically, however, despite growing international concern (UNICEF, 2003; 2006), there has been surprisingly little research on national policies related to African orphan children and on the everyday lives of these children. Narratives of the "African orphan crisis," usually found in journalistic and donor agency reports, often rest on latent Northern assumptions about the nature of childhood, family, and community, and on the premise that the death of biological parents almost inevitably results in children's helplessness and abandonment. Although appeals to "save" orphans tend to accentuate what are generally assumed to be their impoverished and isolated circumstances, too little thought is paid to the possibilities of support networks at local levels (Bray, 2003; Meintjes & Giese, 2006). Such crisis narratives are unfortunate, for not only is orphanhood in SSA diverse and complex, but as well there is growing evidence that young orphans and the communities in which they reside often possess resources that foster resilience and facilitate adaptation to difficult circumstances (Abebe & Aase, 2007; Ennew, 2005; Meintjes & Giese, 2006; Panter-Brick, 2000). Indeed, studies that examine the lives of orphans and the ways communities and institutions are striving to respond to their unique needs can help to transcend the implicit "helplessness" articulated in crisis narratives.

This chapter draws on one such study conducted in 2007 in Malawi, a small landlocked and largely rural country in central Africa which has one of the lowest per capita Gross Domestic Products (GDP) in the world. With a total population of approximately 14 million, Malawi is home to an estimated 950,000 orphans aged 17 years and under (Government of Malawi, 2008). It is estimated that slightly more than half this population has been orphaned due to HIV/AIDS. Although the HIV prevalence rate in Malawi has recently stabilized at 12 percent of 15–49 year olds, the enduring impact of AIDS, coupled with the effects of chronic poverty, means that even with a reduced infection rate, the orphan population will continue to grow for some time to come (UNAIDS, 2007).

In this chapter we contend that in Northern countries popular perceptions of orphanhood in Malawi today are overly influenced by a crisis narrative that obscures the significance of communities, extended family networks, and the resilience of orphans themselves. This crisis narrative presupposes that when children lose their parents they have little option but to fend for themselves in a dog-eat-dog world (Abebe & Aase, 2007; Ennew, 2005; Meintjes & Giese, 2006). This narrative has also tended to fuel institutionalized interventions that often fail to account for, and build on, the resilience and energy inherent among the people closest to orphans such as extended family members, friends, and concerned community inhabitants (Chirwa, 2002; Cook, Ali, & Munthali, 2000). Following from such assumptions, the emphasis of international assistance is to *save* orphans by removing them from their families and communities rather than to *help* them by strategically investing in the capacity of their communities to provide care. We consider this to be a counterproductive narrative that depicts orphanhood in contemporary Africa as devoid of support from extended families and communities. In response, we present evidence from a case study in Malawi demonstrating that sustainable, effective, and culturally appropriate approaches to orphan care frequently emanate from within local communities, and that this has implications for externally sponsored orphan care programs.

Field research for this study, which was conducted by the two authors, a Canadian and a Malawian, was inspired by perspectives emerging from the new social studies of childhood, an interdisciplinary field that has emerged from criticisms of "adultist" research approaches that tend to frame children as *becoming* adults, whose experiences and opinions have less validity than those of adults. These perspectives are in turn linked to a broader shift in social research that has resulted in close scrutiny of the conventionally marginal voices of women, the poor, indigenous peoples, and the disabled. Accordingly, this approach to research has repositioned children as social actors who have distinct experiences and viewpoints that deserve as much scholarly attention as those of adults (Aitken, 2001; Hill, 2006; Holloway & Valentine, 2000; Prout, 2005).

In order to contextualize our discussion, we begin by considering the conceptualization of orphanhood in a cross-cultural and global context. We then review both the situation of orphanhood in Malawi and national policy related to Malawi's orphans, highlighting in particular the role of Community Based Childcare Centres (CBCC) as a focal point for orphan care. We conclude by considering the situation of a cohort of orphans in Northern Malawi whom we interviewed in order to elicit an understanding of their daily lives and relationships.

Assumptions and Misassumptions about Orphanhood in Sub-Saharan Africa

Childhood is a central element of social and cultural reproduction. Debates concerning the treatment of children are often, therefore, colored by the lenses of cultural diversity. This extends to the notion of child "vulnerability" and to orphanhood, which can have different manifestations and effects in different times and places. For many years, the conventional view of orphans was that they were children under the age of 18 years who had suffered the loss through death of one or both biological parents (Government of Malawi, 2005; UNICEF, 2003). Yet this definition, which centers almost entirely on parameters of age and biological parenthood, has been challenged on several fronts, largely because of its culturally limited connotations. In many societies, for example, generational categories are not assigned simply on the basis of years lived, but rather are considered in relation to lineage within families or to social events or characteristics such as initiation ceremonies and marriages (Aitken, 2001; Holloway & Valentine, 2000; Prout, 2005). Within such contexts, formal age boundaries are constructs that have relatively little meaning. In addition, the assumption that biological parenthood is essential for child welfare overlooks the potential significance of other care-givers who may or may not be extended family members. This presupposition regarding the centrality of one or both biological parents for children's wellbeing and development resides on the perception of the social primacy of the nuclear family. Throughout much of SSA, however, this is far from an accurate depiction of family and parental relations for it has resided on the perception of the social primacy of the nuclear family and tends to marginalize potentially supportive mechanisms that are associated with nonnuclear families and community relations (Abebe & Aase, 2007; Madhavan, 2004; Nyambedha & Aagaard-Hansen, 2003).

The propensity to focus almost exclusively on the vulnerability of children whose parents have died, and consequently overlook the diversity and complexity of orphanhood in SSA, echoes a populist Euro-American imagination of orphanhood that was initially formed during the late nineteenth century. Then, as now, attention was directed almost exclusively to individual orphans who were seen to be in need of salvation through acts of charity (Ennew, 2005; Panter-Brick, 2000). This focus on orphan children alone effectively ignored the facts of class-based poverty and the potential capacity of family members and communities to care for children. Furthermore, in many circumstances children were deemed to be orphans when living parents were perceived as unfit to care for their children because of their impoverishment (Panter-Brick, 2000). Poor single mothers were especially singled out in this regard. A similar narrow focus on orphaned African children has likewise tended to overlook the structural conditions of poverty that exacerbate the disadvantages of poor children, the limited life expectancy of poor parents, and the rights of poor, yet loving relations to raise orphan children.

In addition to these longstanding conventional perceptions of orphanhood, several comparisons of human development indicators among orphans and nonorphans in contemporary SSA have generated conflicting findings. Some studies have found that orphans generally have minimal access to education, health care, and adequate nutrition (Bicego, Rutstein, & Johnson, 2003; Makame, Ani, & Grantham-McGregor, 2004; Monasch & Boerma, 2004). A recent analysis of Demographic Household Survey (DHS) data in 10 countries in Africa, including Malawi, observed that orphans were less likely to be enrolled in school than nonorphans, even when both groups were living in the same households (Case, Paxson, & Ableidinger, 2004). The overall conclusion was that children's opportunities for education are diminished following the death of biological parents. Yet DHS data are limited since they rely on cross-sectional information only and, therefore, give no indication of the prior duration of school attendance or whether orphans have abandoned school before or after their parents have died (Sharma, 2005). Indeed, other studies using the same DHS data have indicated that although school attendance among single orphans (i.e., with one biological parent still living) is lower than the average for all children, this is not the case among children who have experienced double orphanage (i.e., those whose biological parents have both deceased) (Guarcello, Lyon, & Rosati, 2004). Moreover, a recent study in Northern Malawi has shown that when orphans and nonorphans are attending school, there is in fact little difference in achievement levels between the two groups (Floyd et al., 2007). These results clearly contradict the perception that orphanhood has a consistently negative effect on school access and achievement.

Concerns about AIDS-induced orphanhood continue to be a preoccupation, particularly among international donors. Bray (2003) has identified four assumptions that reinforce these predictions:

1. High AIDS mortality rates will produce high numbers of orphans;
2. These orphans will not be able to live in appropriate social environments capable of equipping them for adult citizenship;
3. Lack of adequate socialization among children orphaned by AIDS will mean that many will not live within society's moral codes, and they will, therefore, be more likely to end up as street children or juvenile delinquents; and
4. Large numbers of such delinquent orphans risk precipitating a breakdown in the social fabric (p. 7).

While the first assumption is undoubtedly true, it must be qualified in relation to the varying definitions and associated meanings of orphanhood. For example, it is a moot point as to whether a child who has lost her parents and is currently living in an extended family situation should be considered an orphan. The second assumption underscores the view that a household with two biological parents, essentially the Western nuclear family model, is the only appropriate social environment for children. There is ample evidence that this household structure has not been the norm in southern Africa, particularly in areas with high levels of male labor outmigration (typical of communities in northern Malawi) (Henderson, 2006; Madhavan, 2004; Meintjes & Giese, 2006), or in societies where childrearing by people other than the biological parents is common practice (Abebe & Aase, 2007; Madhavan, 2004; Nyambedha & Aagaard-Hansen, 2003). The third assumption rests on a similar precept as the first, implying that only biological parents can properly socialize their children. It also negates the agency of children—orphans and nonorphans alike—as they grow and mature (Bray, 2003). The fourth assumption concerning ultimate societal deterioration can be linked to apocalyptic social attitudes that reflect popular uneasiness about young people who are not integrated into society through established institutional structures such as families or schools (Matthews & Limb, 1999b). Invariably, however, the logic supporting the view that large numbers of AIDS orphans will tear at the social fabric of southern Africa does little more than reinforce unreflective anxiety and fear. It also fosters the widely held perspective that interventions from outside, directed at individual children who have lost their parents, are vital if these children are to be rescued from the risks of orphanhood.

In contrast to this type of crisis narrative that leads inexorably to the conclusion that aid from sympathetic outsiders is necessary to "save" orphan children , an alternative perspective points to the imperative of supporting those communities that are striving to provide for orphans' needs on a small scale. From this perspective, policy approaches to assist orphans and other vulnerable children must be based on an affirmation of the concept of social resilience and the supposition that social groups, be they extended families or broader community neighborhoods, are capable of adapting to adverse circumstances in accordance with the means at their disposal (Abebe & Aase, 2007; Chirwa, 2002; Government of Malawi, 2005). Viewed in this light, community-based orphan care systems should be neither static nor uniform, nor centered solely on the welfare of individual children. Instead, by focusing attention on a multitude of factors such as poverty, gender inequality, child abuse, and lack of formal education, all of which not only decrease the quality of life of millions of orphans, but of millions of nonorphans throughout sub-Saharan Africa as well, interventions should ideally be highly adaptive and oriented toward enhancing the broad social networks within which orphan children are situated (Kesby, Gwanzura-Ottemoller, & Chizororo, 2006; Madhavan, 2004).

In the specific context of Malawi, Chirwa (2002) has pointed out that indigenous conceptualizations of orphanhood are wide-reaching and can include the rupture of social bonds, limited family support, and even situations of socioeconomic deprivation. These perspectives suggest that while orphanhood may or may not be defined by the death of biological parents, it is a concept that is directly rooted in broad social conditions and corresponding risks of social stigmatization and marginalization. Since Malawian kinship structures situate children within a mutually reliant family network that reaches beyond biological parents and siblings, Chirwa sees hope that the majority of Malawi's orphans will be included in extended families and communities. If orphanhood is viewed as a *process of social exclusion* rather than as a *fixed state of being* for a predetermined period of time, then the binary categorization of orphans and nonorphans can be diminished. By refuting narrow definitions, this broader perspective of orphanhood draws attention to more contextually relevant signs of child vulnerability such as age, gender, local food security, and proximity to social services. It thus lends itself to a social resilience approach to policy formulation, one that is based on a "tacit admission that families and communities have the potential to rebound and reconfigure themselves in the face of crisis" (Chirwa, 2002, p. 110).

Fortunately, within the past decade, academic and policy-oriented literature has begun to adopt a broader conceptualization of orphans in recognition of the fact that the death of biological parents in and of itself does not necessarily relegate children to outright deprivation, and should not, therefore, automatically set off populist angst. The crudeness of the universal definition of orphanhood has prompted a shift toward an endorsement of the term "orphans and other vulnerable children" (OVC), an acknowledgment of the similar circumstances facing many children, those who have lost their parents, but as well those whose parents are alive but may lack resources, be absent from home, or be abusive. This shift in perception can be seen in the way UNICEF has reported on AIDS-induced orphanhood in SSA over time. In contrast to its 2003 report, *Africa's Orphaned Generations,* which began with the alarmist statement, "The HIV/AIDS epidemic in sub-Saharan Africa has already orphaned a generation of children—and now seems set to orphan a generation more" (UNICEF, 2003), in 2006 UNICEF adopted a more nuanced tone, reflecting a broader view of the complex ways that the HIV/AIDS epidemic has affected young people:

> The AIDS epidemic in Africa puts children at risk physically, emotionally and economically. All children are indirectly affected when their communities, and the services these communities provide, are strained by the consequences of the epidemic. Nurses, doctors, teachers and others can become ill and die from AIDS, affecting health care, education and other basic services. (p. iv)

This broader perspective of the HIV/AIDS pandemic accounts for the community context of the disease and its impact on the local circumstances in which children live. From this viewpoint, vulnerability can take different forms, both tangible (e.g., food insecurity, and lack of health care and education) and intangible (e.g., neglect, emotional abuse, and lack of positive role models).

The reconceptualization of orphans as embedded within a social fabric, whether or not they are part of a nuclear family, is a necessary first step to addressing the urgent need for supportive and sustainable policies. In this light, the promotion of children's rights cannot be construed as simply a matter of changing orphans' circumstances by relocating them to orphanages or providing handouts. Rather, it is a matter of addressing the broad issues affecting their communities—including the extensive range of people who are there to look after them—because these are the communities children will one day inherit. It is against this conceptual backdrop that community-based approaches to orphan care have emerged in Malawi.

Community-Based Orphan Care in Malawi

In the spirit of building community-based capacity to provide care for orphans, in 2005 the government of Malawi launched the National Plan of Action (NPA) for Orphans and Other Vulnerable Children (OVC) (Government of Malawi, 2005). Preparation of the plan, which connected guiding principles, strategic objectives, and proposed activities with anticipated funding sources and timelines, involved a technical working group comprising representatives from the government of Malawi, the UN, several international aid agencies, and the National AIDS Committee (NAC). Most of the activities outlined in the NPA were designed to provide strategic support to orphans and vulnerable children living in communities, usually with extended family members. Within the terms of the NPA, the government's role has primarily been to coordinate, monitor, and provide support to community-based organizations (CBOs) and NGOs which are regarded as the main executing agencies of the Plan.

A key component of the NPA has been the establishment of Community Based Childcare Centres (CBCC), of which there are now several thousand nation-wide (Government of Malawi, 2005). Similar in some respects to nursery schools, the CBCCs are equipped with books, games, and learning materials, and are open to orphans and nonorphans of preschool age. CBCC caregivers receive basic training in early childhood education. These centers constitute an important initiative in reaching out to orphaned and vulnerable children in Malawi, providing them with food, early education, and a nurturing environment that helps them to develop within their communities. Nonorphans as well as orphans are welcomed. This is not only because both orphans and nonorphans may live in circumstances of poverty, but because it helps to reduce the potential stigmatization of socially separating orphans from other children and the broader community.

In principle, CBCCs are heavily reliant on volunteer energy, and each is governed by a committee of local people. These committees are responsible for allocating resources that will assist OVCs, usually through means of support for households, and for ensuring the sustainability of the CBCCs through fund-raising and various income-generating activities. These sources of revenue are especially helpful in offsetting the costs associated with raising children in indigent households. Nevertheless, many CBCCs have also required external financial and technical assistance, particularly in their initial stages of existence.

Ekwendeni Hospital AIDS Programme

In the Ekwendeni area in northern Malawi, where we conducted most of our research fieldwork, CBCCs receive substantial support from the Ekwendeni Hospital AIDS Programme (EHAP). Established by Scottish missionaries in 1889, Ekwendeni Hospital is currently administered by the Church of Central Africa Presbyterian (CCAP). In the early 1990s, with assistance from several international donors, EHAP initiated an orphan care program in order to extend a range of services for households and communities caring for orphans and other vulnerable children. The program is organized within the framework of a governing structure that seeks to maximize input from the many villages in the Ekwendeni Catchment Area. Each village has a committee of approximately 10 people who are charged with mobilizing available resources to support local OVCs. Wherever possible, EHAP's orphan care program works in conjunction with local CBCCs. As elsewhere in Malawi, CBCCs in the district are staffed by community inhabitants and provide a range of services, including the provision of food, clothing, blankets, fertilizers and other farming inputs, early child development activities, and the subsidization of school fees and uniforms for older children.

While CBCCs strive to mobilize local resources for these services, a substantial proportion of assistance for community-based orphan care in Ekwendeni originates from outside local communities. At the time of our research fieldwork, EHAP was supplying capital funds and business management training to assist CBCC members in establishing income-generating activities such as maize mills and piggeries. EHAP has also provided business training to dozens of individuals so that they can increase profits and help ensure the sustainability of OVC support activities. Other external charitable donations provide seed money for various small-scale cooperative food and condiment retail enterprises to support CBCC activities. Through this combination of external assistance and mobilization of local resources, it was clear that in Ekwendeni the care of OVCs depended substantially on the resilience of communities to adapt to new challenges and to invest time and resources into caring for these children. It was also evident that training and business experience gained through these programs can have a side benefit for the entire community by enhancing local capacity for long-term economic independence.

Research Methodology

The research project did not endeavor to test the effectiveness of community-based care systems per se. Instead, our intention was to assess orphans' perspectives on the social and spatial contexts of their daily lives. We, therefore, interviewed a cohort of 25 orphans between the ages of 7 and 14 years, posing questions that would encourage them to articulate how they feel about the places where they live and the people taking care of them. As outlined in table 10.1, 20 of these young people, all of whom who were purposively selected in order to ensure diversity in terms of age, gender, access to services, and type of parental loss, were living in extended family circumstances or in single parent households in the Ekwendeni Catchment Area. The remaining five young people were resident in three different orphanages in Blantyre, the major commercial city located in southern Malawi. Interviews with these children required sensitivity because of occasional references to the emotionally charged issue of parental loss. Neverthelesss, we felt that the risk of emotional disturbance was balanced by the value of giving the children the opportunity to tell their stories and talk about their problems (Robson, 2001).

All the children selected for this study fell under the international definition of an "orphan." Yet despite this common epithet, they had had diverse experiences with parental loss and were living in variable conditions and receiving different types of care and support (table 10.2).

Table 10.1 Descriptive statistics of orphans interviewed in Malawi, June–July 2007 (n=25)

Characteristic	*Category*	*Frequency*
Gender	Male	13
	Female	12
Age	7–10	5
	11–14	20
Type of Parental Loss	Maternal orphan	5
	Paternal orphan	9
	Double orphan	11
Type of Care	Institutional	5
	Community-based	20

Table 10.2 Primary caregiver (n=25)

Caregiver	*Frequency*
Single mother	7
Institutional	5
Single grandparent	3
Multiple adult relatives	3
Aunt and uncle	3
Parent and stepparent	2
Single father	1
Elder sibling	1

Because of this diversity of circumstance and care,we soon discerned that orphanhood itself is generally not a primary cause of child vulnerability. Rather it is one component of a broad set of factors that are related to household income, place of residence, relationship to caregivers, age at the time of a parent's death, and gender of the deceased parent. This last factor—the gender of the lost parent—was significant in terms of the major source of current support. While men have greater access to resources such as land and wage labor in Malawi (Bezner Kerr, 2005), paradoxically children who have lost their mothers are classified as more vulnerable than those who have lost their fathers largely because fathers are seen as less suited for caregiving than mothers or even women who are unrelated to the children (Government of Malawi, 2005).

Among the cohort of children whom we interviewed, the most common source of care was from (seven) single mothers whose spouses (the father of their children) had passed away. These children were referred to as "paternal orphans." That most of them continued to live with their mothers was a reflection not only of the conventional role of women as caregivers, but of the difficulty that widows generally face in finding new husbands or other partner relations who will assist them in caring for their children. In contrast, of the five children who were "maternal orphans," that is, had lost their mothers, only one lived with her father. This girl indicated that she did much of the housework and had taken on a large part of the adult female role in the household. In the other four cases of maternal orphanhood, either the father had remarried or the child was staying with other relatives. "Double orphans," or those who have lost both biological parents, are classified by the government as the most vulnerable group of orphans. Yet among the children whom we met and interviewed, there was no categorical predictability about their circumstances and overall welfare.

Perspectives of the Children: Difficulties and Challenges

During the interviews, the children explained to us both the positive and negative aspects of their daily lives. Hunger, the need to work, and the difficulty of dealing with memories of their deceased parents were the key negative aspects affecting them, whereas friendships, playing, and love from caregivers were commonly the positive aspects of their daily lives. Adopting the geographic significance of place, we were interested in knowing how children felt about the places in which they lived, and particularly the extent to which these places felt familiar and safe. In response to the general question "How do you feel about the place you live?" 19 of our respondents expressed a sense of general satisfaction with their situations, 3 indicated that their living conditions were fine or better than where they had lived before, and only 3 did not like where they were living. Of the 5 orphans in institutional care whom we interviewed, all said that they liked where they lived, citing the profound difficulties they had experienced prior to residing in the orphanages. These responses should be qualified, however, by the fact that we were granted access to children in orphanages via the management of the orphanages and government social workers. Possibly as well, our perceived link to authority figures might have influenced the way children described where they were living. In other circumstances we accessed the children through local volunteers associated with EHAP, who would have been less directly perceived as authority figures than managers of orphanages. Of the orphans receiving care primarily from someone other than a parent or grandparent (n=7), only two complained that they were treated unfairly, and this related to the distribution of food or domestic work. The others (n=5) said they felt that they were treated the same way as others in the family, and that this made them feel loved.

Of the three children who indicated that they were unhappy with their current situations, we present brief descriptive synopses of two (using pseudonyms) drawn from summative notes of the recorded interviews.

> Sam's father died when he was young, and when his mother remarried, he was sent to live with extended family members because, as he said, his stepfather was unfriendly and did not want to live with his wife's children. Sam was living in a village near Ekwendeni, which, because of its lack of water and poor soil conditions, was prone to food insecurity. In his interviews with us, he complained of hunger, how he sometimes went without eating a meal for an entire day, and how his family sometimes had to rely on wild fruit for sustenance. He further indicated that if he spoke about his hunger in his household, he was frequently told to be stoic, because "that's how life is." Poverty and malnutrition were an ever-present fact of life for Sam, but this was less because of his status as an orphan, and more because of the overall indigence of the household and community where he lived.
>
> Wilson, a 12-year-old boy who had lost both of his parents, worked for tobacco farmers throughout the year to support his younger sister and elderly grandmother. He reported that he would earn between 100 and 150 Malawian kwacha per week (US$0.75–US$1.00). His situation was tantamount to that of a child-headed household because his grandmother was ill and he was the only one able to work. Their house was by far the most meager in the village; surrounding homes had metal roofs and solid foundations, while their home was barely five feet high with no foundation and a poorly thatched grass roof—a situation that is reflective of the high levels of poverty in rural Malawi. When we asked what happened to him after his father died, he said, "I was very worried. We didn't receive any help from neighbors or relatives." In addition to working for tobacco farmers and attending school, Wilson farmed his own plot to feed his household. During our visit, we noticed a granary about one-third filled with maize and inquired as to whether that was his harvest. He said it was their harvest for the entire year, even though it was the amount one adult would normally consume in a month. He said they would normally eat twice per day, but they were always worried about food. He said Christmas was the last time he felt full, because he "worked extra hard and was able to save enough to buy some meat in town." We asked if he was looking forward to the same this year and he said, "No, I don't think it will be possible. It was so much work." Despite these difficulties, he said he was proud of his ability to provide for his family.

These two vignettes illustrate the significance of food insecurity for rural orphans and the tenuous extent to which some communities and neighborhoods are able to provide for their basic needs. Sam's rejection by his stepfather and Wilson's lack of support from relatives and neighbors who seemed to be profiting from tobacco production suggest that orphan children risk falling through the cracks of traditional childcare systems. Sam's separation from his mother due to her choice to remarry can be construed as the result of the low status of women in their community. Without speaking to her directly, but drawing on other research on gender relations in the Ekwendeni area (Bezner Kerr, 2005), it seems apt to assume that Sam's mother faced limited options following the death of her husband. His example draws attention to the array of social issues contingent on the realization of children's basic rights .

These vignettes also illustrate how the vulnerability of orphans in Malawi can largely be linked to the socioeconomic marginalization of many rural communities. In such circumstances the restricted access of orphans to social services such as education, health care, and nutrition are mainly factors of the status of the communities in which they live, rather than to their status as orphans per se. In the poorest village we visited, there were over 1,000 students at the local school with only three teachers and a headmaster. We were told that because the local educational facilities were remote and poorly funded, parents were required to send their children to town to prepare for final examinations, a venture that required either cash for lodgings or personal connections that would enable their children's access to room and board. In this context, orphans' disadvantage had less to do with their *orphanhood* than it did with the broader context of poverty and social inequality in Malawi. Rural orphans and nonorphans alike were at a disadvantage because of the poorly funded local school. In contrast, orphans living in towns attended better schools than nonorphans in the rural community. These examples serve as cautionary notes, highlighting the link between children's rights and the need for the social and economic advancement of women in Malawi, and the imperative ofsustainable food security programs and strengthened capacity of communities to provide care for orphans.

Children' Perspectives: Contextualized Resilience

Despite these difficulties, however, most of the young people whom we interviewed expressed relative satisfaction with their lives. While many indicated that they were satisfied with the availability of food and material goods, and that they had access to schools and clinics, one of the most striking responses among these children was their reference to the significance of play. For example, in response to a question regarding personal concerns, a 12-year-old girl in a rural community who had lost both her parents replied that she was sad about the loss of her parents and that there was no one to whom she could communicate this sadness. We then asked her, "How do you deal with these thoughts?" and she replied simply, "I just go play." Having friends and a space to play was an important means to relieve sadness and stress. Among the boys, not surprisingly, football was overwhelmingly popular. One village boy indicated that he was happy where he was residing because there was space for him to play football. Another village boy indicated that football was everything to him.

These narratives about play also highlighted the value of peer friendships as a source of psychosocial support for orphans—both in institutions and in community-based care. When asked whether they felt loved, and by whom, six of the respondents quite specifically indicated that they were loved by friends. One of the boys in an orphanage spoke emphatically about how close he was to his best friend there, claiming that they shared everything and would be friends for life. Another boy in a rural village talked warmly about the friends with whom he played, herded livestock, and attended school. He said he could share all his thoughts and worries with these friends because they played together and he trusted them. These accounts expressed a sense that friends could really understand each other.

Statements concerning the significance of friends corroborated findings by van Blerk and Ansell (2006) who found that friendships with peers were crucial for identity formation and the overall well-being of children who had experienced AIDS-related migration in Malawi and Lesotho. Many of the children participating in van Blerk and Ansell's study had indicated that the most challenging aspects of migration were missed friendships and the hardship of having to make new ones. Curiously, while most orphan care policies recognize that separation from siblings is an undesirable outcome for orphans, few acknowledge the significance of children's bonds with their friends.

From our summative notes of recorded interviews, we can draw two further vignettes that exemplify how social environments tended to be more important for children than the specific status of orphanhood per se:

> Jennifer was born in Mzuzu, a small city in northern Malawi, where her father had been a teacher and her family enjoyed a humble but comfortable lifestyle. When she was six years old, her father died and

> so her mother took Jennifer and her three siblings to Blantyre to live with relatives. Within two or three years her mother also fell ill and the family moved to their ancestral village near Ekwendeni. A short while later Jennifer's mother died, and the siblings were thereupon separated. The elder sister was sent to a boarding school, the two younger brothers remained in the village, and Jennifer herself was sent to live with her grandparents and other adult relatives in Ekwendeni in order to attend primary school. In speaking with us, Jennifer complained about the physical abuse she experienced at school and the drudgery of agricultural work, and the superstitions that kept her housebound most of the time. Such complaints are not unique to orphans, but are sadly common among vast numbers of youth in Malawi and elsewhere in sub-Saharan Africa. Apart from the unfortunate loss of her parents and the separation from her siblings [clearly difficult experiences for any young person], in the context of Malawi she nonetheless had several advantages: adequate food and care in her extended family home, and a willingness on the part of family members to invest in her education in a context where all too often parents favor boys' enrolment in school over that of girls. Equally evident was the extent to which Jennifer had developed a palpable spirit of independence and defiance as a result of the very adversities that had confronted her.
>
> Annie's father had died when she was still too young to remember him and her mother then moved away to work in Blantyre. She herself was raised by her aunt and uncle in Ekwendeni. Her mother would send money and gifts, but she rarely visited her daughter. Nevertheless, the gifts meant a great deal to Annie, and when her mother died she was distraught. Yet her mother's death did not alter her day-to-day circumstances, for she continued to live in her extended family household, the only home she had known since the death of her father when she was very small.

Although orphaned and obliged to live with extended families, both of these girls were living in circumstances that were as accommodating as could be expected. Both were attending primary school, and they looked forward to eventually attending secondary school and pursuing careers as nurses.

Conclusion

The limited scope of our research is not adequate to conduct an in-depth comparison of the relative merits and drawbacks of institutional and community-based care approaches. Nonetheless, it does suggest that a community-based approach generally provides a better opportunity for a holistic response to the advancement of children's rights in Malawi. The most pressing problems faced by orphans in rural Malawi—hunger, lack of access to quality education, and the need to work—affect whole communities and, therefore, are not resolved by removing orphans from their place of belonging. Furthermore, the value of interpersonal relationships, as the cohort of young people in this study articulated, can be compromised by their removal from their communities. Community-based approaches, such as the EHAP orphan care program, can provide multiple benefits to orphans, their households, and communities, and hold the potential for a more sustainable and wide-reaching impact. In contrast, heavy reliance on institutional approaches may result in the isolation of orphans and the diminishment of the right of orphans and nonorphans alike to social development and their long term well-being.

In terms of a *global* response to orphans in Malawi, the crisis narrative and the corresponding emotive impulse to "save" children by removing them from perceived spaces of impoverishment must be channeled through a sober examination of the social, cultural, and economic context in which these children live. Future research should recognize the contingency of orphans' rights, and the rights of their caregivers and nonorphaned contemporaries. The conceptual isolation of orphans from their families and communities risks repeating the mistakes of the past by disrupting the social and cultural reproduction of vulnerable societies far removed from the global centers of power, whose values and practices are assumed to be the norm. At the same time, we acknowledge that local community contexts are not idyllic counterpoints to broad institutional policy responses. In our case study, communities were constrained by lack of sensitization of children's rights, by the low status of women, and by the persistent problem of food insecurity. Therefore, future research and policy efforts should be directed at identifying and grappling with these obstacles as a way forward rather than assuming a hopeless situation. Community-based orphan care still holds the best hope for holistic and sustainable care for the greatest number of OVCs in Malawi.

References

Abebe, T., & Aase, A. (2007). Children, AIDS and the Politics of Orphan Care: The Extended Family Revisited. *Social Science & Medicine, 64*, 2058–2069.

Aitken, S. C. (2001). *Geographies of Young People: The Morally Contested Spaces of Identity*. London & New York: Routledge.

Bezner Kerr, R. (2005). Food Security in Northern Malawi: Gender, Kinship Relations and Entitlements in Historical Context. *Journal of Southern African Studies, 31*, 53–74.

Bicego, G., Rutstein, S., & Johnson, K. (2003). Dimensions of the Emerging Orphan Crisis in Ssub-Saharan Africa. *Social Science & Medicine, 56*, 1235–1247.

Bray, R. (2003). *Predicting the Social Consequences of Orphanhood in South Africa* (CSSR Working Paper No. 29). Cape Town: University of Cape Town.

Case, A., Paxson, C., & Ableidinger, J. (2004). Orphans in Africa: Parental Death, Poverty, and School Enrolment. *Demography, 41*, 483–508.

Chirwa, W. C. (2002). Social Exclusion and Inclusion: Challenges to Orphan Care in Malawi. *Nordic Journal of African Studies, 11*, 93–113.

Cook, P., Ali, S., & Munthali, A. (ca. 2000). *Starting from Strengths: Community Care for Orphaned Children in Malawi.* Retrieved from www.uvic.ca/icrd/graphics/Malawi%20Report.pdf.

Ennew, J. (2005). Prisoners of Childhood: Orphans and Economic Dependency. In J. Qvortrup (Ed.), *Studies in Modern Childhood: Society, Agency, Culture* (128–146). New York: Palgrave Macmillian.

Floyd, S., Crampin, A. C., Glynn, J. R., Madise, N., Mwenebabu, M., Mnkhondia, S., Ngwira, B., Zaba, B., & Fine, P. E. M. (2007). The Social and Economic Impact of Parental HIV on Children in Northern Malawi: Retrospective Population-Based Cohort Study. *AIDS Care, 19*, 781–790.

Government of Malawi. (2008). *Malawi HIV and AIDS Monitoring and Evaluation Report 2007.* Retrieved July 22, 2008 from http://data.unaids.org/pub/Report/2008/malawi_2008_country_progress_report_en.pdf

Government of Malawi. (2005). *National Plan of Action for Orphans and Other Vulnerable Children, 2005–2009.* Lilongwe, Malawi.

Guarcello, L., Lyon, S., & Rosati, F. (2004). Orphanhood and Child Vulnerability: Malawi (Understanding Children's Work Project Working Paper Series). Retrieved July 22, 2008 from http://ideas.repec.org/p/ucw/worpap/26.html.

Henderson, P. C. (2006). South African AIDS Orphans: Examining Assumptions Around Vulnerability from the Perspective of Rural Children and Youth. *Childhood, 13*, 303–327.

Hill, M. (2006). Children's Voices on Ways of Having a Voice: Children's and Young People's Perspectives on Methods Used in Research and Consultation. *Childhood, 13*, 69–89.

Holloway, S., & Valentine, G. (Eds.), *Children's Geographies: Playing, Living, Learning.* London & New York: Routledge.

Kesby, M., Gwanzura-Ottemoller, F., & Chizororo, M. (2006). Theorising Other, "Other Childhoods": Issues Emerging from Work on HIV in Urban and Rural Zimbabwe. *Children's Geographies, 4*, 182–202.

Madhavan, S. (2004). Fosterage Patterns in the Age of AIDS: Continuity and Change. *Social Science & Medicine, 58*, 1443–1454.

Makame, V., Ani, C., & Grantham-McGregor, S. (2002). Psychological Well-Being of Orphans in Dar El Salaam, Tanzania. *Acta Paediatrica, 91*, 459–485.

Matthews, H., & Limb, M. (1999a). Defining an Agenda for the Geography of Children: Review and Prospect. *Progress in Human Geography, 23,* 61–90.

Matthews, H., & Limb, M. (1999b). Reclaiming the Street: The Discourse of Curfew. *Environment and Planning A, 31,* 1713–1730.

Meintjes, H., & Giese, S. (2006). Spinning the Epidemic: The Making of Mythologies of Orphanhood in the Context of AIDS. *Childhood, 13,* 401–430.

Monasch, R., & Boerma, J. (2004). Orphanhood and Childcare Patterns in Sub-Saharan Africa: An Analysis of National Surveys from 40 Countries. *AIDS, 18,* S55–S65.

Nyambedha, E. O., & Aagaard-Hansen, J. (2003). Changing Place, Changing Position: Orphans' Movements in a Community with High HIV/AIDS Prevalence in Western Kenya. In K. Fog Olwig & E. Gullov (Eds.), *Children's Places: Cross-Cultural Perspectives* (pp. 162–178). London & New York: Routledge.

O'Kane, C. (2008). The Development of Participatory Techniques: Facilitating Children's Views about Decisions Which Affect Them. In P. Christensen & A. James (Eds.), *Research with Children: Perspectives and Practices* (pp. 125–155). New York: Routledge.

Panter-Brick, C. (2000). Nobody's Children? A Reconsideration of Child Abandonment. In C. Panter-Brick & M. Smith (Eds.), *Abandoned Children* (pp. 1–26). Cambridge & New York: Cambridge University Press.

Peters, P. (2006). Rural Income and Poverty in a Time of Radical Change in Malawi. *Journal of Development Studies, 42,* 322–345.

Prout, A. (2005). *The Future of Childhood: Towards the Interdisciplinary Study of Children.* London & New York: RouteledgeFalmer.

Robson, E. (2001). Interviews Worth the Tears? Exploring Dilemmas of Research with Young Carers in Zimbabwe. *Ethics, Place, and Environment, 4,* 135–142.

Sharma, M. (2005). *Orphans in Malawi: Prevalence, Outcomes, and Targeting of Services.* Washington, DC: International Food Policy Institute.

UNAIDS. (2007). *AIDS Epidemic Update: December 2007.* Geneva: United Nations.

UNICEF. (2003). *Africa's Orphaned Generations.* New York: UNICEF.

UNICEF. (2006). *Africa's Orphaned and Vulnerable Generations: Children Affected by AIDS.* New York: UNICEF.

UNICEF. (2009). *The State of the World's Children: Special Edition.* New York: UNICEF.

van Blerk, L., & Ansell, N. (2006). Children's Experiences of Migration: Moving in the Wake of AIDS in Southern Africa. *Environment and Planning D: Society and Space, 24,* 449–471.

CHAPTER 11

The Fluctuations of Child Worker Support: A Study of Female Domestic Workers in Senegal

Daniel Lavan and Richard Maclure

Introduction

In Senegal, as elsewhere across sub-Saharan Africa, the population is heavily skewed toward youth; 50 percent of the country's inhabitants are under 18 years of age (UNICEF, n.d.). Equally striking is that an estimated half of all children aged 5–14 years in Senegal are involved in "productive activity"—in other words, they work. Approximately 85 percent of this activity is nonremunerated family-based domestic labor and farm work. A recent study estimated that there are more than 450,000 *economically active* children in Senegal between the ages of 5 and 14 years, with half of those being under the age of 12 years (UCW, 2010).[1] Among girls who are involved in some form of productive activity, 10.1 percent are estimated to be working as remunerated child domestic workers outside the home, a category of work that has been characterized as often qualifying under ILO Convention 182 as one of the least protected forms of child labor (e.g., Black, 2005).

Since the mid-1980s, in an effort to redress the exploitative conditions within which many children have been working, Enda Jeunesse Action (EJA), which is a unit of the national NGO, ENDA Tiers-Monde, has supported working children on the basis of the concept of *child protagonism*. Essentially this is the precept that actions must be led by children, with adults playing a supporting role and helping to strengthen children's collective agency. Among the earliest child workers targeted by EJA were female domestic workers[2] employed in urban households and recognized as being among the most vulnerable of working children. Through methods of urban outreach and animation, structured to accommodate child workers' lifestyles and objectives, EJA's mandate has been to foster and strengthen organization and solidarity among working children and youth, and to cultivate their capacity for reflection, planning, and action. EJA's overall goal has been to promote the establishment of quasi-autonomous associations of working children and youth capable of collectively asserting their status as bona fide workers, and hence improving their conditions of work and health.

By the mid-1990s, against the backdrop of the rising discourse of child rights following the promulgation of the United Nations Convention on the Rights of the Child (UNCRC), the actions of EJA and its partner organizations in West Africa led to the founding of the African Movement of Working Children and Youth. Continually mentored by EJA, this movement has expanded as a federated organization in many African countries, mainly in francophone West Africa, but in the eastern and southern regions as well (notably in Angola, Zimbabwe, and Kenya). Over the past decade and a half, this federation of child worker associations has contributed to global discussions related to child rights and children's work and has enhanced the lives of many working and under-schooled children and adolescents.

Yet there are now concerns that EJA's effectiveness in organizing youth workers and advocating for working children's rights has diminished. This applies in particular to young female domestic workers. Drawing upon a recent ethnographic study conducted in Dakar over a period of four months (2008–2009), we present evidence that working and living conditions for domestic workers have not significantly improved over the past decade, and that the groups and associations facilitated by EJA have recently experienced a marked loss of organizational cohesion and vigor. We trace this decline in collective activity to EJA's perceptible shift away from the concerted grassroots action which has been the basis of its earlier support of child workers' rights. While we argue that this change in focus and in the *modus operandi* of EJA is partly rooted in the dynamics of international aid, we also point to what we consider are fundamental flaws in the assumption underlying EJA's reliance on child protagonism as an operational approach to intervention.

To contextualize this discussion we begin with a review of the evolving nature and context of child work in Senegal. Specifically we focus on the working and living conditions of female domestic workers, which served as the impetus underlying EJA's formation of associations designed to foster solidarity and collective action among these young women.

The Advent of Urban Child Work in Senegal

Nearly all economically active Senegalese children living in urban areas work informally, either in independent petty enterprises, or, as in the case of domestic workers, in employment relationships that are not legally regulated or protected. As in most developing countries, the informal sector in Senegal is the country's foremost provider of employment, goods, and services. Historically, of course, in agrarian economies children have worked in the fields and participated in household labor alongside their parents. Yet children's work in urban settings is altogether different. As early as 1981, Morice (1981) observed that children's work in the urban centers of Senegal could not be regarded as reflecting the survival of an agrarian past, but was rather rooted in processes of rural pauperization that had come about through a combination of persistent drought, structural adjustment policies, and the absence of a coherent national agricultural policy. The demographic impact of this rural demise has been an ever-expanding rate of rural–urban migration and the subsequent emergence of a massive pool of unskilled labor and the imperative to produce and consume at the lowest possible price, thus minimizing the value of labor (Morice, 1981). In a globalized world economy, debtor countries with minimal regulatory controls such as Senegal provide contexts for paternalistic production and reproductions systems that have remained functional and sustainable only with ever-intensifying exploitation of children's work (Cabanes, 2000; Cunningham & Stromquist, 2005; Nieuwenhuys, 1994).

A further factor that has fostered an expansion of urban children's work in Senegal has been the relative stagnation of the country's formal education system. The quality of primary schooling is generally poor, and secondary school placements are nowhere near adequate to accommodate appropriate age groups. Consequently, primary school completion rates are low, illiteracy levels are high, and more than half of all Senegalese children aged 5–14 years are not enrolled in the school system (United Nations Educational, Scientific and Cultural Organization [UNESCO], 2010). Moreover, despite the vast numbers of young people out of school, the government devotes only a miniscule proportion of its educational budget to nonformal education (African Economic Outlook [AEO], 2010). Consequently, with a weak education system and limited occupational opportunities in rural areas, children and adolescents have increasingly gravitated to cities in search of informal sector jobs. For most of these young people, if work is to be found at all, it lies in petty informal enterprises and domestic work (Diallo, 2008; Dimé, 2007).

Female Domestic Workers in Senegal: The Historical Backdrop

Similar to the historical phenomenon of children's work in agrarian societies, the movement of female labor among households to assist with domestic tasks has long existed among extended families in Senegal, and has generally been construed as a process of socialization for purposes of preparing girls for their future roles as homemakers.[3] In traditional rural contexts, girls working as domestic help in households other than their own generally enjoyed the right of recourse in cases of conflict, thus attenuating any exploitative tendencies (Jacquemin, 2006; 2009). Yet as with other forms of child labor, growing impoverishment has compelled many rural families in Senegal to abandon this form of intrafamilial socialization in favor of the more pecuniary strategy of sending girls to work in urban households for modest pay (Coalition Nationale des Associations et ONG en Faveur de l'Enfance au Sénégal [CONAFE-Senegal], 2006).

This option has nonetheless proved to be attractive for many rural girls, especially those who were faced with little or no local opportunities for education and training, or for remunerative rural work. The appeal of the assumed marvels of Dakar, Senegal's capital (*les merveilles de Dakar*) and of other urban centers—that is, the commodities, fashions, and independent urban lifestyles that tend to figure in the stories of those who have returned from towns and cities to their home villages—often became intermingled with girls' practical desire to contribute to family revenue and to prepare for their own futures as wives and mothers. As early as the 1980s, jobs for female domestic workers were plentiful. Even modest urban households generally had the means to hire girls for basic domestic chores. In more affluent households, or in homes where female members were themselves working or pursuing their education, it was not unusual to find two or three domestic workers sharing the tasks of childcare, cleaning, and cooking. Although in earlier years most of these girls had no formal schooling, by the mid-1990s it had become more common for some to have attended several years of primary school before leaving home in search of work (Diaw et al., 1996).

Yet despite the attraction of obtaining independent income, female domestic working conditions were generally far from ideal. Two early studies of female domestic workers revealed that despite national legislation codifying the rights and obligations related to domestic employment, most employers were either ignorant of, or indifferent to, labor legislation, and rarely did they bother to hire domestic workers on the basis of written contracts (Diawet al., 1996; Ndiaye-Kane, 1985).[4] Verbal contractual agreements were the norm, and not surprisingly allotted tasks, hours of work, and regular payment of mutually determined salaries were often not respected. Although procurement of a paid job was clearly the goal of most domestic workers, complaints about their treatment as employees were common. These centered on issues such as lack of respect, excessive workloads, nonpayment of salaries, risks of assault and sexual abuse, unwarranted mistrust and accusations of theft, and no time off for illness or for one day of rest per week. Girls who protested such conditions were often threatened with dismissal, and where this occurred, salary arrears were typically forfeited (Diaw et al., 1996, p. 26). In view of these working conditions and the precariousness of employment relations, the turnover rate among domestic workers was relatively high (Diaw et al., 1996).

Living conditions for many female domestic workers were likewise difficult, although these often varied according to different working circumstances. Girls who lived in the homes of their employers tended to have access to basic amenities such as running water, electricity, and more nutritious food, and they were spared a daily commute to and from their places of work. Yet there were disadvantages in living with employers, notably the susceptibility of being pressed into longer hours of service, and prolonged isolation from relatives and friends.

Girls who did not live with their employers frequently lived together in groups based on common village or ethnic origins. Typically 8–15 girls (sometimes more) would share rented quarters that often lacked electricity and fresh water (Diaw et al., 1996). When not engaged in their regular employment, some girls commonly undertook other types of revenue-generating activity such as sewing, hairdressing, embroidery, millet grinding, or small commercein order to add to their earnings from domestic household work. Sometimes the youngest among them would provide infant and childcare for the older domestic workers. Since medical expenses were very rarely covered by employers, and were generally beyond the means of most low-paid domestic workers, the girls tended to rely on wider ethnic solidarity networks for the cost of medical treatment or other forms of urgent expenditure (Diaw et al.,

1996, pp. 20–24). In the 1980s, these wider supportive urban networks of relatives or individuals sharing common community or ethnic origins were relatively strong and offered significant assistance for groups of girls first arriving in the city.

Enda Jeunesse Action and "Child Protagonism": Support for Child Domestic Workers

In 1985, in response to the growing numbers of vulnerable out-of-school Senegalese children drifting into potentially exploitative informal work in urban streets and households, EJA was established as a new unit within ENDA Tiers-Monde. Building on a development approach first pioneered by ENDA in the early 1970s that focused on empowering marginalized groups through participatory reflection, capacity building, and collective grassroots action, EJA adopted the concept of "child protagonism" as a basis for assisting working and street children. Rejecting the internationally predominant view that all forms of child labor were pernicious and hence should be abolished, EJA espoused a more nuanced approach rooted in their experience-based conviction that children are capable of understanding the options available to them, and thus have the *right to choose* to be engaged in informal work activity as a rational survival strategy for themselves and their families. Accordingly, EJA adopted a mandate of facilitating reflections among working children as a basis for mobilizing to improve their working conditions and increase their earnings. According to this child protagonist approach, the working child or the street child "must be the subject and not the object of any program or project. He must play the leading role in the entire process, from start to finish" (Enda Jeunesse Action [EJA], 1985). In line with this logic, EJA eschewed common charitable and paternalistic aims of many NGOs and state agencies to integrate street and working children into institutional environments, notably schooling and nuclear family situations, that were deemed to be "normal" for children and adolescents (Terenzio, 1992).

In many respects, established as it was in the mid-1980s, EJA was ahead of its time as a children's development assistance program. By seizing upon the notion of working children as *social actors*, which was essentially an extension of the conventional roles of children within many traditional family and kin-based production systems, EJA effectively rebuffed the dominant Western "folk view" of childhood as merely a "a kind of rehearsal for adult life" (Schildkrout, 1981). Within a decade, EJA's perspective of children as *subjects* rather than *objects* of development assistance had not only been implicitly endorsed in Western scholarship, as exemplified by the "new paradigm for the sociology of childhood" (Prout & James, 1997), but it was also reinforced by the nearly universal affirmation of the 1989 UN Convention of the Rights of the Child. Increasingly, mainstream development discourse came to accept the idea of children, particularly young adolescents, as capable of exercising agency in constructive and beneficial ways. Concurrently, and largely drawing upon these insights, a growing faction of development actors also came to align itself with EJA's view that support for working children should focus on eliminating the harmful aspects of children's work rather than on removing children entirely from work that might be beneficial to them when judged holistically and contextually.

EJA's strong thesis of child protagonism was initially held to be consistent with a reliance on adult-directed programs of outreach and education aiming to foster the collective capacity to promote and defend their own basic rights (Terenzio, 1992). In adherence to this child protagonist approach, EJA devoted considerable attention to the training of EJA staff, particularly the street-level animators who connected with child workers. EJA reports produced in the early to mid-1980s convey a rich understanding of how the attainment of even modest goals with marginalized working children required strong capacities of reflection, patience, and dedication to the almost paradoxical ideal of directing young people into their own authentic leadership role.

EJA and Support for Young Female Domestic Workers

From its inception in 1985, EJA worked with various categories of informal child workers, both female and male, including shoeshine boys, market porters, and itinerant road sellers. However, young female domestic workers quickly became the most important target group of EJA's support. Consistent with its child protagonist approach, EJA strove to facilitate a sequence of critical reflection and dialogue among domestic workers in Dakar neighborhoods, with subsequent support for collective actions based on objectives set by the domestic workers themselves. Such objectives tended to center on lobbying employers for job security and more hours and days of rest, and on collectively seeking opportunities for literacy and training, and development initiatives in their home villages (Diaw et al., 1996).

In response to their ambitions for literacy and manual skills acquisition, between 1986 and 1994 EJA established educational spaces for neighborhood groups of domestic workers. There they were able to attend classes in basic literacy and French, and in various marketable skills such as hairdressing, knitting, crocheting, and dressmaking. In addition, EJA regularly organized discussion sessions with these working girls on issues such as family planning, hygiene, childcare, and domestic economy. As the number of EJA-supported groups of domestic workers and their centers expanded in the early 1990s, other unemployed girls having no access to education also began to attend the literacy and skills-training courses, as did young adult women who worked in trades such as laundry and grain pounding (Diaw et al., 1996).

In 1994, EJA-supported domestic workers participated in the creation of the Dakar Association of Working Children and Youth. To demonstrate the significance of national and regional solidarity among working children, Workers Day demonstrations were organized by associations in several cities of Senegal and in other regions where EJA had established a network of partner organizations. In 1995 various groups of domestic workers marched in the annual Dakar May Day parade, carrying signs with slogans such as *Nit du masin* (Wolof for "Human beings are not machines"), some of the girls marched alongside their own employers

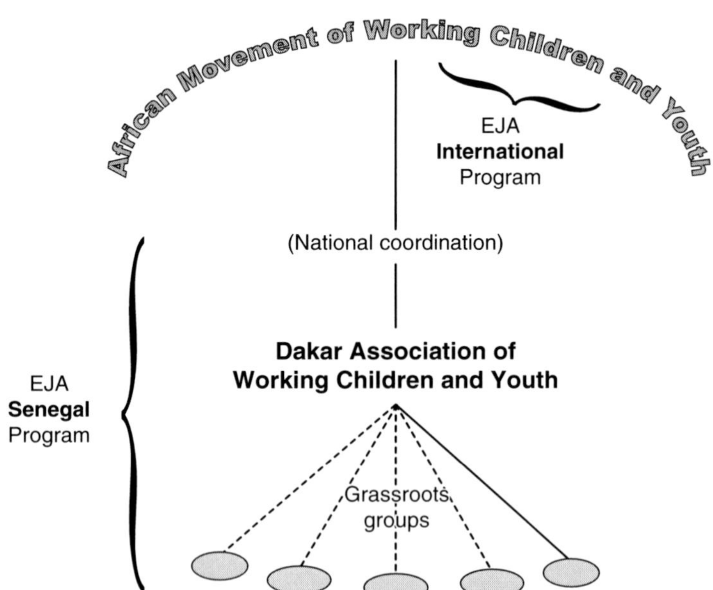

Figure 11.1 Organizational structure of the African movement of working children and youth (showing areas of support from two EJA program offices).

who themselves were union members in formal sector employment (EJA, 1995). From EJA's perspective, this was something of a breakthrough—a symbol of working children's empowerment combined with public recognition of their legitimate status as workers with rights. This May Day march provided the impetus for the creation, shortly thereafter, of a more permanent solidarity network of working children's organizations, the African Movement of Working Children and Youth.

Four years later a UNESCO report on EJA initiatives with children and adolescents in the informal economy asserted that there were approximately 800 working children affiliated to the grassroots groups of the Dakar Association of Working Children and Youth, and that these groups had achieved a number of modest goals: "[They have] set up mutual health insurance groups for common diseases financed through membership fees. Certain groups have also managed to obtain discounts for medications and consultations at health posts. Reading and writing is also an achievement for all of them" (de Ravignan, 1998, p. 24). The study also attributed to a female domestic worker the general claim that there had been an improvement in relations with employers of domestic workers. The author of the study cautioned, however, that more needed to be done to formalize and guarantee contractual arrangements for girls working as household help (de Ravignan, 1998).

A broad sense of grassroots collegiality also underlay EJA support for young female domestic workers. Manual skills trainers and literacy teachers with group animation skills continued to be hired and trained to work with groups of domestic workers. This connection with EJA helped to ensure that the domestic workers gained a sense of safety in the workplace and solidarity with one another. For example, a 1999 newspaper report recounted a series of activities involving domestic workers and EJA animators that included trips to the historical island of Gorée[5] and to the park and zoo in Hann[6] (Fall, 1999). Likewise, during the course of fieldwork for this study, a former EJA animator who had worked with groups of domestic workers in Dakar recollected how such activities and connections contributed to feelings of solidarity and self-esteem among the girls, and to an increase in their capacity for self-expression. As she explained (as translated from the French),

> The strength was [in] communication, the ability to say: "I want this" or "I don't want that." This was already something—for the child and adolescent workers . . . to express themselves. I really think that was strong [significant]. Because if one considers that in the context of our culture and their [young] age—such oral expression—for children to

> be able to say what they think without fear—I think that is strength [accomplishment].

The Limitations of Support for Child Domestic Workers

Despite indications of progress, the sustainability of associations of young workers, and of the local groups to which individual workers were affiliated, was never assured. An abiding question, for example, was whether domestic workers could maintain organizational activity and group solidarity without sustained EJA support.[7] Reports of early EJA experiences acknowledged the challenge in adopting a collective approach designed to foster solidarity among as many working children as possible while accommodating extensive differences in age, gender, type of work, hours of work, and the discrete goals and interests of child workers (Coly, 1999; EJA, 1985). As one EJA animator in the late 1990s observed, in the event that young people's affiliation to EJA-sponsored groups and to the broader Association of Working Children and Youth did not result in additional income-generating activities, or enable them to progress financially, many of these young people would begin to lose interest in the burgeoning child worker movement (de Ravignan, 1998). While EJA discourse periodically acknowledged the complex and evolving distinctions between *leading* a working children's social movement and *supporting* such a movement (e.g., Save the Children, 2002; Terenzio, 1992), in hindsight its child protagonist approach appears not to have satisfactorily addressed deeply rooted norms and structures of the adult world and the conventions of adult authority.

Such inherent tensions have come to a head in recent years, and this has had the effect of diminishing the earlier momentum of child worker organization and action in Dakar and elsewhere in Senegal. Erstwhile markers of progress pertaining to child worker rights have faded, and on the whole the conditions of working children, notably young females, have not substantially improved since the late 1990s. As outlined in a recent EJA document (translated from the French):

> Their living conditions are worse because they do not eat enough and they are poorly housed. Some of these girls, such as domestic workers . . . are at risk of unwanted pregnancy because of the advances of their (male) employers or others who are closely connected to their employers. When this happens the girls are usually dismissed from their jobs, and this often creates problems with their families who are generally conservative in outlook. Consequently the girls find themselves in

> difficult circumstances, without jobs and with loss of family ties. (EJA & Mouvement Africain Enfants Jeunes Travailleurs [MAEJT], 2006)

In recent years as well the Senegalese media have routinely presented *exposés* of the exploitation and poor working conditions of urban children. Newspaper reports of domestic workers under the age of 15 years (a contravention of Senegal's Labour Code), and of instances of employer maltreatment, are commonplace (e.g., Alissoutin, 2006; Ndiaye, 2010). Such anecdotal accounts were reinforced by a joint government / ILO survey of child work, which reported that there were over 21,000 child domestics in Dakar and that in Senegal child domestics worked an average of 50.6 hours per week (L'Agence Nationale de la Statistique et de la Démographie [ANSD] & Bureau International du Travail (BIT)/ Programme International pour l'Abolition du Travail des Enfants [IPEC], 2007). Similarly, an NGO study of children's working conditions in 2006 summarized the problems confronting many child domestic workers as follows: very young ages (some household domestics as young as six years); sexual harassment, rape, and unwanted pregnancies; denial of opportunities for education or training; false accusations of theft; lack of medical coverage; no days of rest or paid holidays (CONAFE-Sénégal, 2006). The same study indicated what has clearly been a loss of momentum in the advancement of the rights and working conditions of children in Senegal, particularly those of young female domestic workers. While observing that each year groups of domestic workers participate in May Day celebrations and in the National Day of the African Child, the study concluded in an ironic and understated manner that "*despite this organizational beginning*... numerous obstacles remain" (CONAFE-Sénégal, 2006, p.22; as translated from the French, italics added). The irony lies in the fact that the "beginning" occurred approximately 20 years previous to this study, and that long sought objectives, such as the right to universally applied job contracts between employers and child employees, remain unattained.

Female Domestic Workers: Evidence from the Field[8]

Qualitative fieldwork for this study focused on the current conditions of female domestic workers in Dakar and the activities of domestic workers' associations under the auspices of EJA and donor-sponsored support. Undertaken in Dakar from early November 2008 through to the end of February 2009, field research primarily involved observations and informal interviewing on a regular basis with two grassroots groups of child domestic workers. A key component of fieldwork consisted of six weeks' observation of literacy training, held twice weekly for two groups of domestic workers. Besides the training activities, the sessions also offered opportunities for the girls to speak about their working conditions and social environments, and hence to gain a sense of solidarity and confidence in having a collective voice. These discussion sessions thereby enabled us to gain insights into the lives of these domestic workers.[9] Between the two groups, we interacted with approximately 40 female domestic workers over the course of 35 meetings. In addition, we benefited from the knowledge of the literacy teachers who had regularly interacted with over 80 domestic workers during the previous two years.

Somewhat less systematically, research fieldwork also involved observations of meetings and activities, and informal interviewing with the following: a) other groups of youth workers who were affiliated with the Dakar Association of Working Children and Youth; b) current and former EJA staff, animators, and literacy teachers; and c) representatives of several child assistance NGOs in Dakar. Once it became clear that hopes for improvements in the conditions and the organization of female domestic workers had faded, the focus of our investigation turned to exploring the factors that have resulted in this loss of momentum.

Present Conditions of Female Domestic Workers

As described above, regular visits over the course of fieldwork to two neighborhood groups of domestic workers, facilitated by two experienced literacy teachers, allowed us to gain insights into the lives of these girls and young women. Most of these domestic workers indicated that they had had either no formal schooling at all, or just a few years of primary school education, which was consistent with their minimal competence in French literacy and conversation, even among the oldest (those over 18 years). Most of these domestic workers were living together in cramped quarters in mixed-age groups of up to 10 girls. Several others were living in temporary encampments on the street with their mothers or other female relatives. A few of the domestic workers were residing in their employers' houses, but the relative comfort of such living conditions was outweighed by increased employer scrutiny, long working hours, and risks of harassment from the household male members, especially during evening hours.

Despite such varied living conditions, none of these domestic workers regarded their current employment status as secure. None had written contracts, and none of them were familiar with national legislation pertaining to domestic employment. When asked to recount personal experiences that had marked their working lives, most spoke about physical and verbal abuse, threats and intimidation, and disputes over salary arrears. One described how, at the culmination of a long salary dispute, "My boss's mother slapped me in front of everyone, and then many piled on blows." Another recounted how her employer had asked her to do laundry at 11:00 pm as she was just finishing bathing. "When I said, 'No, I've just taken my bath', she said I was being insolent and ungrateful after all that was provided for me and that I had no dignity because I spent week nights in the house. I became angry and asked to be paid out. My employer refused, but eventually one of her sons convinced her to. I walked home at midnight with all of my bags." Several of the girls felt that visits to home villages could easily lead to dismissal.

A number of girls recounted how they had been pushed at an early age into domestic work in the city, and expressed fear that this would be the only employment they would ever have. In hopes of eventually shifting into a different line of work, several explained that they had enrolled in EJA-sponsored classes in order to acquire basic skills such as reading, writing, and arithmetic, and occupational skills such as weaving, beading, and crochet. Our observations of group activities and dynamics indicated, however, that the most meaningful group function for the domestic workers was simply to meet informally, and to chat and commiserate with one another. These field insights were confirmed by the literacy teachers whom we interviewed.

Understanding the Declining Collective Engagement of Child Domestic Workers

During the course of fieldwork it also became clear that coinciding with the ongoing difficulties confronting female domestic workers in Dakar, there had been a general decline in membership in the EJA-sponsored working children's groups and increasingly sporadic attendance at scheduled meetings.[10] In fact, in 2008 alone, more than 10 of the neighborhood groups of domestic workers had become inactive and thus were no longer considered as part of the Dakar Association of Working Children and Youth. These included several of the groups that had existed since the early 1990s and that had participated in the founding of the African Movement of Working Children and Youth. Underlying this decline was the interplay of three significant factors:

1. Breakdown of the Core Educational Model

In recent years, numerous difficulties with EJA's basic education for child workers, and particularly for female domestic workers, has led to criticisms and doubts about the viability of its educational program. EJA literacy teachers have long pointed out the deep-seated problems associated with irregular child and youth worker attendance at scheduled classes, often due to the demands of their employment. Literacy teachers themselves have become dispirited, complaining about very low remuneration and lack of administrative supervision and support. By way of contrast, however, citing a recent European-funded program framework with a binding target to provide literacy training to 600 working children in Dakar, EJA administrators espouse a conviction that effective education can be extended to child and youth workers if sufficient funds are available to ensure adequate pedagogical space and material, and payment of literacy instructors.

Yet during research fieldwork, it was clear that achieving both quantity and quality objectives would require a much more fundamental reconception of EJA's educational program. Several EJA field staff expressed doubts that resources of the new program would be sufficient in attracting more working youth, or in ensuring better quality instruction. Indeed, our own field observations indicated that literacy teaching tends to be tediously didactic. Despite offering a venue for female domestic workers to gather together and talk about their daily lives and the challenges that they face, there was no evidence of a tangible connection between literacy acquisition and larger goals of collective action aimed at improving their working conditions. In fact, in keeping with a rising emphasis on attaining measurable medium term learning outcomes, there is little likelihood of a "new and improved" educational program attracting groups of female domestic workers in the future. As EJA has acknowledged, there has always been a high turnover among domestic worker group members, often as high as 80 percent in some groups.[11] Since EJA has no requirement or incentive to continue supporting neighborhood groups of workers with whom it has historically been engaged, its educational outreach has shifted to worker populations that are potentially easier to organize than female domestic workers.

A further consideration with regard to EJA support for child worker education is the current shift of EJA resources toward support for the expanding population of Senegalese *talibés* (Koranic pupils forced to beg in the streets). With the rising international profile of this highly visible and clearly exploited group of children in Dakar, EJA's European donors have indicated a strong preference for directing assistance towards the *talibés* of Senegal. This is a significant factor for EJA program activity which has come to rely on substantial external donor funding. With a shift of resources away from child worker education and training in favor of more extension work directed at *talibés*, an undoubtedly needy group of children, regular gatherings of child workers has eroded.

2. Program Criteria for Direct Group Support: Age and Working Status

With its scope of targeted intervention expanding in response to international donor interest, at the time of research fieldwork EJA announced that henceforth its direct support could be offered only to groups in which at least two-thirds of the members were 17 years or younger, and in which most were *economically active*, rather than involved only in productive activities in their own households.[12] This created a twofold difficulty for the neighborhood groups of domestic workers, first because of the large numbers of nonworking girls who had joined the groups, and second because approximately half of the domestic workers who attended the meetings of the neighborhood domestic worker groups were estimated to be over 18 years. In an effort to enrol more young female domestic workers, EJA accordingly undertook a recruitment drive. Through subsequent postresearch fieldwork correspondence, we learned that while there was some initial success in domestic worker recruitment, under-18 attendance in EJA-sponsored meetings of domestic workers had faltered, and hence there was little hope of reviving literacy and skills training for these young women.

Commenting on the conditionalities regarding "child" group membership, one domestic worker in her 30s who had regularly attended neighborhood group literacy and skills classes strongly criticized the age requirement (two-thirds under the age of 18) as a basis for group legitimacy and continued EJA subsidization of literacy classes and skills training. In her view, the age distinction between "child" domestic workers and many female domestic workers was artificial, and hence an unjustifiable criterion for group membership. Her viewpoint was reiterated by another over-18 member who said that the imposition of an under-18 limit was a discriminatory rule, and that all female domestic workers should be given an opportunity to learn literacy and other skills regardless of their age. Both of these comments, articulated during a meeting, elicited applause from all other domestic workers in attendance, both young and over 18 years in age.

At the time we conducted research fieldwork, EJA was still far from meeting its program target of enrolling hundreds of under 18-year-old child workers for its externally funded literacy classes, regardless of the fact that there is an abundance of working girls and boys in surrounding streets and markets.

3. Questions about Child Protagonism

The EJA national program office has acknowledged that despite its intentions of cultivating self-directed management among the neighborhood groups of child and youth workers that it has helped to form over the years, and despite its encouragement of support for neighborhood groups from the Dakar-based Association of Working Children and Youth, organized groups of working children have declined in the past few years. This has raised questions about the viability of child and youth group capacity building. As discussed above, the high turnover in group membership among young female domestic workers was regarded as a serious obstacle to the development of group autonomy and hence group legitimacy.

When the decline of EJA-sponsored groups of child domestic workers was discussed at a national meeting in November, 2008, representatives of female domestic workers complained of their inability to contribute even 1000 CFA (slightly less than US$2) monthly toward compensating the groups' teachers.[13] On this occasion, however, an EJA program officer who had limited direct familiarity with neighborhood groups' activities and challenges stressed the distinction between *actors* and mere *beneficiaries,* and forcefully argued that the solution lay in reinvigorating the ideal of child protagonism. From his perspective, child workers who had benefited from EJA support had become too dependent on external support. He especially criticized the Dakar-based Association of Working Children and Youth for having failed to actively recruit a new generation of younger workers, thereby reinvigorating what risked becoming a moribund child worker movement. Although articulated as a critique in a public forum, this interjection accorded with a growing concern that children and adolescents were either unable or unwilling to assume collective autonomy for group activity. Our own observations confirmed this impasse, particularly among female domestic workers for whom interest in collective activity stemmed largely from the informal nature of the gatherings and the training activities that were sponsored by EJA. Beyond this, however, domestic workers demonstrated little interest in assuming voluntary responsibilities for autonomous group development and longevity. As one of the experienced literacy teachers suggested, many child domestic workers, migrating as they have from different rural areas and ethnic communities, have little interest and confidence in being leaders—protagonists—of a child-led collective social action.

Of the two neighborhood groups of domestic workers that we visited regularly, only one had even nominal officers associated with the African Movement of Working Children and Youth, and very few of these workers were apprised of the nominal structure and vision of a child workers movement. Indicative of how little had changed within the past decade, neither of the neighborhood groups had set up cooperative health insurance schemes or had negotiated discounts at health service centers, two goals that de Ravignan's 1998 report had indicated was a burgeoning accomplishment of children's working groups. In effect, the ideal of child protagonism has not been realized as an effective strategy for enhancing the rights of female domestic workers in Senegal.

Conclusion: Child Protagonism and the Dynamics of External Aid: Conflicting Agendas

At the time of research fieldwork it was clear that EJA's adoption of child protagonism as an operational approach to child workers rights had met with limited success. In particular, in relation to the status of young female domestic workers in Senegal, a key underlying weakness of this approach has been the inability to adapt it to the situation of domestic workers and to the nature of the groups that they tend to form. Not only do their working conditions heavily constrain their individual ability to participate in associational activities, but it has proven unfeasible to instil permanent organizational capacity in groups whose most senior members typically return permanently to their home villages rather than remaining in urban areas and are, therefore, unable to transfer the organizational competence and memory to their juniors. Skills and capacities for acting independently from adult involvement are not easily retained among groups of children whose engagement is not assured for long periods of time.

Consistent with many mainstream development initiatives, the goal of the child protagonist approach has not only been to enhance the immediate conditions of children, but also to strengthen their capacity so that they themselves are capable of generating resources to sustain their own group activities, most centrally by paying for the services of their teachers and trainers. Yet the neighborhood groups of domestic workers that we encountered in Senegal had no adequate means to solicit or generate such resources on a collective basis, and most of the adherents to these groups were either unable or unwilling to make personal contributions to cover the honoraria of the teachers and trainers. This then led to an awkward patron-client relation that stemmed from EJA's intial role as an external catalyst of change. It is, in fact, a commonplace conundrum that arises from many such externally initiated interventions. From the beneficiaries' perspective, the main attraction lies in the services and training that are provided to them, and the potential opportunities from which they may benefit. Accordingly, when the external resources begin to diminish, or when pressures are brought to bear on the beneficiaries to contribute more of their own resources for the same externally initiated services, interest in group activity may easily wane. As one EJA animator candidly admitted, suggesting sentiments of aid recipients, "If I am in a group and I don't see any benefits in that group, I think I have to leave."

There is nonetheless a risk in employing the patron-client dichotomy too crudely. EJA did not conceive of education as a service to be received passively by working children as a "benefit." Indeed, it was generally understood that a working child who commits herself to, and persists, in a challenging educational course is already *acting* courageously. If she overcomes her inhibitions, channels her remaining daily energy towards the attainment of specific educational goals, and is engaged in collective learning activities with her peers in solidarity, she is already an agent and beneficiary of her own actions.

The issue of resources required to sustain local activity and social support is nonetheless critical, and clearly there is something to be said for diminishing the dependency of beneficiary groups on external aid. Yet in view of the paucity of resources available to many working children, particularly to female domestic workers, and the diversity of constraints and challenges confronting indigent individuals who are struggling to survive, it is often a moot point as to whether poorly paid young workers—or local people in general—are capable of sustaining mobilization and grassroots actions for collective advancement. This is particularly so among the protagonists of the groups considered in this study—the young female household workers and their literacy and manual skills teachers, none of whom had either the personal resources or the necessary contacts to autonomously sustain the activities of the neighborhood associations they had formed. As one youth respondent queried rhetorically, "[For youth]to find sponsors [for education and training centers] would be very, very difficult [for us]. [But] ENDA [staff] know the [donor] partners. Why don't [they] talk to [the partners] and say we want you to help this [youth workers] group?" Viewed from this perspective of child workers and their relatively low-paid literacy teachers alike, the notion of *autonomisation* (group self direction) was tantamount to being cast adrift by EJA. As another former animator stated, "It's fine to *autonomise* them, but it's also necessary to accompany [support] them" (translated from the French).

A second emerging factor in the overall decline of the neighborhood groups of female domestics that we observed is that the original vigor of grassroots solidarity and modestly remunerated activism on behalf of child domestic workers has also diminished. Increasingly, a nominal monthly stipend is insufficient to retain the caliber of individuals who formerly served as qualified literacy trainers. To a large extent this is because the sense of mission and grassroots *militantisme* embraced by EJA field staff during the early years of their work with child domestic workers has been progressively displaced by ambitions of more secure and lucrative employment. Many of the original literacy trainers have left EJA, and those who remain or who have been recently hired no longer retain a high professional morale. Partly in response to this situation, EJA attempted to reinvigorate its animator training program so as to strengthen basic education for child workers. Yet there has been a decided divergence of agenda, and hence a gap in communication, between field staff who are connected with working children and more office-bound EJA staff who tend to be more preoccupied with the requirements and periodical shifting interests of international donors.

Overall, there has been very little reflection on how the prevailing discourse of the international aid industry, which heavily influences national and local development policies and programs, has had an impact on aid effectiveness among local beneficiaries and the organic workings of neighborhood groups such as those of female domestic workers. One long-term effect of inattention to such interactions is the intensifying difficulty in reconciling the prioritization of *child* domestic workers as a relatively homogeneous category of working girls, and the evolving reconfiguration of groups of neighborhood girls and women, for example, those who work as household servants regardless of age (ranging in our study from 11 to 35 years), and those who are unemployed, but are keen to benefit from possible learning opportunities. EJA's original mandate explicitly included "youth," as its title reminds us ("Jeunesse"), but with the formal emergence of the African Movement of Working Children and Youth it became increasingly embedded in international networks of *child*-centered activity, *child* rights, and nongovernmental as well as governmental *child* protection organizations, all concerning themselves with children as defined in the UNCRC (individuals who are categorized as 18 years old and under). As a result, EJA did not explore the possibility of supporting an emerging network of local *women* (preteen, teen, and adult) in a manner that might effectively heed local realities and needs. Under increasing pressure to isolate *child workers* (under strict UNCRC and ILO definitions) as program beneficiaries, from the perspective of EJA the "creeping" inclusion of non-economically active girls and older domestic servants has emerged as a *problem* that requires an organizational policy adjustment reasserting the singular focus on assisting under-18 children. Unfortunately, what has been overlooked in this readjustment process is the strengthening of local female solidarity that cuts across externally defined boundaries of age and employment status.

The influence of shifting donor priorities as exemplified by increased attention to the plight of *talibés* as opposed to the circumstances of child workers, coupled with current international emphasis on *child-centered* development, are consistent with a broader pattern of development discourse that has affected the priorities and program decisions of EJA and other NGOs. With civil society in Senegal still relatively weak, international donors have emerged as key actors in advocating the cause of child rights and in setting the agenda of child development assistance. Foreign aid now accounts for an estimated 23 percent of government spending (US$361.0 million in 2007 for operating costs and capital investments), much of it directed toward social services. In response to the donor emphasis on "partnership," national NGOs have grown in stature as civil society actors in Senegal. Yet in doing so they have come to rely on donor largesse and are thus compelled to accommodate donor conditions, reporting requirements, and policy directions. As many critics have observed, this has tended to diminish the sensitivity and responsiveness of national NGOs to shifting local circumstances and to the voices and needs of intended beneficiaries (Bebbington, 2004; Ebrahim, 2003; Ogunseye, 1997). In line with this trend, EJA staff themselves have vehemently complained about donor demands for quantitative information, and the way that such demands have distracted organizational attention from working children's associations, and diverted personnel and resources away from direct engagement with children and adolescents.

On the other hand, we are cautious about attributing too much weight to EJA's shifting relationship with female domestic workers and other child worker groups. As we discerned in the research outlined in this chapter, an exaggerated faith in the ideal of child protagonism remains at the core of EJA's strategic approach. There continues to be an assumption that established neighborhood groups of working children should strive to function autonomously, and that the wider Associations of Working Children and Youth should be able to independently support neighborhood groups of working youth and to develop the capacity of newly formed groups. Building upon this assumption, EJA has transferred its attention to more centralized levels of the regional African Movement of Working Children and Youth, confident that capacity building can be effectively cascaded downward to the neighborhood group level by child and youth delegates. Yet reliance on volunteer children and youth to assume autonomous responsibility as child protagonists for local training and other neighborhood group activities has proven tenuous at best. As one advocate of the African Movement of Working Children and Youth has acknowledged, the movement has been "a bit top-heavy... [and] top driven, and as a result, there isn't much happening at the grassroots level... There is a very strong regional or even pan-African body, but a very weak grassroots organization. And it should be the other way around in my opinion." In our view, the strengthening of grassroots organizations, and of neighborhood groups of working children and adolescents such as female domestic workers, requires *ongoing* support, mutual interaction, and mutual flexibility between local protagonists and those outside agencies that strive to assist them.

In broader terms, in seeking to account for the tenuous sustainability of the neighborhood groups of domestic workers that we have described in this chapter, and the overall lack of significant improvements in their livelihoods, it is important to keep in mind that NGO efforts to achieve stable and permanent advances in the rights of working children in Senegal are severely constrained by broader structural obstacles. Senegal's political economy is extraordinarily weak. In 2007 it ranked 166th out of 182 in the UN's Human Development Index, and in 2008 its unemployment rate was estimated at 48 percent, exceeded by only 9 other countries. In this context of profound structural weakness, family survival often depends on children working in jobs where there is little leverage over employment conditions. In this economic environment, with its overlay of complex cultural and social factors, the strategies for realizing the best interests of children are by no means self-evident. EJA's chosen strategy of support to child domestic workers can be credited, at the very least, with enriching the lives of hundreds of these children over the years by reducing their isolation, reinforcing a sense of solidarity, and contributing to their learning. That this support has not developed into collective associations that are durable, nor systematically improved the overall conditions of child domestic workers in Dakar, illustrates not only the limits of child protagonism as a conceptual strategy, but also the limits of adult-directed interventions.

On a more positive note, however, the experiences described in this chapter also point to the possibilities of progress when adults and children, and local and "nonlocal" people, are able to work together. We believe that improvements in the conditions of female domestic workers will require a more concerted, cooperative, and comprehensive strategy of intervention, important elements of which have been suggested, and in some cases already put into practice, by a range of concerned actors. More systematic research, both in villages and in urban centers, is necessary to establish accurate baseline data regarding the numbers and age distribution of girls migrating to cities for domestic work and returning home later on. This would allow for much more accurate monitoring of the migration of female domestic workers rather than reliance on impressionistic and anecdotal reports. It is also necessary to ascertain both the real numbers and the proportion of young female domestics who have no opportunity to participate in any form of organized educational or leisure activity, or to otherwise benefit from organized support.

As we have shown in this chapter, creating a framework in which to sustainably provide such activities and services for domestic workers has been a key challenge for EJA, particularly when subject to the shifting demands of donors. The provision of "second chance" basic education and job training must, therefore, be built upon an ever more solid basis of permanent state-NGO cooperation, with the state (assisted by international donors) allocating increased resources for the nonformal education of child workers, and NGOs assisting in the delivery and evaluation of educational and training interventions. It is here that EJA's early methods of intensive animation and support for domestic workers can offer important lessons. Such adapted education and training approaches surely have an application in rural areas as well, where ideally they can contribute to the perennial goal of improving rural livelihoods and thus rendering village life more attractive for young girls and reducing the difficulties attendant with early female migration to the cities.

Finally, improvements in the working conditions of child domestic workers, including their time available for education and training, will be accomplished through improvements in the working conditions of *all* domestic workers regardless of age. In this sense, we believe that NGOs should not be constrained by a singular focus on child protagonism, or narrowly defined conceptions of child-centered development approaches, but rather should support efforts to facilitate the unionization of child workers and/or to legitimize the status of child workers as members of established (adult) workers' unions in Senegal.[14] So doing would help in advancing the goals of ensuring legal contracts and the regularization of working conditions for child workers, and a broader understanding of child worker rights among their employers. In this way, too, we believe that under the umbrella of union activity, children's agency could be more effectively incorporated into a broader integrated struggle for rights that unites informal sector workers, the poor, and children together.

Notes

1. The categories of "economically active" and "productive activity" have been defined by the ILO. The figures for economically active children are based on a Nation Study on Children's Work reported in ANSD/BIT-IPEC (2007).
2. All of the domestic workers discussed in this chapter, both in the historical accounts and the present research findings, were females. The term "child domestic worker" is used throughout the chapter to refer to the subset of these workers who were under 18 years of age.
3. In *rural* Senegalese culture the gendered division of labor remains rigid within patriarchal family structures, dictating a predominantly domestic role for females. As a result, among rural children 5–17 years old, roughly twice as many boys are economically active as girls, but much higher percentages of girls are involved in significant productive activities in the home (i.e., from 56 percent of 7-year olds up to 90 percent of 13-year olds) (UCW, 2010). Moreover, while civil and political liberties for women in the country are viewed as relatively advanced for the region, cultural attitudes toward women's status continue to place them on a severely unequal footing and thus foster systematic violations of the internationally recognized rights of girls and women. Excision (female genital mutilation), though formally illegal and now decreasing, is still widely practiced. A 2004 study found that 29 percent of girls aged 15–19 years were already married, divorced, or widowed. Furthermore, roughly half of all marriages are polygamous, inheritance and property rights for women are negligible, and domestic violence is frequent (SIGI, n.d.).
4. Both of these studies were produced by Enda Jeunesse Action largely to serve as baseline analyses for planning the forms of organization and action with young female domestic workers.

5. Gorée is an island accessible by ferry from downtown Dakar. It is a popular tourist destination for its well-preserved colonial architecture, in particular its slave fort.
6. Hann is a neighborhood on the eastern edge of Dakar that houses a forested park and zoological garden.
7. The most that could be claimed was that the members negotiated learning objectives according to their own aspirations and perceived needs, and that they contributed small monthly sums toward the compensation of their instructors.
8. Methods used included semi-improvised dramas, neighborhood mapping, and topic-specific discussions (e.g., "an experience that has marked my working life," or "why I value education"). These methods were deemed preferable to standard interviews with child and youth domestics for their greater potential to permit relatively free expression, as well as out of the ethical consideration of using the workers' extremely limited free time to at least partially mutual benefit. As all of the domestic workers spoke in Wolof, we relied on the literacy teachers/research assistants for translation, which often necessarily took the form of paraphrasing an extended anecdote, remark, or section of a drama (so as not to interrupt it). As a result, we employ limited use of direct quotations in presenting what the domestic workers expressed.
9. Field research was conducted by Lavan as part of his doctoral research under the supervision of Maclure who also spent time in Senegal conducting a related project.
10. The Dakar association's own figures claimed 1,000 members for March 2008 and then only 700 for September 2008. From visiting most of the active groups and viewing their membership lists, our own estimate was between 300 and 400 for the period of the fieldwork.
11. The literacy teachers we interviewed agreed that the migration patterns of domestic workers create significant obstacles both to their own literacy progress and to the overall conduct of the literacy courses. Despite the risk of losing their positions, nearly all domestic workers visit their home villages on important holidays. However, both literacy teachers and the girls themselves asserted that most "shuttle" back and forth over the course of several years.
12. Donors had tightened the criteria for their Senegal program in the wake of a negative 2004 report from the Foundation for International Research on Working Children that had found a high percentage of Dakar association members who would not qualify as child laborers under ILO definitions (Nimbona & Lieten, 2004). The African Movement of Working Children and Youth as a whole has also made it a priority to increase the proportion of child membership in all Associations.
13. Strangely, no one at this meeting mentioned the issue of the national program's membership critieria for direct support to groups' literacy and skills training.

14. The expansion of union membership to include child workers is a recently articulated agenda of the National Coalition of Senegalese Workers.

References

African Economic Outlook (AEO). (2010). *Senegal: Social Context and Human Resource Development.* Retrieved June 28, 2010 fromhttp://www.africaneconomicoutlook.org/en/countries/west-africa/senegal/

Alissoutin, R. L. (2006). *La problematique des employées de maison*. Dakar: Groupe de recherches d'études et de formation (GREF). Retrieved from http://www.grefonline.org/problematique%20des%20employ%E9es%20de%20maison.pdf

L'agence Nationale de la Statistique et de la Démographie (ANSD) & Bureau International du Travail (BIT)- Programme International pour l'Abolition du Travail des Enfants (IPEC) & (ANSD/BIT-IPEC). (2007). *Enquête Nationale sur le Travail des Enfants (E.N.T.E.S–2005): SENEGAL: Rapport National d'analyses*. Ministère de l'économie et des finances, Agence nationale de la statistique et de la démographie/BIT/IPEC.

Bebbington, A. (2004). Theorizing Participation and Institutional Change: Ethnography and Political Economy. In S. Hickey & G. Mohan (Eds.), *Participation: From Tyranny to Transformation?* (pp. 278–283). London: Zed.

Black, M. (2005). *Child Domestic Workers: A Handbook on Good Practice in Programme Interventions* No. 17. London: Anti-Slavery International.

Cabanes, R. (2000). Family versus the Logic of the Market. In B. Schlemmer (Ed.), *The Exploited Child* (pp. 263–267). London: Zed.

Coly, H. (1999). Annexe IV: Éxperience d'un animateur. *Voix des enfants d'Afrique*. Dakar: Enda TM.

Coalition Nationale des Associations et ONG en Faveur de l'Enfance au Sénégal (CONAFE-Sénégal). (2006). *Rapport complémentaire élabore par la CONAFE-Sénégal au Comité des Nations Unies pour les Droits de l'Enfant.* Dakar: Coalition Nationale des Associations et ONG en faveur de l'Enfant-Sénégal.

Cunningham, H., & Stromquist, S. (2005). Child Labor and the Rights of Children: Historical Patterns of Decline and Persistence. In B. H. Weston (Eds.), *Child Labor and Human Rights: Making Children Matter* (pp. 55–83). London: Lynne Rienner.

de Ravignan, A. (1998). *Working and Inventing on the Streets of Africa: Education to Fight Exclusion*. Paris: UNESCO.

Diallo, Y. (2008). *Les activités des enfants en Afrique subsaharienne: les enseignements des enquêtes sur le travail des enfants en Afrique de l'Ouest*. Rome: UCW Project.

Diaw, B. e. a. (1996). *Les Mbindaan sans Mbindou: Étude avec les petites bonnes à Dakar (*Jeuda No. 99). Dakar: Enda Jeunesse Action.

Dimé, M. (2007). Galérer, bricoler, partager, contester et rêver: figures de la précarité juvénile à Dakar. In Y. Assogba (Ed.), *La jeunesse en Afrique subsaharienne* (pp. 123–143). Québec: Université Laval.

Ebrahim, A. (2003). NGOs and Organizational Change: Discourse, Reporting, and Learning. Cambridge: Cambridge University Press.

Enda Jeunesse Action (EJA). (1985). *Street Children and Youth: The Grand Bassam Approach (final report, Jeuda 27e)*. Dakar: Enda Jeunesse Action.

Enda Jeunesse Action (EJA). (1995). Le 1er mai 1994 et la défense des droits en Afrique de l'Ouest. In Enda Tiers-Monde (Ed.), *Enfants en recherche et en action: Une alternative africaine d'animation urbaine* (pp. 208–215). Dakar: Enda Tiers-Monde.

Enda Jeunesse Action (EJA) & Mouvement Africain Enfants Jeunes Travailleurs (MAEJT). (2006). *Notre programme pour 2007–2011*. Project Proposal.

Ennew, J., Myers, W. E., & Plateau, D. P. (2005). Defining Child Labour As If Human Rights Really Matter. In B. H. Weston (Ed.), *Child Labor and Human Rights: Making Children Matter* (pp. 27–54). Lomdon: Lynne Rienner.

Fall, D. M. (1999). Dakar: les domestiques à bonne école. *MEDIAF/Le Soleil.* Retrieved from http://www.syfia.info/index.php5?view=articles&action=voir&idArticle=663

Jacquemin, M. (2006). Can the Language of Rights Get Hold of the Complex Realities of Child Domestic Work? The Case of Young Domestic Workers in Abidjan, Ivory Coast. *Childhood, 13*(3), 389–406.

Jacquemin, M. (2009). « Petites nièces » et « petites bonnes » à Abidjan: Les mutations de la domesticité juvénile. *Travail, Genre et Sociétés, 22*, 53–74.

Morice, A. (1981). The Exploitation of Children in the "Informal Sector": Proposals for Research. In G. Rodgers, & G. Standing (Eds.), *Child Work, Poverty, and Underdevelopment* (pp. 131–158). Geneva: International Labour Organization.

Ndiaye, A. (2010). Travail des enfants : Dans l'enfer silencieux des enfants travailleurs. *Walf Fadjri.* Retrieved from http://fr.allafrica.com/stories/201003260619.html

Ndiaye-Kane, Y. (1985). *Les "Mbindaan" ou employées de maison de HLM Montagne s'organisent* (Jeuda No. 42). Dakar: Enda Tiers-Monde.

Nieuwenhuys, O. (1994). *Children's Lifeworlds: Gender, Welfare, and Labour in the Developing World.* New York: Routledge.

Nimbona, G., & Lieten, K. (2004). *Child Labour Unions: AEJT Senegal.* Amsterdam: Foundation for International Research on Working Children.

Ogunseye, B. (1997). The Voluntary Sector and Sustainable Development in Africa: NGO Dilemmas. International Institute for Environment and Development (African NGO Networks).

Prout, A., & James, A. (1997). A New Paradigm for the Sociology of Childhood? Provenance, Promise and Problems. In A. James, & A. Prout (Eds.), *Constructing and Reconstructing Childhood: Contemporary Issues in the Sociological Study of Childhood* (2nd ed.), (pp. 7–33). London: Falmer.

Save the Children. (2002). Strengthening Child-Led Organisations: Report of a Supporting Event Organized by International Save the Children Alliance and Girl Scouts of the USA under the Umbrella of the Under 18 Participation Task

Force (U18PTF) during the United Nations Special Session on Children, New York, May 2002.

Schildkrout, E. (1981). The Employment of Children in Kano (Nigeria). In G. Rodgers, & G. Standing (Eds.), *Child Work, Poverty, and Underdevelopment* (pp. 81–112). Geneva: International Labour Organization.

Terenzio, F. (1990). *Enfants en situation difficile: quelques axes de réflexion* (Jeuda No. 77)

Terenzio, F. (1992). Chargeurs de briquets à gaz, cireurs ambulants, porteurs de marchés, employées de maison, accompagnateurs de touristes: quelques exemples d'appui aux enfants et jeunes travailleurs au Sénégal et ailleurs (Jeuda No. 83). Dakar: Enda Jeunesse Action.

Understanding Children's Work (UWC). (2010). *Comprendre le travail des enfants et l'emploi des jeunes au Sénégal.* Rome: Understanding Children's Work.

United Nations Children's Fund (UNICEF) (n.d.). *Senegal Statistics.* Retrieved March 25, 2010 from http://www.unicef.org.proxy.bib.uottawa.ca/infobycountry/senegal_statistics.html

United Nations Educational, Scientific and Cultural Organization (UNESCO). (2010). *EFA global monitoring report 2010: Reaching the Marginalized.* Paris & Oxford: UNESCO & Oxford.

CHAPTER 12

Circles of Care: Community-Based Child Protection in South Africa

Philip Cook and Lesley du Toit

Introduction

Research on human development has consistently demonstrated that children require a strong foundation of physical, emotional, cognitive, and social supports to reach their maximum potential (Rogoff, 2003; Shonkoff & Phillips, 2000). Different cultures weave the strands of these supports together in varied patterns that have evolved in response to diverse natural and social environments. Concurrently, however, despite differences in culture and socioeconomic context, children have similar basic needs. These include proper nutrition; stable, loving relationships; education that fosters cognitive, emotional, and social development; positive role models; and safe, effective transitions from childhood through adolescence to adulthood and parenthood (Myers, 1992). In recent years, particularly since the promulgation of the United Nations Convention on the Rights of the Child (UNCRC), many of children's needs have been recognized as fundamental rights. Accordingly, while there is also widespread acknowledgment that children possess the inherent capacity to defend their rights, it does not shift the burden of responsibility away from adults, and particularly from governments, as duty bearers to ensure that these rights are realized. Indeed, children are dependent upon surrounding "circles of care," that is, layers of adult support provided by individuals, communities, and institutions that contribute to the protection and enhancement of children's basic rights and help to ensure secure social environments that guarantee the realization of these rights.

For children in Southern Africa, however, a catastrophic obstacle to the sustainability of systems of support for children's development has been the AIDS pandemic that has swept across the subcontinent with devastating effect on communities and families. Among the countries most affected by the disease, South Africa is experiencing the crushing burden of having the highest number of persons living with HIV of any country in the world—5.7 million in 2007. In that same year, over 1.4 million South African children had lost one or both parents to AIDS (UNAIDS, 2008). Compounded with, as well as exacerbating, widespread poverty, these extraordinary losses have disrupted the circles of care that children need to both survive and thrive. With illness and death among young and middle-aged adults, AIDS has unraveled the web of communal protections for children provided by parents, relatives, teachers, nurses, social workers, and other caregivers, rendering many youth vulnerable to abuse and exploitation. In fact, neglect, exploitation, and the physical and sexual abuse of children have reached epidemic proportions in South Africa (Guthrie, 2000; UNICEF 2003). In light of these realities, local communities and all levels of government are confronted with the profound challenge of mending the social fabric necessary to meet the needs and protect the rights of South Africa's children.

In terms of legislation and policy, the South African government has attested to the imperative of promoting the protection of the rights of children. The Constitution of South Africa (Section 18) is quite clear that the "Best Interests of the Child shall be Paramount," thus enshrining the survival and protection of children in the country's founding principles. The work of the Inter-ministerial Committee on Young People at Risk, established by Nelson Mandela in 1996, has sought to shift the formal childcare and protection system away from models based on pathology toward early intervention programs and the strengthening of families and communities. South Africa has also ratified the UNCRC and promulgated numerous legislative protocols concerning children's rights, including the Child Care Act, a Children's Bill, and the Declaration of Commitment to Children Affected by HIV/AIDS. Unfortunately, despite these formal commitments, in practice, support for vulnerable children remains fragmented, piecemeal, and largely ineffective (Guthrie, 2003; Meintjes, Budlender, Giese, & Johnson, 2003). For example, the Foster Child Grant and the Child Support Grant, both social security funding mechanisms for caregivers of vulnerable children, have come under increasing criticism for either not reaching the intended beneficiaries, or in some cases placing vulnerable children at further risk of abuse and exploitation (Meintjes, Budlender, Giese, & Johnson, 2003). Overall, a significant gap still exists between the rhetoric and reality of rights for South African children who are most in need of protection, support, and services.

Consequently, as in many other countries attempting to move the UNCRC from policy to practice, it has been necessary to rebuild circles of care in South Africa and to develop child protection capacities at the local level through direct support for vulnerable children, their caregivers, and the communities most affected by HIV/AIDS. This has necessitated identifying and building on existing capacities of potential caregivers and local communities that are in a position to foster children's individual and collective self-efficacy and resilience. This in turn requires the use of innovative, participatory research strategies that seek to better understand the comprehensive dimensions of poverty and AIDS that affect children's well-being and so contribute to an expanding knowledge base for effective child support systems. In short, efforts to bridge the gap between far-sighted child rights policies and effective rights-oriented practices in the context of the AIDS pandemic in South Africa requires a combination of rigorous research, community empowerment, good governance, and a culturally sensitive approach to working in the collective African context. These considerations underscored a community-based "Circles of Care" research project, described in this chapter, that sought to address child rights and protection in South Africa's Free State. By encouraging the participation of children, their families, and their communities, the project aimed to promote existing community strengths and capacity to ensure the realization of the rights, care, and protection of children.

The "Circles of Care" Project

The Circles of Care project was an effort to merge children's rights policy and practice, with special attention to mitigating the suffering and social pressures stemming from HIV/AIDS. In building on their cultural capital and inherent resilience, at-risk children, their families, neighbors, and local governments collaboratively developed a community-based child protection model, informed by a participatory research strategy. Between August 2002 and July 2004, nine municipalities in the Free State, a chiefly rural province in the heart of South Africa, participated in the project (Free State Provincial Government, 2008).

The Free State was chosen because of the high levels of HIV, as well as the minimal systems of support available to populations at risk, particularly children. Communities participating in this initiative included Bluegumbosch, Mbeki Park, Disaster Park, Bolata, Makwane (Maluti-A-Phofeng); France (Sasolberg); Hani Park, Tenneseun (Welkom); and Tstesing (Batlokwa traditional tribal area). HIV infection rates in these communities were approximately 10–25 percent and unemployment was very high (40–75 percent). The selection of these communities was based on the recommendations of the South African Ministry of Local Government that singled out high levels of poverty and HIV in these communities.

The Circles of Care approach was driven by three objectives: (1) to examine support and protection strategies specifically targeting vulnerable children, especially those directly affected by the HIV/AIDS pandemic; (2) to develop local human resources by strengthening the resilience of community leaders, families, and children, and enhancing their capacities to contribute to both the development and implementation of child protection policies; and (3) to strengthen the action research capacities of local government officials and community leaders. The sum of these objectives is the "circle of care" itself—a vision for the protection and development of children and youth within the immediate context of their families and communities. The overarching vision of the Circles of Care approach is that within each municipal area the rights of young people surrounded by a circle of care are likely to be sustained and strengthened. Specifically they are likely to be physically, socially, and emotionally secure; their basic needs will be met; they will be consistently supported and guided by adults; their personal identities and cultural heritage will be respected; and they will be able to participate in matters directly affecting them. The vision further includes the stipulation that municipalities will critically assess established services, and where necessary consider new services and plans through the lens of the UNCRC, the South African Constitution, and the African Charter, particularly as they relate to vulnerable children and youth. In essence, the comprehensive vision of the Circles of Care approach is to foster a commitment among all community and local government actors to establish "circles of care" as a basis for the protection and promotion of children's rights.

Framework and Approach

In order to achieve this vision, the Circles of Care project was informed and guided by a social ecology framework, a child-based approach to

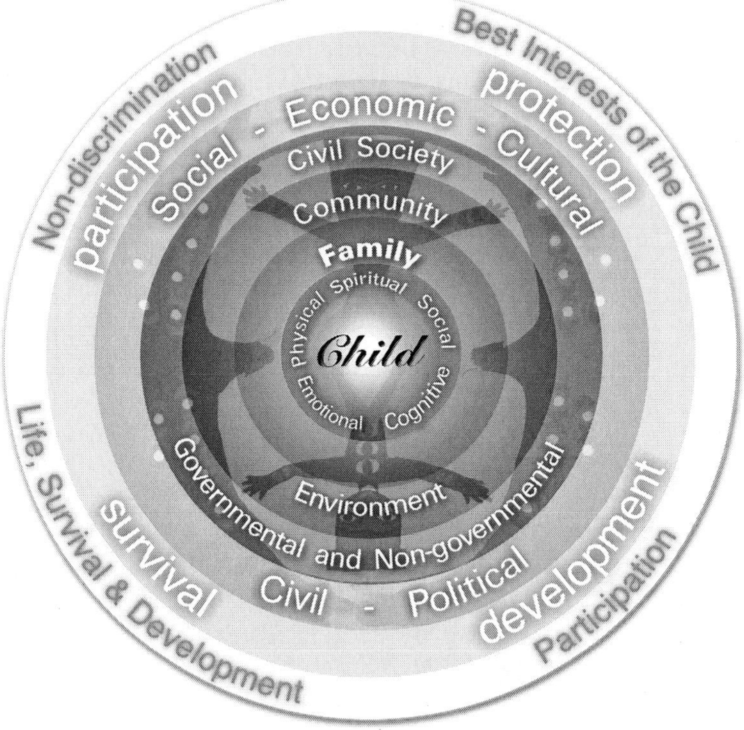

Figure 12.1 The developmental rights-based framework.

intervention that entailed a commitment to community participation and action (figure 12.1).

Drawing on Urie Bronfenbrenner's (1979) social ecology of childhood, the above diagram represents a "developmental child rights framework" and can be used to conceptualize and implement a rights-based approach. The model places each child at the center of a series of concentric, nested circles that represent differing layers of support networks—resources that may be mobilized to create a "circle of care." The child's basic human developmental needs—physical, cognitive, emotional, and social—are represented in the inner quadrants. These developmental needs are supported by the immediate social nexus of family and/or other caregivers. At the next level, the community is the site of social structures (e.g., housing, schooling, recreation, and water sources) and the infusion of sociocultural *morés* to which each child is exposed. This level also includes the local natural environment. Extending further outward are diverse levels of governance (e.g., specific policies that determine the range and quality of social services available for children) and the broader sociocultural environment and overall political economy that impinge on systems of support for children. The final level of the framework represents the presence of ideas, values, and beliefs that either enhance or undermine a child's right to safe and healthy development.

The four guiding principles of the UNCRC, participation, protection, development, and survival, are included in the outer layers of the diagram and represent cross-cutting themes that emerge across levels as either strengths or weaknesses insofar as they promote a rights-based approach. These include, for example, cultural attitudes that encourage or restrict open discussion about HIV/AIDS with young people and children's right to information that can facilitate safe healthy choices.

Typically, the stronger the interconnectedness there is between each concentric circle, the healthier will be children's relationships with their human and natural environment, and thus the increased likelihood of their resilience and long-term development. Conversely, when these concentric circles are disconnected and undermined by risks from within, the protective relationships upon which children depend for their development are easily eroded, thus jeopardizing their chances of achieving lives that are healthy and fulfilling.

Community-Based Participation and Action

From the perspective of the Circles of Care research project, a community-based, bottom-up approach necessitates the adoption of participatory child-focused research that engages young people in narrative discourse that pays particular attention to their personal experiences and relationships with immediate family and caregivers, peers, and other community members. Given the objective of fostering and strengthening circles of care for vulnerable children, their narratives should be encouraged to proceed as far as possible in a three-step progression: (1) elucidation of the *risks* that affect children's well-being and long-term development; (2) emphasis on *recovery* through the identification of community mobilization strategies that can facilitate the establishment or improvement of children's protective networks; and (3) encouragement of a process of restoration whereby communities concerned with the protection and support of vulnerable children are open to communication and action with governmental and nongovernmental organizations that share a common interest in children's rights.

A Culturally Grounded, Child Rights-Based Approach
This approach to research acknowledges that there is an dichotomy between a rights-based approach and an approach that recognizes cultural differences. However, by adopting the premise that inquiry should focus not only on children's needs and rights, but should also foster an understanding of the broad cultural underpinnings of their unique lives and the social contexts within which they are growing up, this dichotomy can be properly addressed. In pragmatic terms this means engaging children and cultural experts such as traditional elders as participants in the inquiry process, both through narration of their own concerns and perspectives, and through their identification of problems and potential ways to resolve them. In the context of children affected by HIV/AIDS, a rights-based approach also places an obligation on local government and all involved in the lives of these children (including international relief agencies) to assume their responsibilities in protecting and promoting the rights of children affected by the widespread impact of HIV/AIDS at the level of child, family, community, and society. Child rights–oriented programs thus entail holistic and inclusive measures implemented by children's "duty bearers" (governments, NGOs, communities, and families) while involving children as active "claim holders" (Knutson, 1997). This approach also entails an obligation on the part of researchers and other stakeholders to genuinely listen to children, to appreciate their reasoning, and where possible to act upon their input and suggestions.

The rights-based approach views rights as indivisible and interdependent. Thus, no one right is seen as more important than another, and action to realize these rights must simultaneously address various groups of rights. AIDS protection programs, for example, should consider children's long-term protection and psychosocial needs. A child rights–based approach should likewise engage children and their guardians as stakeholders in actions that aim to generate outcomes that adhere to the standards set forth in the UNCRC. In particular, it should aim to increase children's participation by building on their resilience and agency.

Despite its obvious merits, the limitations of the Circles of Care approach must also be acknowledged. One limitation stems from the UNCRC itself, which, although almost universally ratified, has nonetheless come under critical scrutiny, particularly in relation to its applicability across cultures. Burr (2002), for example, on the basis of her fieldwork with street-involved children in Viet Nam, provides a particularly useful discussion on global and local approaches to children's rights and the role of international agencies that strive to assist these young people. As she points out, rights-based approaches often presuppose a Western conception of the primacy of the individual as the bearer of rights, which may conflict with ideas of communal rights held by other cultures. In contexts where children are valued essentially as members of the rights-bearing family collective, the "best interests of the child" (Article 3 of the UNCRC) may be interpreted differently and the obligations of children to family welfare may take on greater importance than common Western perceptions of children's "best interests."

In the Circles of Care project in South Africa, focus groups held with community Elders revealed that externally held conceptions of child rights were often controversial because they were perceived to undermine the authority of traditional leaders, disempower parents, challenge community discipline, and reduce responsibility among children (Cook & White, 2006). In addition, because childhood is culturally constructed and quite specific to the particularities of time and place, there were difficulties in arriving at a common understanding of the very meaning of childhood. In certain respects, the "childhood" prescribed by the UNCRC is an idealized modern Western one, and as a result may have limited force in other cultures. Boyden (1990: 208, in Burr, 2002) notes that this "globalized" Western model of childhood has, for example, made it "problematic for children to work or to show a level of independence that is now deemed inappropriate in the West." Finally, the involvement of international agencies in the application of the UNCRC may likewise reinforce the perceptions within affluent nations that children in the South need to be "rescued" by outsiders who are better equipped to offer support than communities in the South (Holland, 1992, in Burr, 2002). Cognizant of these perceptual barriers, we attempted in this project to bridge the divide between child rights as exemplified by the UNCRC and local cultural perspectives concerning the best interests of the child through a comparative assessment of children's perceptions of their rights, well-being and protection, and the perceptions of community elders (traditional cultural experts) concerning children's rights and obligations. This information-gathering process was critical as a first step towards the development of actions that would build on cultural and community strengths.

Methodology: The "Triple A" Participatory Action Research Method

> The complexity of the ideological and methodological nuances subsumed under the term *participatory action research* belie an approach to inquiry and action that on the surface seems natural, human, and intrinsically sensible. Put colloquially, you get the people affected by a problem together, figure out what is going on as a group, and then do something about it. (Kidd & Kral, 2005, p. 187)

The "Triple A" participatory research approach of the Circles of Care project was pioneered by UNICEF, and later refined by the International Institute for Child Rights and Development (IICRD) in addressing the question of community support for vulnerable children in Malawi (Cook, Ali, & Munthali, 2000). In the Circles of Care project, the "Triple A" was further adapted to specifically build on South African traditional governance systems by exploring cultural beliefs, practices, and customs affecting children. Specific examples of cultural practices include child custody for orphans, dispute resolution practices in mediating family violence, and the initiation of girls and boys. This methodological approach connects research to practice through three sequential "A's." The first step consists of an *assessment* of strengths and weaknesses as these relate (as in the case of Malawi, for example) to the care and support of orphans and other vulnerable children. Second is the *analysis* of information collected during the first step, with an eye to identifying underlying causes and prospective problem-solving strategies. Generally, the preliminary data analysis is conducted by local project facilitators. The results are then presented to community representatives who participate in another stage of analysis in order to discuss the causes of community problems and their potential solutions. The final step consists of the establishment of plans of *action* that can assume a number of different forms, for example, advocacy and public consciousness-raising; development of local capacities; service delivery; mobilization of resources; or monitoring and evaluation. Action plans may also initiate linkages with local government, community-based organizations (CBO's), international nongovernmental organizations (NGOs), and international agencies (e.g., UNICEF).

The main purpose of the "Triple A" approach, as with other participatory action research processes, is to stimulate the capacity of local communities to mobilize local resources in response to locally identified needs. It is also an approach that is attuned to the nuances of culture and language, to the need for safe environments in which to conduct discussions, and to principles of dignity and mutual respect among all participants.

Project Activities

The three Triple "A" stages of the Circles of Care project in Free state were completed between August 2002 and July 2004. Each stage was led by teams of three local facilitators per community who were hired, trained, and supervised by the authors. The assessment phase lasted from October 2002 to June 2003, the analysis phase from July 2003 to December 2003, and the action phase was completed by September 2004. During the assessment phase, three sets of focus groups were conducted with groups of children, care providers, elders, and local professionals working with children (e.g., teachers, day care workers, community health care workers, and social workers). Details of each of the phases are addressed below.

Training

Because a singular objective of the project was to enhance local research capacity and to avoid an overly professionalized approach to the study, training local research facilitators was a key component of the project. Training sessions conducted by the authors focused on four inter-related areas:

1. understanding the premises of the Circles of Care project;
2. understanding children's psychosocial development processes;
3. learning critical self-awareness that would affect facilitator relations with children, youth, and adults alike;
4. learning the methodological skills necessary to implement participatory action research, and the techniques of interviewing, focus group coordination, and community asset mapping.

Particular emphasis was placed on relating facilitators' personal experiences and values to the community members with whom they would be working. Training for the "Triple A" activities (key informant interviews, community mapping, and "Triple A" focus groups) was carried out in three stages:

- *Formal training in a 4-day workshop*. Themes included Defining Circles of Care; A Culturally Grounded Rights-Based Approach; Defining Vulnerability and the Needs of Children; Understanding

Culture; Communication and Facilitation Skills; Children's Psychosocial Development; Children's Grief; and Implementation of the "Triple A" Process.

- *In-service training over the course of the research.* Topics covered included Mapping; Selecting and Setting up Community Groups; Introduction and Orientation of the Groups to the Process; Gathering and Recording Data Using the "Triple A" Handbooks; Analysis of the Data; Implementing the Action Phase of the "Triple A"; and Monitoring the Action Phase.
- *Ongoing supervision*: Topics covered the following: Engaging Community Members, Children and Youth; Assisting Groups to Understand the Developmental Nature of the "Triple A" Process; Dealing with Group Dynamics; Relations among Team Members; and Team Support.

Fieldwork and Data Collection

Approximately 400 adults from the 9 municipalities participated in focus groups, community mapping, and advocacy workshops. Representatives from local and traditional governance systems were involved in various stages of the research. Approximately 40 community leaders and 30 municipal leaders from the 9 municipal areas took part in numerous "Triple A" action planning stages and government workshops.

In adopting the "Triple A" approach to research, the Circles of Care study in South Africa undertook four sequential methods of field-based inquiry in each of the research sites.

Key Informant Interviews

The first methodological step was to identify key individuals who were knowledgeable and had extensive appreciation of the vulnerability and lack of fundamental rights of children living in poor, HIV/AIDS-affected communities. Through these interviews the research team was able to gain a solid grounding of the problems and challenges confronting vulnerable youth in the different sites of the study. The numbers of key informants interviewed in each study site ranged from 10 to 15. These included municipal bureaucrats, traditional community leaders, social service personnel (social workers, community development specialists, teachers, and health care workers), local child rights advocates, and adolescent youth.

Focus Groups

In order to facilitate a deeper understanding of issues, follow-up focus group discussions were held with some of the key informants who participated in the first stage of one-to-one interviews. Additional focus group interviews were conducted with community elders (*Morena*) and traditional healers (*Dinaka*), and with several others involved in the support of youth recreation and sports. Approximately 400 adults from the various communities took part in focus groups, as well as 40 community elders and healers and 30 municipal leaders. Focus groups proved to be a critical community forum for dialogue on rights and responsibilities, harmful and helpful cultural activities, and the future of young people.

Community Asset Mapping

Based on the initial round of key informant interviews, the researchers then conducted community asset mapping exercises in order to ascertain the locally based assets or social networks and resources, such as schools and health clinics, that could potentially be mobilized to assist destitute children (Kertzmann and Mcknight, 1993; Veale, 2000). One-day community mapping workshops were carried out with children, adult caregivers, and local community leaders. Specific assets identified in the mapping workshops included places of safety and available services for children (e.g., clinics, schools, and clubs), and sources of child rights advocacy and support within the community (e.g., church groups, community centers, and women's associations).

Engagement of Children and Youth as Research Participants

The Circles of Care team sought to involve children and youth throughout the project, partly for purposes of enhancing their resilience and agency, and partly in order to identify their specific needs and the gaps in developmental supports and local resources necessary for their welfare. Over 700 children and youth between the ages of 12 and 25 participated in the focus groups and community mapping workshops. Most of the children were identified by the research facilitators as in need of protection services within their home communities. These included young people living in extreme poverty, those who were not in school, those who had been orphaned by the AIDS pandemic, and children with disabilities. Despite a lack of direct evidence, it was assumed that a sizeable number of these vulnerable young people had suffered abuse and/or exploitation. Among the older youth (aged 15–25 years), several were recruited to participate as mentors of younger children in the mapping workshops.

While adhering to the principle that young people can contribute actively to processes of analysis and action, the research team nonetheless acknowledged the diversity that exists between young people of different ages, gender, interests, and capabilities. The participation of children and youth in the Circle of Care project required training and sensitivity to ensure representation across such diversity. Care was taken to ensure that boys and girls participated in equal numbers, although certain focus groups included only girls in order to allow for more candid and specific discussion of issues related to gender and female risk.

Alongside their participation in focus groups and community mapping workshops, young people were also engaged in role-playing and dramatized stories, in artwork, and in various games. In all circumstances, efforts were made to ensure that children's participation was conducted in environments where they felt safe and comfortable, and where they could speak freely and pose questions to facilitators who were interested in them and listened to what they had to say. On occasion, a respected traditional leader or trusted community adult was invited to participate along with the children and youth so as to provide support and assurance.

Training was not provided solely on a one-time basis to hired research facilitators before the start of the project. Instead, throughout the duration of the project training continued to be a principal component linking research with action. As the research progressed, increased attention was directed toward children's and youth learning. As such, in all municipalities where the project was conducted, youth workshops covered the following topics: AIDS prevention and treatment; strategies for personal wellness and healing; community wellness; healthy child development; support for orphans and vulnerable children; mobilization of communities; and cultural roots.

Results: A Community-Based Child Protection Model

A three-stage model for community-based child protection emerged from the participatory research process. The first stage involved the identification of risk and protective factors contributing to child well-being. During the second stage, participants assessed ways to mobilize communities for the promotion and protection of children's rights. The third stage then centered on measures capable of enhancing methods of governance that are more favorable to the well-being of children and youth. Derived through the "Triple A" process, each of the three stages of the model built on one another. The next section examines the outcomes of each of these stages as developed through the Circles of Care project.

Stage 1: Risk: Assessing Children's Vulnerability and Resilience

One self-evident finding that emerged through an examination of the evidence obtained from interviews, focus groups, and community asset mapping was that the children who are most affected by HIV/AIDS are also likely to be exposed to a host of other risk factors that jeopardize their general well-being. This in turn necessitates the urgency of enhanced protective factors for these children.

Risk Factors

The risk factors identified through the "Triple A" process were analyzed through the lens of the social ecology framework of childhood discussed previously. At the level of the *child/family nexus*, participants identified notable problems such as alcohol abuse (which can result in fetal alcohol syndrome), family violence, child neglect, and abuse of child support grants. Also discussed were parental unemployment, hunger and poor health, lack of funds and proper health necessary to attend school, and early pregnancy and subsequent teen parenthood. Participants also reported unsettling family situations—increasingly common in light of the HIV/AIDS pandemic—that exposes them to the following risks: orphanhood that renders them susceptible to neglect, transience, and abuse; situations where older siblings must care for younger siblings; and those in which grandmothers, or other elderly relatives, must care for their grandchildren. One 14-year-old girl aptly expressed the feelings of isolation and vulnerability in such risk-oriented circumstances:

> It doesn't feel safe in the community – everybody thinks too much of themselves. Once I saw a child sexually abused by an older child. It's scary in our community because a hearse drives around all night and we don't know what it does. It would be safer if we just stayed indoors. Outside the world is too bad for us children. There are some kind people in our community, but not enough to keep us safe. (Disaster Park Community Interview)

Many young males also reported that in response to parental neglect or abuse, or to outright family breakdown, and to the perpetual cycle of unemployment and poverty, they were easily drawn into criminal activity as a way to gain money, status, and respect that would otherwise be unattainable for them. For similar reasons, many girls with virtually no prospect of legitimate employment were often drawn toward prostitution. Yet the great majority of these young people also recognized that crime and prostitution constituted a downward spiral of ever-deepening risk. In these circumstances, their sense of alienation had easily become mutually reinforcing, with parents frequently expressing a loss of positive influence and control over their children. In turn, adult attitudes toward antisocial youth were generally antagonistic, with most seeing punishment and retribution rather than rehabilitation as effective responses to youth delinquency.

At the level of *community relations and structures*, participants identified lack of preschool and childcare facilities, a paucity of organized recreation and recreational facilities, and inadequate connections between home and school that fostered early school abandonment. In particular, school abandonment and the absence of recreational possibilities were seen to be directly linked to children's susceptibility to alcohol, illicit drugs, and unprotected sex. These behaviours in turn contributed significantly to negative community attitudes regarding perceived youth delinquents and corresponding popular support for policy responses oriented towards arrest and prevention rather than measures of prevention and protection. As expressed in the following interview excerpt, guardians were deeply concerned about these cumulative risks confronting children:

> In the past 4 years we have seen many more deaths in the community. As a result of the loss of their breadwinners and caregivers, children don't have enough to eat. Many drop out of school, some turn to crime or drugs. The traditional protection of children is eroded. We need stronger support from our community leaders, especially from local government. (Orphans' Guardian, Blue Gum Bosch Community Interview)

At the level of policy *formulation and governance*, participants noted that the lack of a birth certification system has resulted in many marginalized children being ineligible for full citizenship rights (e.g., full public education and health care). They also noted a lack of government services designed to interrupt cycles of risk and self-destruction among adolescents (e.g., organized recreational programs and a restorative youth justice system); a lack of program follow-up to national policies stipulating the protection of orphans and other high-risk children; inappropriate targeting and delivery of child welfare grants; poor (or lack of) coordinated services with community and traditional leaders; and poor coordination of HIV/AIDS programs for children and youth. Participants also reported the following: a) insufficient consultation with local people concerning policy formulation and program development; b) poor communication on child rights issues, resulting in frequent local misunderstanding of, and resistance to, child rights as an approach to children's development; and c) a widening gap between government authorities and local/traditional leadership. Overall, as indicated by social workers in the pilot communities, there was a need for greater capacity development for professionals working with children.

> Community social workers and community development workers often feel overwhelmed at the scale of these vulnerable children's problems, as a result of HIV/AIDS and poverty, so that they don't know where to start. We need practical tools to help us protect children and their rights. (Government Social Worker, Welkom Interviews)

Finally, risk factors at the *sociocultural environment/political economy* level were also noted. These included: a) a decline of traditional initiation ceremonies and corresponding diminishment of formal guided transitions from childhood through adolescence into adulthood; b) skewed resource distribution and high levels of unemployment, resulting in a rising spiral of risk behaviors among youth—for example, crime, prostitution, violence, and drug and alcohol abuse; c) a lack of coordinated national programs focusing on HIV/AIDS prevention and treatment, and on safe sexual relationships; and d) the rising cost of living, translating into insufficient family funds for basic foodstuffs and medicines for children.

Protective Factors

Protective factors were noted at only two levels of the social ecology of childhood. At the level of the *child/family nexus*, participants noted assets such as traditional birth ceremonies aiming to strengthen mother/child bonds; the presence of extended family in the community; close sibling relations; and affection for animals. At the level of *community relations and structures*, participants reported a number of cultural strengths, such as traditional initiation ceremonies; community-endorsed cultural taboos, particularly with respect to male/female relations; the reinforcement of the traditional authority of elders within families and communities; communal support mechanisms for orphaned and abandoned children; child-focused rituals (e.g., naming ceremonies and girls' initiation); strong community leadership; and cultural activities (e.g., dance, songs, and games). Participants also noted that supportive schools, sports clubs, church groups, community gospel choirs, AIDS clubs, constructed recreational spaces, and natural spaces also served as protective factors. Significantly, participants did not identify any protective factors emanating from government policies and services, or from the broader sociocultural environment. This is most likely a result of the relative social isolation of many of the participants and a corresponding lack of services in many of the project communities. Indeed, many participants commented on the erosion of already weakened services resulting from HIV/AIDS.

Regardless of gender, many youth indicated that the cycle of AIDS and poverty fueled a propensity to engage in drug and alcohol abuse, in part as a form of temporary escape, and in part because it emulated the behavioral patterns that they perceived among many adults, frequently within their immediate families and in the larger community. Having been subjected to perceived injustices inflicted by parents, older family members, teachers, and police, many indicated feelings of isolation and a deep distrust of adult authority figures. Inevitably, therefore, most sought solace with groups of peers with similar experiences and perceptions.

As this information suggests, although the litany of risks identified in the interviews, focus groups, and community mapping was bleak, the social ecology of youth in the Free State is not entirely dispiriting. Participants in the interviews and focus groups also highlighted a range of factors within the social environment of youth that served as factors of protection and helped to foster youth capacity for resilience and recovery. In addition, as many of the participants indicated, the research process itself became something of a positive force. As many young people in particular commented, through the games and experiential activities that were an integral part of the action research process, and through the very act of collectively discussing their situation in safe environments in the company of trusted and supportive research facilitators, involvement in the research itself constituted a therapeutic process.

Stage 2: Recovery: Mobilizing Communities for Children's Rights

Following the identification of risk and protective factors extending across the social ecology of young people in communities affected by poverty and HIV/AIDS, children, youth and other community participants developed action plans designed to reduce risk and enhance protective factors beneficial to young people and their families. Four categories of action resulted from this process: (1) advocacy; (2) capacity building; (3) community service projects; and (4) monitoring and evaluation. Each of these is summarized with several examples of proposed initiatives in corresponding areas:

Advocacy
Actions within this category consisted of efforts to increase public awareness of specific issues and to lobby local officials to direct more attention and resources towards these issues. For example, in *Blugumbosch* (Maluti-A-Phofeng), participants created plans that led community leaders to petition school principals and educational administrators to accept greater enrolment of orphans in schools and to clamp down on mistreatment of children by teachers. Likewise, the *Batlokwa* elders negotiated grants with the provincial Department of Social Development for improvements in the care and feeding of children orphaned by HIV/AIDS. In *France* (Sasolberg), local parents and caregivers of disabled children lobbied faith-based organizations and municipal officials to fund the establishment of a daycare center for these children and the provision of special education training for daycare staff.

Capacity Building
In order to strengthen the capacity of local civic groups and municipal authorities in promoting and protecting child rights, a number of actions were proposed. The development and delivery of child rights education programs designed to augment awareness of child protection laws and awareness of child rights principles were suggested in Maluti-A-Phofeng. In Welkom, proposals were put forward for the training of community leaders in aspects of child development and in ways to recognize instances of abuse and other indicators of risk among HIV/AIDS orphans, disabled children, and those unable to attend school. In *France* (Sasolberg), participants expressed the need for the training of parents, caregivers, and teachers on issues related to the learning needs of disabled children and ways to address these needs. In *Disaster Park* (Maluti-A-Phofeng), participants argued for the creation of a local support group for parents of children with disabilities.

Community Service Projects
Following these action-oriented recovery programs, several community service projects in support of vulnerable children were developed. At the time of writing, these included the establishment of a feeding program for undernourished children in the *Batlokwa* tribal area; the development of sports and recreational programs for children in Maluti-A-Phofeng, Welkom and Sasolberg; and the establishment of "culture clubs" in the *Batlokwa* tribal area and in

Maluti-A-Phofeng and Welkom to serve as venues for traditional stories, songs and dance, which could help to strengthen children's connection with local cultural values and traditions. Participants also suggested projects such as leadership and development training for youth in Maluti-A-Phofeng; HIV/AIDS awareness for adolescents, youth and elders in *Batlokwa* and Maluti-A-Phofeng; the creation of food gardens for orphans and undernourished children and family members living with HIV/AIDS (*Disaster Park, Blugumbosch, France, Hani Park)*; and the opening of a daycare center for single working parents in *Blugumbosch* and *France.*

Monitoring and Evaluation

Participants' action plans also included strategies for monitoring progress and reassessing their objectives and the strategies for achieving these objectives. In the *Batlokwa* communities, scheduled home visits by volunteers and community social workers to monitor the well-being of at-risk children were carried out, complemented by a system of reporting to community or tribal leaders in the event of needed interventions. During the two years of the project, community leaders and local project stakeholders in all the municipalities met each month with local government representatives in order to identify children in need of support, to locate gaps in service delivery, to examine ways of strengthening local government responsibility for children, and to assess the impact of community-based projects. Annual workshops involving children as well as adults were also held in order to assess the success of community child protection interventions.

Stage 3: Restoration: Strengthening Responsive Local Governance

The final stage of the community-based child protection model that emerged from the Circles of Care project involved efforts to strengthen local government support for child protection strategies. Children, caregivers, and community leaders were connected with local government officials who might contribute more effectively to the enhancement of children's rights, ideally by building on initiatives either proposed or enacted in the Circles of Care project. At this stage, the aim was to enhance the capacity of duty bearers to assume greater responsibility for children's rights. Activities resulting from the interactions among the groups were placed in four categories.

In the area of child rights capacity building, a training program for caregivers who were involved in feeding undernourished children was established in the *Batlokwa* communities. The building of child rights capacity was further facilitated by ongoing in-service training workshops for local and provincial government departments. These workshops were provided by the Child and Youth Care Agency for Development (CYCAD) which also facilitated the development of municipal child rights committees that linked community researchers with responsible government agencies responsible for education, health, citizenship, agriculture, and immigration.

Participants also identified the need to refine the responsiveness of the childcare and foster care grants so as not to place children at further risk. To this end, a special project was initiated in the *Batlokwa* community to help families and communities in directing assistance for locally identified vulnerable children. In addition, building on existing local systems of accountability and good governance, the provincial government helped to create pilot projects exploring the potential for community-managed grants for children. Representatives of provincial and local governments began to work together with local leaders in providing sustainable support for community owned and managed day care centers for vulnerable children and their caregivers.

In order to enhance forms of traditional governance, the provincial government supported the reinforcement of communal modes of social support. For example, in *Batlokwa,* following their partnership with CYCAD, traditional governance structures voluntarily took on the monitoring and care of many severely marginalized children, including orphans and children with disabilities. Similarly, the *Batlotkwa* Elders group assisted in overseeing a community grant for orphans based on an action plan supporting youth-led initiatives. The establishment of orphan culture programs is one such supportive measure.

In the area of youth development, local government supported the training of youth to mentor and care for younger children in their communities. CYCAD facilitators worked with local government representatives to engage vulnerable youth through experiential, culturally grounded, wilderness leadership activities in the Drakensberg Mountains. These training programs encouraged both personal and community-based growth and internally generated "bottom-up" development.

Conclusion and Lessons Learned

The Circles of Care project helped to reduce vulnerability and risk among many South African children and youth affected by HIV/AIDS by building on their inherent resilience and that of their families and communities (Werner and Smith, 1992; Fraser, 1997). The "Triple A" approach drew on the strength of traditional African cultural values, beliefs, and practices by better understanding communal practices such as music and initiation ceremonies as bases for supporting children's healthy development. By striving to enable communities and local governing structures (municipal, provincial, and traditional) to support children most affected by HIV/AIDS, the project attempted to reverse negative development trends caused by HIVS/AIDS.

One of the primary lessons to emerge from this action research project is that simple, low-cost participatory interventions such as the "Triple A" can be an effective tool in supporting children living in contexts of HIV/AIDS and poverty. In this particular study, the methodology allowed for the identification and creation of local assets to support vulnerable children and youth. The process of carrying out the steps of the "Triple A" enabled beneficiaries, including children, to gather and apply local knowledge as protagonists in their own lives. Not all local government ministries (notably those of child protection, health, and education) initially embraced the Triple "A" actions suggested by children, guardians, and communities. Over time, however, most municipalities have adopted the proposed actions that emerged from the research, and all of the communities have implemented various bottom-up developmental approaches in support of the rights of children affected by HIV/AIDS and poverty. It was essential, however, to allow participants the time (typically one year) to critically reflect on the implications of research findings concerning children's risks and their capacity for resilience, and to assess the extent to which communities and local government bodies were capable of reducing these risks and augmenting children's resilience.

At the microlevel of the child, the research indicated that when young people are able to participate in discussions concerning their rights in the context of poverty and HIV/AIDS, there is a marked propensity for an increase in their self-efficacy and a desire to contribute to actions aimed at enhancing their own welfare. This was exemplified by the active involvement of children and youth in assessing their challenges and assets, in analyzing the root causes of the problems they faced, and in working with their communities to create action plans that benefited them and their peers. A central theme that emerged from the discussions with young people was that the very act of *collectively discussing* their situation in safe environments, in the company of trusted adults, was highly beneficial. This revealed the power of personal narrative as a restorative tool in supporting children's self-identity and in reinforcing their resilience in the midst of HIV/AIDS. This positive sentiment was well captured by a 16-year-old boy:

> Before this process [the Triple "A"], many of us were lost, [but] now we have found unity amongst ourselves, we have tools to address our problems, we have the strength to help ourselves and ours peers." (Participant, Blugombusch focus group)

Yet not all children who participated were able to benefit from the project. As previously observed by others who have assessed children's resilience (Garbarino, 1999), a small percentage of young people connected to this study were clearly overwhelmed by the adversity of their circumstances, and consequently appeared to be either perpetually despondent or were susceptible to involvement in criminal activity, prostitution, or other forms of risk behavior. This underscores the need to further strengthen government and community programs reaching the most vulnerable and marginalized children and youth, and to augment iterations of the Triple "A" in order to effectively assist these groups.

At the broader community level within the social ecology framework, the "Triple A" approach appeared to be a useful tool for reinforcing collective adult self-efficacy in support of vulnerable children. It also highlighted the merits of tripartnership involving community members, and representatives of local and provincial levels of government. This was exemplified in Batlokwa where such a partnership was instrumental in policy formulation and the mobilization of resources designed to reduce levels of child exploitation and to assist children suffering HIV/AIDS.

Ultimately the "Triple A" approach of the Circles of Care project, while useful as a participatory research tool aiming to foster children's resilience in the context of HIV/AIDS, is limited in its overall effectiveness. While a number of policies, legislative reforms, and practices are in place to address the many risk factors these youth face, a critical problem rests with the difficulties local government and communities have in realizing many of these initiatives in a sustainable fashion. Perhaps one measure of the efficacy of the Circles of Care model is its ability to further inform future policy and legislation by effectively identifying strengths and challenges of these initiatives. In addition, in the context of HIV/AIDS in sub-Saharan Africa, legal measures must be reinforced by community-driven restorative practices that engage the participation not only of local leaders and enabling organizations such as CYCAD, but as well encourage the active involvement of children, adolescents, and their immediate adult caregivers.

References

Bronfenbrenner, U. (1979). *The Ecology of Human Development.* Cambridge, MA: Harvard University Press.

Burr, R. (2002). Global and Local Approaches to Children's Rights in Vietnam. *Childhood, 9*, 49–61.

Cook, P., Ali, S., & Munthali, A. (2000). *Starting from Strengths: Community Care for Vulnerable Children in Malawi.* University of Victoria: Unpublished research report.

Cook, P., Blanchet-Cohen, N., & Hart, S. (2004). *Children As Partners: Child Participation Promoting Social Change.* Victoria, Canada: IICRD, University of Victoria.

Cook, P. & White, W. (2006). Risk, Recovery and Resilience: Helping Young and Old Move Together to Support South African Communities Affected by HIV/AIDS. *Journal of Intergenerational Relationships, 4*(1), 65–77.

Fraser, M. (1997). *Risk and Resilience: An Ecological Perspective.* Washington, DC: NASW Press.

Free State Provincial Government. (2008). "*General Information.*" Retrieved from *http://www.fs.gov.za/GeneralInfo.htm* on June 22, 2010

Garbarino, J. (1999). *Lost Boys: Why Our Sons Turn Violent and How We Can Save Them.* New York: Anchor Books.

Guthrie, B. L. (2003). *A Rapid Assessment: The Situation of Children in South Africa.* Cape Town, South Africa. Save the Children and the Children's Institute, University of Cape Town.

Kidd, S. A. & Kral, M. J. (2005). Practicing Participatory Action Research. *Journal of Counseling Psychology, 52*(2), 187–195.

Knutson, K. (1997). *Children: Noble Causes or Worthy Citizens.* Aldershot, UK: Arena.

Meintjes, H., Budlender, D., Giese, S., & Johnson, L. (2003). *Children in Need of Care or in Ieed of Cash? Questioning Social Security Provisions for Orphans in the Context of the South African AIDS Pandemic.* Cape Town, South Africa: Children's Institute and the Centre for Actuarial Research, University of the Cape Town.

Myers, R. (1992). *The Twelve Who Survive: Strengthening Programming of Early Childhood Development in the Third World.* New York: Routledge.

Rogoff, B. (2003). *The Cultural Nature of Human Development.* Oxford, UK: Oxford University Press.

Shonkoff, J. & Phillips, D. (Eds.) (2000). *From Neurons to Neighborhoods: The Science of Early Childhood Development.* Washington, DC: National Academy Press.

Super, C. & Harkness, S. (1986). The Developmental Niche: A Conceptualization at the Interface of Child and Nature. *International Journal of Behavioral Development, 4*, 545–569.

UNAIDS (Joint United Nations Program on HIV/AIDS). (2008). 2008 *Report on the Global AIDS Epidemic*. Geneva: UNAIDS. Retrieved from http://www.unaids.org/en/KnowledgeCentre/HIVData/GlobalReport/2008/2008_Global_report.asp on May 2, 2010.

United Nation's Children's Fund (2003). *Africa's Orphan Generations*. New York: UNICEF.

Veale, A. (2000). Dilemmas of Community in Post-emergency Rwanda. *Community, Work and Family*, *3*, 233–239.

Werner, E., & Smith, R. (1992). *Overcoming the Odds: High Risk Children from Birth to Adulthood*. Ithaca, NY: Cornell University Press.

Author Biographies

Juan Albarracin-Jordan holds a PhD in anthropology with a specialization in conflict resolution and environmental and natural resources management. He is a consultant in policy strategic environmental and social assessment. His professional experience focuses mainly in the mining sector, covering countries and regions in Latin America and West Africa. He was technical advisor in intercultural issues to three committees of the Constituent Assembly of Bolivia, in 2007, and international observer with the Carter Center. He was visiting senior research fellow at the Center for the Advanced Study of the Visual Arts, National Gallery of Art, in Washington DC, and member of the Academic Committee of the 53rd International Congress of Americanists. Dr. Albarracin-Jordan has written numerous books and articles on the evolution of human settlement patterns, cultural adaptation, strategic environmental and social assessment, as well as indigenous issues. Currently, he is president of the Bartolome de Las Casas Foundation and professor at the Universidad Andina, in La Paz, Bolivia.

Julie Bergeron graduated as Attorney at Law in Quebec, Canada, and gained a masters degree (LLM) in human rights and humanitarian law from Essex University, United Kingdom. She has over 10 years of experience in the area of human rights and children's rights, particularly with UN agencies in Asia and the Pacific Region. She has been working as Attorney at Law/Child Protection Officer for UNICEF since 2000. She was a Child Protection Specialist for UNICEF Viet Nam between 2003 and 2008. She is currently working as Chief of Child Protection for UNICEF Haiti.

Isabel A. S. Bordin, MD, MSc, PhD, is an affiliated professor of the department of psychiatry in the Escola Paulista de Medicina at the Universidade Federal de São Paulo. She is a child psychiatrist, head of the Social Psychiatry Division and member of the International Clinical

Epidemiology Network (INCLEN). Her primary research interests are focused on children at high-risk for mental health problems, including antisocial behavior, pregnancy in adolescence, disadvantaged youth, and exposure to domestic violence.

Thérèse Bouchard has studied both praxeology and educational psychology. In the past 30 years she has worked in the international development community. She spent seven years in Chile working in communications and directly with the local people. She was the director general of Development and Peace for five years, and has worked at the Canadian Centre for International Studies and Cooperation (CECI) since 1993. Thérèse has followed up the democratic processes in Chile, Namibia, and Haiti, and has worked as a consultant in this field in Japan, Haiti, and the Great Lakes region in Africa. She has taught conflict-resolution negotiations since 1995, notably in Burundi, Nepal, and Burkina Faso. She has also worked as a trainer for CIDA in the area of human rights since 1992.

Beatriz Caicedo is an auxiliar professor in the School of Public Health at the University of Antioquia. She is a PhD candidate in human geography from the University of Bristol, UK with a specialization in multilevel statistical methods and geographical information systems. Her masters training was in epidemiology, with a specialization in lifecourse epidemiology from the University Federal of Pelotas, Brazil. Her undergraduate study was in Management of Health Information Systems from the University of Antioquia, Colombia. She has published articles in national and international scientific journals concerning youth mortality, the right health and access to health services in Colombia, the evaluation of early prevention programs of aggressive behaviors, and the long-term effects of early risk factors on aggressive behavior. In 2007, she was a recipient of a full scholarship to pursue studies on Epidemiology by the Wellcome Trust Foundation.

Kathryn Campbell is an associate professor in the department of criminology at the University of Ottawa. Her research and teaching interests are mainly in the area of social justice and include studies examining miscarriages of justice, youth justice, and Aboriginal justice. In the past eight years, Kathryn Campbell's research has examined the nature and extent of wrongful conviction in Canada; in particular, how the wrongly convicted cope with imprisonment, Canadian policy responses to this problem, and the impact of medical errors in pediatric forensic pathology on convictions. Kathryn Campbell is also involved in a large international study funded by the International Development Research Centre that examines how social capital may mitigate against youth involvement in gangs; the three research sites of the study encompass Ottawa-Carleton, Canada, Managua, Nicaragua, and San Salvador, El Salvador. Finally, after completing a Social Sciences and Humanities Research Council funded study examining family violence in a northern Aboriginal community in 2007, Kathryn continues to be interested in Aboriginal justice initiatives.

Philip Cook holds a PhD in cross-cultural psychology from Queen's University, and is the founder and current executive director of the International Institute for Child Rights and Development (IICRD). The IICRD is part of the Centre for Global Studies at the University of Victoria, and is recognized to be a Canadian leader in community-based, national, regional, and international applications of the United Nations Convention on the Rights of the Child. During this time the Institute has been working in partnership with a cross-section of UN agencies, governments, and international nongovernmental organizations, and children's organizations. These partnerships have resulted in policy design, community-based research initiatives, school-based programs and projects with marginalized children, youth and their communities on various issues including child participation in local governance, youth leadership and development, support for Indigenous children, child participation monitoring and evaluation, intergenerational programs, promoting the rights of sexually exploited children and caring for children orphaned by HIV/AIDS.

Myriam Denov is an associate professor in the School of Social Work at McGill University. She holds a PhD from the University of Cambridge, where she was a Commonwealth Scholar. Her research and teaching interests lie in the areas of war and political violence, war-affected children, postconflict reconstruction and peacebuilding, and gender and security. She has worked nationally and internationally with former child soldiers, survivors of sexual violence, and people living with HIV/AIDS. Her current research, supported by the Social Science and Humanities Research Council of Canada (SSHRC), is exploring the militarization and reintegration experiences of former child soldiers in Sierra Leone and Colombia. She has presented expert evidence in court on child soldiers and has served as an advisor to government and NGOs on children in armed conflict, and girls in fighting forces. She is the author of *Child Soldiers: Sierra Leone's Revolutionary United Front*.

Prof. Luis F. Duque, MD (U de Antioquia), MPH (Johns Hopkins), is researcher and professor at Universidad de Antioquia School of Public Health. He has ample experience in health services direction (Deputy Minister of Health, Director National Institute of Health, Advisor to the President of Colombia in Public Health policy), direction of higher education institutions and academic life (President U de Antioquia, Director Higher Education National Institute of Colombia, Dean National School of Public Health, faculty member at U de Antioquia, Colombian School of Medicine, Visiting Scholar at Harvard), advisor on health matters for more than 15 years (World Bank, IADB, WHO, UNICEF, US AID). Prof. Duque has experience on aggression and related risky human behaviors research, and in public policy adoption to promote resilience and to prevent violence. Since the past 10 years he has been leading the PREVIVA Program (Violence and risky conducts prevention) at the School of Public Health, University of Antioquia. Medellin, Colombia.

Lesley du Toit was appointed deputy minister of the Ministry of Children and Family Development in British Columbia, Canada on April 18, 2006. Prior to that, she was executive director of the Child and Youth Care Agency for Development in South Africa. An internationally recognized leader in working with children and youth at risk, she has over 25 years of child welfare and child and youth care experience. She is an expert in the transformation of government service systems for children and youth at risk, particularly those involving indigenous and nonindigenous communities with direct responsibility for service delivery, including capacity building and accountability. In 1988, Ms. du Toit was awarded a master of science degree in child and youth care administration (with distinction) from Nova University, United States. She also holds bachelor degrees (Hon.) in social work and psychology from Unisa, South Africa. In 1996, she received the Spirit of Crazy Horse Award, an international award for leadership and work with troubled young people.

Dr. Christine Gervais is a sociologist working as an assistant professor in criminology at the University of Ottawa. Her teaching and research areas include children's and women's human rights, crimes against humanity, education and development in Latin America, social justice, human trafficking, and feminist spirituality. She is a member of both the Interdisciplinary Research Laboratory on the Rights of the Child in the faculty of law and the laboratory for justice studies and research in the faculty of social sciences at the University of Ottawa.

Daniel Lavan has taught in public primary schools and organized out-of-school learning interventions in Ghana, Nigeria, and Uganda. After MA coursework in the Comparative International Development Education programme at OISE/U Toronto he returned to Tamale for field research toward his MA thesis on basic education reform and teachers' classroom practice in Ghana. During his doctoral studies at the University of Ottawa he continued to pursue an interest in the influence of international aid frameworks and global Child Rights discourse both at the classroom level in formal schools and within NGO interventions for out-of-school children in postcolonial nations. With a Doctoral Research Award from the International Development Research Centre he conducted his doctoral thesis fieldwork in Senegal in 2008–2009, examining the *African* Movement of Working Children and Youth and its relations with international NGOs.

Esther Lupafya is acting director of the Ekwendeni Hospital Primary Health Care Division and the Ekwendeni Hospital AIDS Programme. She began her career at Ekwendeni Hospital as Maternal and Child Health Care Coordinator in 1989 and in 1990 became the Orphan Care coordinator. In 2001, Mrs. Lupafya became the HIV/AIDS coordinator. She holds a bachelor's degree in community health and in 2008 she completed a master's in social development and health at Queen Margaret University in Edinburgh, Scotland. Mrs. Lupafya is actively involved in promoting social research related to health, livelihoods, orphanhood, and food security in the Ekwendeni area.

Richard Maclure is a professor in the Faculty of Education at the University of Ottawa. He holds a PhD in international development education from Stanford University. He teaches in the field of comparative and international education, and conducts research pertaining to basic education, marginalized youth, and the evolving role of civil societies in addressing youth issues. He recently completed a SSHRC-funded study on youth participation in Senegal, and is currently coordinating a research project on youth social capital formation, with case studies in El Salvador, Nicaragua, and Canada. His publications have appeared in journals such as *Comparative Education*, *Journal of Latin American Studies*, *Harvard Educational Review*, and *Journal of Youth Studies*.

Fahmida Mariam is a former project officer for Save the Children, Canada, Toronto. In March of 2010, based in Dhaka, Bangladesh, Fahmida joined Sightsavers as the South Asia program director. She also has a degree from Ryerson University in Toronto.

John D. McLennan, MD, MPH, PhD, FRCPC(C) is an assistant professor in the departments of community health sciences, paediatrics, and psychiatry in the faculty of medicine at the University of Calgary. He is also a practicing child psychiatrist. Dr. McLennan's primary research interests include life trajectories of children at high-risk, societal efforts to improve children's outcomes, and the effectiveness of these efforts.

Herbert Muyinda is an anthropologist at the Child Health and Development Center, College of Health Sciences, Makerere University, Uganda. He has conducted research on disability in conflict situations, among children in rural areas, and other vulnerable populations. He has written a number of publications on HIV/AIDS and STDs, disability, conflict, and poverty. Before, Herbert was a researcher at the Medical Research Council on AIDS in Uganda. The project focused on the potential of traditional institutions in the control of HIV/AIDS among young people in rural areas. His current research is on the supply chain of Malaria, AIDS, and TB (MAT) in rural health facilities in Uganda. Herbert holds a PhD in anthropology from the University of Copenhagen, and a masters in public administration and management from Makerere University.

Geoffrey Oyat is an Acholi from Northern Uganda who has over 10 years experience in child protection work with field experiences in Northern Uganda, Sri Lanka, and Liberia. He has worked with Save the Children since 2001 and while working in Northern Uganda, was instrumental in developing and executing programs for children caught up in the conflict. He was part of the effort that brought the voices of affected children internationally galvanizing a sizeable international response for what was for many years a forgotten conflict. He was also the pioneer national coordinator for the Coalition to Stop the Use of Child Soldiers in Uganda for the period 2002–2006 equally playing a leading role in mobilizing like-minded human and child rights organizations in Uganda and beyond for better protection and reintegration response for children associated with armed groups. He has also been working with communities in particular with women and children to cope up with development challenges in a situation of conflict.

Sheetal Patel is a PhD candidate at the School of Population and Public Health, University of British Columbia. She is currently conducting her doctoral research, which seeks to determine HIV vulnerabilities among young people in postconflict Northern Uganda. Sheetal's research interests include infectious disease surveillance and HIV/AIDS prevention and programming for vulnerable populations both in Canada and internationally. Sheetal holds a masters degree in public policy as well as a master of Public Health from the London School of Hygiene and Tropical Medicine.

Inbal Solomon has recently completed her master's degree at the University of Ottawa, where her primary research centered on the impacts of the ongoing Middle East conflict on civil society, particularly its youth. She, alongside Dr. Myriam Denov, has also published a chapter entitled "Militarised Bodies: The Global Militarisation of Children's Lives" in *Contested Bodies of Childhood and Youth*. Prior to this, she took on a lead role in the organization of the "Children's Rights and International Development" conference, showcasing research on children's experiences in contexts of armed conflict, institutionalization, violence and abuse, child labor, exploitation, and HIV/AIDS. Her research interests include civilian militarization, children's rights, peace and conflict studies, and human rights.

Fatima D. Rigato, MD, MSc, is the coordinator of Projeto Quixote, a social project and nongovernmental organization affiliated with Universidade Federal de São Paulo, dedicated to helping marginalized children and youth. She is also a practicing pediatrician. She has worked for years with marginalized children and youth including those involved in the street, those with mental illness, and those who have experienced incarceration in detention facilities.

Liam Riley is a doctoral candidate in geography at the University of Western Ontario in London, Canada. His research interests include childhood, gender, household change, food security, and urbanization in Malawi. The research on orphans included in this volume was conducted as part of his master's degree program at UWO. The research findings have been presented at conferences in Canada, the United States, and South Africa. Liam would like to acknowledge the financial support from the Social Sciences and Humanities Research Council of Canada and UWO, which made this research possible.

Dharshini Seneviratne, was Head, Learning and Impact, at Save the Children in Sri Lanka at the time of writing this chapter. She has a BA in English literature from Colombo, Sri Lanka, and an MA in media studies from New York. She functioned as an internal evaluator and researcher within Save the Children and also managed child rights research consultancies and related advocacy. Also, she engaged in research and evaluation training including on child participation in research, and supported the development of child-friendly research methodologies. She produced research papers/advocacy briefs on child rights topics. Prior to her work at Save the Children, she worked as a media researcher and journalist. Presently, she is employed by the Asian Regional Centre of the Commonwealth Youth Programme (CYP), Commonwealth Secretariat, based in Chandigarh, India.

Nelson K. Sewankambo, MBChB, MSc, M.MED, FRCP, Doctor of Laws, Honoris Causa, professor of medicine is the principal of Makerere University College of Health Sciences. He has devoted his past 13 years of professional life to the advancement of medical education, research, and capacity development. He has led teams of academicians, composed of experts in Europe, North America, and Africa, to develop and manage a very successful model for strengthening a medical school in the developing world—the Infectious Diseases Institute at Makerere and there are now plans to replicate this in Nigeria. He has also initiated a successful research capacity building consortium involving seven African institutions and two universities in the UK. He is providing leadership for an Africa wide initiative for Strengthening Research Capacity in Africa. He was the founder of the internationally reknowned Rakai Health Sciences Program where he has contributed a large volume of scientific publications in peer-reviewed journals together with providing mentorship and development of many Ugandan junior and mid-level researchers.

Vivi Stavrou is a clinical psychologist and social scientist, who has research, evaluation, policymaking, and project management experience in the areas of child protection, mental health and human rights, emergency and postconflict social development programming and the development of community-based psychosocial interventions and services. She is a former researcher at the Centre for the Study of Violence and Reconciliation and the deputy executive director of the Regional Psychosocial Support Initiative, Johannesburg, South Africa. Ms. Stavrou served for three years as a staff debriefer for the *South African Truth and Reconciliation Commission.* She is currently a social development consultant and senior associate with REPSSI and the Columbia Group for Children. She was short-listed for the 1998 Nelson Mandela Award for Health and Human Rights and was awarded the South African Chamber of Commerce and Industries Social Involvement Award. She has a degree from the University of KwaZulu-Natal in South Africa.

Patricia Spittal is an associate professor at the University of British Columbia's School of Population and Public Health. Her areas of specialty include sexual and drug-related harms associated with injection drug use, and vulnerabilities of young aboriginal drug users who live in both Vancouver and in the interior of British Columbia. Dr. Spittal's current work focuses on Uganda, where she examines the special social and cultural vulnerabilities women face in extremely high-risk context such as sex trade, and HIV/AIDS prevention programming needs of children affected by civil strife, including child soldiers.

Sakiko Tanaka graduated with a PhD in social policy in Columbia University. She is trained as a researcher for economic and social policy analysis with a focus on child and family policy issues, including international comparative analyses. She was a child protection officer for UNICEF Viet Nam from 2004 to 2008, working on alternative care projects for orphans and children with disabilities. She currently works for the Asia Development Bank based in the Philippines.

Michael Ungar, PhD, is a professor of social work at Dalhousie University. He has conducted workshops internationally on resilience-related themes relevant to the treatment and study of at-risk youth and families and has published over 70 peer-reviewed articles and book chapters on the topic. He is also the author of nine books including *Counseling in Challenging Contexts: Working with Individuals and Families Across Clinical and Community Settings*; *The We Generation: Raising Socially Responsible Children and Teens*; and *Strengths-Based Counseling with At-risk Youth*. Currently, as the Director of the Resilience Research Centre, he leads a number of studies of resilience involving researchers from more than a dozen countries on six continents. In addition to his research and teaching, Michael is a board member of the American Family Therapy Academy, has sat on the Board of Examiners for the Nova Scotia Association of Social Workers since 2002, and is on editorial boards of four journals, including *Family Process* and the *British Journal of Social Work*.

Index